From Followers to Leaders

Innovation is at the heart of growth. To innovate, firms in newly industrializing countries cannot hope to match the R&D spending of the world's leaders. This book argues that they do not have to. By learning from the best, and focusing innovation effort on design and cultural change, firms from the unlikeliest places can catch up and then move ahead of world leaders.

The last years have seen a profusion of books and articles on managing technology, focused almost exclusively on leading-edge firms in leading-edge countries. The book argues that succeeding as a follower-firm requires learning from many experiences, avoiding simplistic prescriptive approaches. The book brings evidence that follower-firms can begin a catch-up process from whatever position they presently hold. Catch-up involves a range of activities which the book details in a series of case studies. These are drawn from many different firms across twelve countries and five continents, in industry segments as diverse as pharmaceuticals, software, garments, beer and steel. Firms have gone from being followers to become world leaders. Some are on the way, some are just beginning, whilst some stay followers but still try to do better than the local average. All of these show that successful experiences can arise anywhere in the world.

Chapters cover the role of innovation on the shop-floor, the need to combine product and process innovation, the particular role of R&D and of design. The evidence from the book is that there are many ways for followers to turn themselves into leaders, providing insight for public policy in building local technological capacity.

Naushad Forbes is Director of Forbes Marshall, India's leading energy conservation and control instrumentation firm, and Consulting Professor at Stanford University in the Program in Science, Technology and Society.

David Wield is Professor of Innovation and Development at the Open University, and Co-Director of its International Development Centre. He recently directed its Centre for Technology Strategy and chaired its Development Policy and Practice group.

APPRECIATIONS OF THE BOOK BY FORBES AND WIELD

From academics

from Professor Nathan Rosenberg, Stanford University

'This book does an altogether admirable job of bringing together a wealth of information, primarily from the Asian "follower" countries, to demonstrate that there are indeed many possible paths to innovation and economic growth. Along the way the authors neatly puncture a number of venerable myths and stereotypes. The book contains much good, thought-provoking material that should contribute to a serious rethinking of the prospects for development.'

from Professor Ron Dore, Imperial College, London

' ... Packed with fascinating detail, and no-nonsense, feet-on-the-ground commentary – an enormous range of factual detail.'

from Mike Hobday, Science and Technology Policy Research, Sussex University

'There is no book similar to this on managing innovation for development. The book shows that there is much scope for "behind the frontier product innovation" and encapsulates well the arguments for movement from "process to product" in industrial development. It is especially good in bringing such a wide range of cases from different regions and sectors.'

from Gerhard Caspar, recently president of Stanford University

'In a lively and engaging style, Forbes and Wield provide evidence for an important and encouraging message: the designation "developing country" is not a mere euphemism. If they are determined to be innovators, especially on the shop-floor, "followers" can develop into technology leaders. The book has lessons and shrewd insights galore also for industries in the developed world. Its detailed comparative perspective is vastly more rewarding than global "globalization" accounts. This is a refreshing addition to the literature on technology.'

From leading industrialists

from Ratan Tata, Tata Industries Ltd, India

'This book deserves to become prescribed reading for all those interested in technology policy in developing countries. It establishes that those countries, and companies in those countries, must institutionalize innovation if they are to become globally competitive, and goes further to describe, in steps that can be readily understood and implemented, how this can be done.'

from Mukesh Ambani, MD Reliance Industries Ltd, India

'Naushad Forbes and David Wield have, in a very convincing manner, showed how technology followers can innovate to be technology leaders. They provide new insights and ideas for leaders in industry, business and government. This book is a must for all those who are charged to create their future.'

From Followers to Leaders

Managing technology and innovation
in newly industrializing countries

Naushad Forbes and David Wield

London and New York

First published 2002
by Routledge
11 New Fetter Lane, London EC4P 4EE

Simultaneously published in the USA and Canada
by Routledge.
29 West 35th Street, New York, NY 10001

Routledge is an imprint of the Taylor & Francis Group

© 2002 Naushad Forbes and David Wield

Typeset in Times New Roman by Exe Valley Dataset Ltd, Exeter
Printed and bound in Great Britain by TJ International Ltd, Padstow, Cornwall

British Library Cataloguing in Publication Data
A catalogue record for this book is available
from the British Library

Library of Congress Cataloging in Publication Data
Forbes, Naushad, 1960-
   International technology management: from followers to leaders/Naushad Forbes and
   David Wield.
      p. cm.
   Includes bibliographical references and index.
   1. Technological innovations—Management. 2. International business
   enterprises—Management. 3. New products—Management. 4. International trade. 5.
   Competition, International. I. Wield, David. II. Title.

HD45.F66 2002
658.5'14—dc21   2001048586

ISBN 0–415–25175–3 (hbk)
ISBN 0–415–25176–1 (pbk)

Contents

Figures

Tables

Boxes

Preface

Development is all about overcoming barriers to catch-up: at the level of the nation, the firm and individuals. Industrial development is at the heart of any national catch-up process, and firms are at the heart of industrial development. Catching up at the level of the firm means growing value-added faster than leading-edge firms. And growing value-added is all about technical change, about innovation, about doing new things for commercial advantage. This book is about firms that have innovated to climb up the value-chain. This climb begins with the hard slog of getting better at producing, with all the small incremental innovations that involves. Follower-firms therefore learn from leading firms, and develop their own capabilities along the way. As they learn more, they develop new capabilities, which include proprietary technology and new products. Finally, as they close the gap, they emerge as leaders themselves. This book argues that firms must start by being good followers, to learn from the best, but have the ambition to emerge as leaders. Indeed firms must choose to go from followers to leaders, and they must manage innovation to get there.

Some firms, several described in this book, have gone on from being followers to become world leaders. Others are on the way, with some just beginning. Yet others stay followers but still try to do better than the local average. Companies choose to be world-class. Examples from Mexico and Brazil, India and Singapore, South Korea and Taiwan, Tanzania and Zimbabwe illustrate our argument, in industry segments from pharmaceuticals, to software, garments, beer, petrochemicals, glass, bicycles and steel. They show that successful experiences can arise anywhere in the world, in the most unpromising environments.

The initial idea for the book came from ten weeks of fun, team teaching a course called *Comparative Technology Policy* at Stanford University in 1990. The focus was rather different to other technology policy courses, because it attempted to focus on the environment for innovation in firms as the unit of analysis. The seminars attracted economists of technical change, international relations majors and even a lawyer, as well as engineering 'undergrads' and 'grads', and MBA students. They wanted to know about more than the national policy environment, about how and why some firms succeeded and others didn't, wherever they were located. The key ideas in this book were further developed when one of us, Naushad, went on to produce a course, *Technology, Policy and Management in Newly Industrializing Countries,* that more fully met the need for integration of knowledge of innovation theory, technology management and industrial development. Unusually, he tried to address the needs of both practitioners and theorists who understood the main elements of innovation theory and technology management, but were concerned about how to pace, time and choose from the mass of useful ideas and experiences. There was no way, we felt, that any one firm, or even nation, could try to do everything. So how to choose what to do first? In the book we have gone beyond academic convention to argue what not to do as well as what must be done. Most of all, we argue that there are many ways for followers to become leaders, and the best way to learn about them is to look at what firms in diverse settings have achieved.

The authors' home institutions give a rather unusual synergy. First, the mix Stanford/Open University is not an obvious one unless you know that both put huge effort into undergraduate teaching, much of it interdisciplinary. In both, the struggle for interdisciplinary, problem-oriented, research teaching and learning goes on, and there are many colleagues to whom we can turn for support. Second, the mix Stanford University/Forbes Marshall, since one of the authors is both a professor and a hands-on company engineer and director. At these institutions, and others, there are many many people who have helped us. Alex Inkeles and Jim Adams require a special acknowledgement. They have been there from the beginning, offering encouragement and advice, and reading and re-reading drafts. They will notice some of their phrases as they read the final product. Jim Adams, as well, co-wrote Chapter 7. At Stanford Harry Rowen provided invaluable comments on an early draft, and Robert McGinn, the late Steve Kline, Nate Rosenberg, Walter Vincenti and a host of students have debated, added insights and anecdotes, and suggested case studies. Cristina Casanueve kindly allowed us to use her Vitro case study, and also contributed valuable comments on the final draft. At the Open University Robin Roy, Steve Potter, Tom Hewitt, Seife Ayele and Joanna Chataway will recognize some of their thoughts. Many others have read drafts of the book, including Ron Dore, Mike Hobday, Ravi Pandit, Pam Smith, Darius Forbes and Shankar Ranganathan. We are grateful to the great Indian cartoonist, R.K. Laxman, for giving us immediate permission to use the cartoon in Chapter 1. We appreciate the help in putting together case studies, interviews, participation and general brainstorming (including of the book title!) of O.P. Munjal, S.K. Munjal and S.K. Rai at Hero Cycles, Madhur Bajaj and Vasant Rao at Bajaj Auto, Dr J.M. Khanna at Ranbaxy, Venkatesh Desai at Alfa Laval, Keki Dadiseth, Arun Adhikari, D. Shivkumar and Dr Raghupathi at Hindustan Lever and Fali Lord, Mateesh, Satyadeo Purohit and Milind Joshi at Forbes Marshall.

We are indebted to our institutions for allowing us to spend the time on writing, often at very inconvenient times for our colleagues. David is especially grateful to Jim Eitel for his hospitality in the Bay Area over many writing visits. We are also indebted to Seife Ayele for research assistance and to Marie Lacy for her attention to our worst drafts. We are particularly indebted to Aparajita Zutschi for expert field work in various Indian firms, and many insightful case studies extracted from larger bodies of work.

This book has been ten years in the making, five years since we first wrote an outline. It is the contributions and support of many many contributors that makes it so distinctive. We are most grateful for all the inputs provided.

Naushad Forbes
David Wield
June 2001

Acknowledgements

The authors and publishers would like to thank the following for granting permission to reproduce material in this work:

Cambridge University Press for Table 5.1, taken from *Technology, Learning and Innovation*, Kim, L. and Nelson, R.R. (eds), 2000

R.K. Laxman and *The Times of India* for the cartoon used in Figure 1.2

Dra Cristina Casanueva Reguart for the 'Vitro' case in Chapter 2

Princeton University Press for Figure 3.1, taken from *Governing the Market*, Wade, R., 1990

Every effort has been made to contact copyright holders for their permission to reprint material in this book. The publishers would be grateful to hear from any copyright holder who is not here acknowledged and will undertake to rectify any errors or omissions in future editions of this book.

1   Beneath the surface

Introduction

Are developing nations permanently restricted to being simply offshore manufacturing and assembly places for the business of the advanced nations? Are firms in newly industrializing countries limited to local markets or to being subsidiary suppliers to the giant international firms that give the world new drugs, new cars, new watches, new software and new shampoo? This book says 'No!' With rare exceptions the less advantaged cannot count on becoming inventors of wholly new goods, or being world leaders in invention and innovation. There remains, though, much that nations and their firms can do to move up the value-added ladder to become significant contributors to world industry and production, and in the process achieve much success themselves.

Consider the following random series of cases to get a flavour of this diversity:

- In 1938, Byung Chul Lee started a small export business in fruits and vegetables with the name 'Samsung', when Korea was very much a poor developing country. In 1969, Samsung Corporation spun off a subsidiary to capture opportunities in electronics. By 2001, Samsung Electronics was the world's largest manufacturer of microwaves, cellphones and monitors and the world's fourth largest semi-conductor manufacturer.
- The Indian pharmaceutical industry has grown rapidly in the past thirty years, based on the (fully legal) reverse-engineering of new drugs. From 2005, Indian pharma companies must follow the intellectual property rights regime of the World Trade Organization. Far from being wiped out, several Indian pharma companies are preparing to become international players themselves in the global market for drugs. As *The Economist* said, 'Among India's 20,000 or so drug makers, Anji Reddy is the most visionary . . . he thinks Indian firms can capture a quarter of the world market for generics . . . manufacturing costs are perhaps two-thirds of rich-country levels . . . "India is the best place to manufacture pharma-ceuticals", declares Brian Tempest, president of Ranbaxy Laboratories, India's largest drug maker.'[1]
- Taiwan dominates the market for a range of IT products: it has 60 per cent of the market for computer mice, 85 per cent of the market for scanners and 65 per cent of the market for motherboards.
- The country that has emerged as the one where the world's leading car manu-facturers are experimenting with their most innovative ways of making cars is

Brazil. In 2000, more new car factories were built in Brazil than in any other country.

- The Indian software industry has been in the headlines world-wide for the past few years. With exports of software services growing at 50 per cent a year during the 1990s, in 2000 software accounted for 11 per cent of India's total exports of US$38 billion. Projections of the national software association suggest that by 2008 software services will account for exports of $50 billion – about 50 per cent more than India's total current exports, prompting a boom in foreign exchange earnings of Opec 1973 proportion.

- South African Breweries has emerged as the world's fourth largest brewer by volume. It has invested in firms in Zimbabwe, China, India, Germany, and in Eastern and Central Europe, a total of twenty countries. In Central Europe it has become the dominant brewer. It was recently given an 'exemplary practice partner' award for its human relations strategies. United Breweries of India currently has brewing volumes that make it the world's ninth largest brewer.

- In 1999, Reliance, India's largest chemicals firm, began production at the world's largest green-field refinery in Jamnagar. The project was put into commission six months ahead of schedule, beating the world record by some months. The capital cost per tonne of capacity at $116 per tonne was also some 30 per cent lower than comparable plants set up by leading international contractors.

- In June 2000, the Indian chairman of Hindustan Lever Limited, Keki Dadiseth, transferred to the Unilever head office in London as director responsible for Unilever's global Household and Personal Products division. His four years' experience running India's largest and most successful consumer products firm demonstrated that a $2 billion firm employing 36,000 people could be innovative, flexible and quickly responsive to changing market conditions. His brief at the head office in London was to do the same world-wide for the global business.

- In 2000, the UK's fourth richest resident was Lakshmi Mittal, an Indian business-man, who runs the world's first global steel business, with plants operating at bench-mark levels in Mexico, Kazakhstan, Germany and the US.[2]

- In January 2001, Lafarge bought Blue Circle of the UK, making it the world's largest cement group. The company they overtook was Cemex, of Mexico, now the world's third largest cement company and seen by many observers as its most innovative. Its chairman, Lorenzo Zambrano, says 'A Mexican company that's really high-tech is not quite intuitive to people. That perception is something we have to overcome'.

Each of these cases demonstrates that world-beating champions emerge in the most unexpected places. Each demonstrates how firms can come from behind, learn from the best, and then close the gap and even move ahead. Innovation and the effective management of technology is at the heart of these stories of adding value. This book is about how this came to be. What led to the successes that underlie these stories? What can we learn from these firms? But also, these are stories of successful firms, but stories of *past* success. Where do these firms go from here?

Beyond these great successes, there is a whole world of possibilities for less dramatic, but cumulatively enormously important, firm innovation in all parts of the world. In many cases such firms can and do make advances in design and production techniques which generate added value. Innovation moves them beyond being merely the drones who make products according to the strict and narrow confines of the role assigned to them by the multinational technology inventing firms.

This book tells these stories, of the 'nearly best' and the 'it could be the rest'. Technology and innovative capability lie at the heart of growing value-added, of catching up. Lessons have emerged from analysis of innovation that have massively improved the chances of a firm catching up. These lessons have emerged from all over the world. They have come from all kinds of companies, in all sectors and from the most unexpected places. Other books have focused on what countries can do to 'catch-up'. This book asks what firms can do to catch-up. We argue that technology-followers can learn from many leading edges, from best practices in technology-leaders but especially from other technology-followers.

Understanding of innovation and technology management in newly industrializing countries (NICs) have changed dramatically over the past twenty years. We begin by questioning misconceptions about technology, until recently engrained in the habits of policy makers, development agents and companies. We present these misconceptions, or myths, not to 'critique' – on the contrary, the myths are embedded to some extent in us all, as individuals and in our organizations and institutions. The authors' own education as engineers was strongly based on the same ideas. Only in the last couple of decades has a mass of new evidence, together with a series of major failures of policies based on the myths, made it possible for an alternative to emerge. The growing number of anecdotes, experiences and theories have begun to add up to a new paradigm of firm technical capability, which we present next, of what constitutes technology management and how it is applied. We contemplate what catching up is all about: increasing value-added through production of goods and services per employee. What matters is being able to grow value continuously and steadily. Finally, we introduce six key propositions about the technology and innovation management task in a technology-follower firm, which we will pursue in later chapters of the book.

Technology in development – myths and realities

Six myths have long influenced thinking on the role of technology in newly industrializing countries:

1   Technology is (just) applied science
2   Technological self-reliance is key to break out of technological dependency
3   More technology is always good
4   High tech is the best tech
5   Technology is well understood and easily transferred
6   R&D is key to innovation and is led by R.

These myths are much less prevalent today than they were even in the early 1990s. We present them because they have been so powerful and pervasive until recently and continue to strangle the practice of technology management. Shedding these myths is key to building an alternative approach to successful management of the innovation process, though it will become clear during the chapter that neither myths nor their opposite are right. We aim to 'balance' learning from myths and recent practice.

Myth 1: technology is (just) applied science

'New technology always comes from the application of science' is the essence of the first myth. On the contrary, the connection between science and technology is very complex and anything other than simple and linear. Nevertheless, the idea that scientific discovery precedes technical progress has held sway in influential circles.

> I am convinced that of all the big problems that face India today nothing is more important than the development of scientific research, both pure and applied, and scientific method. This is indeed the basis and foundation of all other work. . . . The extensive use of that method can only come through a properly directed education and a large number of research institutions which deal with pure science as well as the innumerable applications of it.*

Against this model can be laid the clear evidence that technology has more often led science rather than the other way around. Through much of human history technology has developed with little, if any, connection to science.† One well-known example of technology leading science is the steam engine which existed for over a century before the science of thermodynamics was developed by Carnot. Carnot's very practical investigations of the efficiency of steam engines (he asked why high-pressure steam engines were more efficient that low-pressure engines) led to the development of the science on which they are now thought to be based. Even a high-technology field like the twentieth-century aerospace industry has countless examples of technical progress either preceding scientific understanding, or proceeding hand in hand with enhanced theoretical understanding. Vincenti uses the example of the shape of an aircraft wing and its ability to generate lift and shows that until well after the Second World War, most airfoils were chosen from catalogues of profiles. These profiles were developed by: first, modifying previously successful forms; second, using rules learned from experience; third (and the only partially scientific process), using such theoretical understanding and methods as were available; and fourth, undertaking a vast amount of wind tunnel testing.[3] By 1936, an estimated 2,000 shapes had been tried in the wind tunnel or in flight. The mix of methods changed over time, with the science of fluid-dynamic theory slowly replacing rules of experience (technology). In aerospace, as in the case of the steam engine, technology contributed at least as much to science as science did to technology.

To expose the myth that technology is simply the application of science is not to deny that the relationship between science and technology is strong: 'Science and technology have become increasingly intimate endeavours . . . [nevertheless] . . . it is a strongly interactive relationship between two semi-autonomous activities.'[4] The implications of following the logic of the first myth are far-reaching. First, scientific knowledge would be valued over technological. But industrial innovation does not usually require prior investment in science.[5] For most industries 'a steady stream of newly minted scientists and engineers suffices to keep the [firm R&D] laboratory

---

* Jawaharlal Nehru, *Selected Works*, 14: 558. Just how prolific a speaker and writer Nehru was can be seen from his *selected* works running to 21 volumes, each 600-plus pages long.
† D.J. de Solla Price made just this point in 1963 in his classic book *Big Science, Little Science,* Columbia University Press.

adequately up to date with the world of science'.[6] Building indigenous industrial technological capacity may require many things in follower-firms, but does not require doing scientific research to build enhanced theoretical understanding.

The key implication of this myth is the importance of funding and doing scientific research. Technology and industrial development are expected to follow automatically. While few believe in this myth today, it led to countries like India and Mexico investing heavily in scientific research in autonomous state research institutions from the 1940s onwards. Through to the mid-1980s, this investment accounted for the bulk of civilian R&D and had little or no impact on the industrial economy.

Myth 2: technological self-reliance is key to break out of technological dependency

Self-reliance is important but 'inter-dependence' is crucial. In Japan and South Korea massive technology import went with strong local effort. Self-reliance fosters local effort so it is good.

However, finding the right balance between self-reliance and copying and buying technology from others is not easy. Dore[7] uses India as an example of erring too far towards self-reliance, what he calls self-reliance as categorical imperative (SRACI). Over a forty-year period in India from 1950, the SRACI syndrome became almost an ideology, best exemplified by Nehru: 'I believe, as a practical proposition, that it is better to have a second-rate thing made in our country, than a first-rate thing that one has to import.' The legacy of such an approach is that everything had to be done in the country. For example, India is one of the few countries in the world that makes zippers using indigenous technology, the rest of the world buying them from the Japanese company YKK. The mostly small-scale Indian zipper companies admit they are years behind YKK but argue that they will eventually catch up.

One implication of this self-reliance as categorical imperative is the constant pressure to 'reinvent the wheel', to design and develop indigenously every new widget from scratch when the technology to produce could be bought more easily and cheaply elsewhere and adapted if necessary. There is another danger. Since there is little or no learning from what already exists (from imitation), much effort is spent making things in the local way, and the country or firm gets locked into an outdated technology. In India, the production of a 1960 Ambassador car continued statically, decades after fuel-efficient, high-quality Japanese models revolutionized global car production.

So although self-reliance can be a virtue, it can also go too far and block innovation. This myth led to technology itself being treated as an infant industry needing protection. Countries from Brazil and Mexico and the Andean Pact in Latin America to India and Korea in Asia to Egypt in Africa passed regulations restricting the import of technology and regulating the terms under which it could be imported. Policies for technology in industrializing economies were dominated by this paradigm until the early 1980s.

Myth 3: more technology is always good

History is littered with examples of 'beautiful' technologies that were massive failures in the market place. Comparing the Hovercraft or Concorde with disposable diapers may seem outrageous, but good technology must be economically successful, and not necessarily technically impressive. Diapers are not, dare we say, technically or even environmentally sweet, but they are a better innovation because they are economically successful. The comparison also illustrates the importance of standards-shaping for successful innovation. The Hovercraft, designed to overcome the separation between land and sea, did not change the standards of either form of transport.

One danger of following the 'more technology is always good' myth is in trying to resolve problems through increasingly sophisticated technical solutions, which move further and further away from what is possible to make cheaply. In the 1970s and 1980s, Honda and Toyota spent a fraction on R&D compared with Ford and General Motors, but they were much more innovative.

Indeed, the key implication of this myth is a focus on R&D spending rather than on the content of R&D. When India's prime minister exhorts the nation (while inaugurating the 2000 Science Congress) to treble the percentage of GDP spent on R&D by 2005, he demonstrates the continuing power of this myth. So too when Korea, in its 25-year science and technology plan, pledges to increase to 4 per cent the proportion of GDP spent on R&D by 2005, which would be the world's highest. A second implication is a focus on big leaps in product technology, rather than on adding value from small improvements in product and manufacturing process.

Myth 4: high tech is the best tech

The view that 'high tech is always better than low tech' goes beyond 'more technology is good'. One common assumption is that the success of Japanese industry is based on high tech. However, there are many success stories based on developing 'well-known' and 'well-used' technologies with better attention to manufacturing organization. These innovative techniques are not capital extensive or high tech in the classic sense, but rather focused on quality issues, rapid turnaround of parts production and distribution, smaller inventories, shorter product life and changed factory layout. Toyota was the first company to implement such an approach and the techniques are sometimes referred to as Toyota-ism, but many other firms have set up their own versions, which have been copied all over the world, and which we will look at in detail later in Chapter 4.

The Indonesian minister for science and technology, Habibie (who succeeded Suharto as president in 1998 until elections were held in 1999), had a pet project: to build a global aircraft company in Indonesia. A World Bank report in 1993 estimated that $1 billion had been spent in subsidies since 1979.[8] Did Indonesia have any basis for entering an industry that had been characterized by the exit of countries like Holland and Sweden? Habibie's logic was that the industry would act as a 'pull' for technological capability building in the country generally.

One danger of following myth 4 is the writing off and relocation of smokestack industries and mature industries for 'industries of the future', rather than rethinking how such industries might be reorganized and transformed. There are examples in Japan where older shipbuilding zones were changed into centres of advanced marine engineering, pottery districts turned into areas of high-technology ceramics, and so on. At a more controversial level, the myth is being played out in India in 2001. The Indian prime minister, voicing a much-expressed view based on the booming software industry, says that India may have missed the industrial revolution but will be in the forefront of the knowledge revolution. There is no doubt that software is a major contributor to the Indian economy, especially to exports. But manufacturing has been the source of every major country's progress, from Britain in the eighteenth century to present-day China. The most ambitious projections of the Indian national software association suggest that the industry will employ over 2 million people by 2008. That is a large number, but it is a fraction of the 80 million people employed in China's export manufacturers in 2000. When China aims at capturing a 50 per cent market share of world textiles, employment and local value-added will dwarf India's software sector. India, meanwhile, has seen a secular decline in its share of world textiles, from 20 per cent in 1950 to around 3 per cent in 2000. If textiles attracted half the public attention of software, perhaps this traditional industry (accounting for over 20 per cent of Indian manufacturing output and employment in 2000) could add a software industry in growth each year.

Myth 5: technology is well understood and easily transferred

Another myth is that technology is 'a piece of kit', easily understood and easily transferred to new locations. But technology is not just products and processes, it is embedded in people. The most distinctive elements of a particular technology are not reducible to blue-prints.

Technological knowledge has many aspects. Nelson[9] distinguishes between public knowledge (that published for public dissemination) and private (proprietary knowledge in a firm). Proprietary knowledge can be documented and codified in the form of drawings, procedures, patents and blue-prints and stored in databases just like public knowledge. But it can also be tacit, contained in the heads, experience and skills of people. Tacit knowledge is the knowledge of how to ride a bicycle or make a soufflé. Tacit knowledge is hard to reduce to a sheet of paper using drawing and text.

Leonard-Barton reports that a close look at Chapparal Steel, famous for its learning culture, reveals an organic learning system so tightly coupled that CEO Forward says he can tour competitors through the plant, show them almost 'everything and we will be giving away nothing because they can't take it home with them'. His confidence derives from the fact that the knowledge management organization is comprehensible only as an organic whole. Moreover it is in constant flux, constantly regenerating.[10]

The constant process of codification of technical knowledge, which happens 24 hours a day all over the world, inevitably leaves behind some tacit parts, often the most important. So technological knowledge is not always generally and easily accessible, and is hard to transfer.

A major implication of this myth was in the technology import regulations of the 1960s, 1970s and 1980s, which were all aimed at getting better terms for technology transfer. For many years the emphasis was on how to change control and lower the cost of technology transfer so that developing countries could obtain it more easily. The logic was based on the understanding that if payments for technology transfer were lowered, the technology could be obtained more cheaply. But in technology quality is everything. As the best multi-country study of technology transfer to a developing country conclusively showed, regulations on technology transfer simply restricted the flow of technology and led to the under-utilization of both imported and domestic technology.[11] In general, nothing like enough effort is normally made in firms to deal with the tacit, embedded aspects of technology, by working on adaptation and learning.

Myth 6: R&D is key to innovation and is led by R

This myth, that industrial innovation requires R&D led by research, implies that companies need to access research if they are to innovate, usually by setting up laboratories of their own or employing scientists to do research before innovation can be achieved. An analysis of what constitutes R&D in practice, even in the leading nations and companies, helps disavow this myth. For one thing, R&D is mostly D, even in advanced countries. Rosenberg[12] suggests that 80 per cent of industrial R&D, even in the technologically advanced US, is to improve products that already exist, not invent new products. But more fundamentally, except in very few science-based industries like pharmaceuticals, most industrial technology can be adapted and innovation can become the core of the firm without any in-house research in the classic sense. This is not to say that firms should not do R&D, but a very different type of R&D is needed in follower-firms.

The implication of this myth led to the setting up of corporate R&D labs in college/campus-type environments, far removed from operations to free up thinking for research. In several famous cases, this led to labs far removed not just from operations but from the company itself. In a backlash, many leading technology firms spent much of the 1980s closing or re-locating or re-focusing corporate research labs – including RCA, Philips, Xerox, Du Pont and AT&T.

In developing countries, this myth led to setting up government labs for industry which focused on basic research that had nothing to do with the needs of local industry, and within industry, to the view that innovation was 'rocket science', not something everyday for every firm.

Box 1.1 Myths and some implications

Myth 1: technology is (just) applied science

- Scientific knowledge is valued over technological.
- Research institutes are set up and funded to do scientific research.
- Wasteful scientific investment is made instead of technology development.

Myth 2: technological self-reliance is key to break out of technological dependency

- Technology is developed in-house, not bought and adapted.
- Local technological effort is wasted on long-term and risky in-house activities.

Myth 3: more technology is always good

- Attempt big leaps in product technology, not 'shop-floor' innovation.
- Focus on R&D spending, not product/process content or increasing value-added in production.
- New technologies are developed to perfection, then marketed, rather than market-tested, then improved.

Myth 4: high tech is the best tech

- Expensive high-tech champions are funded and subsidized.
- Mature and dirty technologies are forgotten.
- Low-tech options are ignored.

Myth 5: technology is well understood and easily transferred

- Focus action on accessing more blue-prints, not on learning and adapting.
- Tacit knowledge is ignored and little effort goes into making up gaps in tacit knowledge when technology is transferred.
- Too much effort on regulatory aspects of technology transfer, not enough on improving the transfer.

Myth 6: R&D is key to innovation and is led by R

- The focus is R&D, not industrial innovation.
- Within R&D, the focus is on Research, not Development.

From myths to building blocks: understanding technical capability in firms

What is technology and why is it so special?

If technology is not just applied science, not just technical, nor high tech, nor well understood and easily transferred, not only produced by hero inventors, what then is it?

McGinn distinguishes between science and technology in the following way:

> Technology is that form of human activity which is devoted to the production of technics [material products of human making or fabrication] and whose root function is to expand the realm of practical human possibility.
>
> Science is that form of human activity which is devoted to the production of theory-related knowledge of natural phenomena and whose root function is to attain an enhanced understanding of nature.[13]

What does this suggest for the meaning of technology?

- Problem solving in technology is very diverse, much more so than in science. Technology requires a broad range of tools, from mathematical to trial and error practice. Reverse engineering, the practice of taking apart and rebuilding a product over and over again, can be more important than any pure scientific theory of why something works. Drawing and redesigning a product, building up knowledge of maintaining and improving products are key activities. Technical progress can require multiple disciplines – such as mechanical engineering plus electrical engineering – and even inter-disciplines – such as mechatronics. Technologists can be engineering and science graduates in a variety of fields, some holding PhDs, or they can be skilled machinists, or anthropologists trying to understand how a new technology will interact with society.
- Tacit and local knowledge is key to technological innovation. 'There is a vast range of technological knowledge embodied not so much in the published literature as in the minds and muscles of many types of working technologists.'[14] Since tacit knowledge is experiential, it is not as easy to transfer as blue-prints. Even when people move with their knowledge from one location to another, it does not guarantee successful transfer, especially of complex technological systems.

- The diverse nature of problem solving in technology includes the key importance of gaining technological knowledge from 'on-the-ground' industrial and non-laboratory situations and production bases. The knowledge built up from local production allows for continuous innovation 'on the job' (the subject of Chapter 4).
- There is a strong relationship between local knowledge 'from the ground' and another key characteristic of technology – its cumulative nature. New technology is almost always built on previous learning and knowledge (including 'on-the-job' tacit knowledge). The competitive advantage of a firm lies 'less in its proprietary knowledge than on its base of tacit competence'.[15] Firms that begin to innovate in a new area, and adopt new technologies, begin a learning process that is related to the skills it already has.

  > The accumulation of skills, experience and technical know-how, whether at the level of firms or of countries, takes time and is a process pertinent to long-run economic development. The heritage of technology and human capital can only increase through a snowball effect, through gradual accretion.[16]

- The management of technology is thus highly firm- and locality-dependent, often locked in people's heads and difficult to write down in blue-prints.

  > Technological change renders equipment obsolete and eliminates the demand for given kinds of worker skills . . . But it cannot *per se* destroy institutions or firms, nor the knowledge that they have built up through technological accumulation and institutional learning. The foundations on which technological learning has taken place can only be destroyed as a result of bad corporate or institutional management.[17]

- Design is central. Although design enters into R&D, most of it is distinct from R&D. Design does not always mean the generation of new knowledge, but it almost always requires a mix of written down, tacit and artistic knowledge. We argue in Chapter 7 that design is crucial in follower-firms.

These characteristics of technology (its heterogeneity – the diversity of its problem solving; the key role of tacit and local knowledge; its cumulative, evolutionary, continuous nature; where management is very firm and locality dependent; and where design is a key activity) make it complex, but point to the capabilities that are needed in follower-firms that aspire to build it. They point to the need to build on existing skills, to continuously improve production rather than looking for miracle 'big bangs'.

Technological capability as adding value

Studies of technical capability within nations and firms that stopped practising the myths were aimed at listing the key attributes of indigenous technological capability (ITC). That is what the subject has been called, but what ITC is really about is the ability of a particular firm or a nation to be competitive by continuously increasing firm or national value-added. Increases may show themselves in some combination of production efficiency, the introduction of new or improved products or processes, or mastery of complementary functions like sales, marketing and purchase. Competitiveness is meaningful only as a relative term, and so also is ITC. Since other nations and firms do not obligingly stand still, competitiveness can only be maintained and increased through continuous improvement and innovation to continuously increase value-added.

Capability building must focus on the firm

Over the past two decades, understanding of the role of technology in newly industrializing countries has undergone a sea-change. Practice of the myths has had disastrous implications, combined with a new interest of looking within the black box of technology to see just what capabilities were developing. Behind the six myths was the biggest myth of all – that technology was a 'policy issue', more for nations and governments than firms. On the contrary, technology is developed largely in firms, and looking within technology's black box means looking within firms. The aim of indigenous technological capability building is to grow value-added.

But where does ITC come from? Figure 1.1 illustrates the dynamic interplay between *access* to knowledge external to the country or firm (international technology transfer), the *endowment* (education, entrepreneurship and culture) that one starts with, and the *effort* put in (learning). While each of these elements is important, the interplay between them is especially important. The policy environment (detailed in Chapter 3) forms the backdrop.

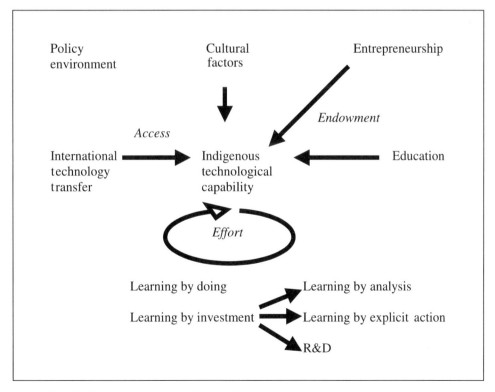

Figure 1.1   Indigenous technological capability.

Endowment

The endowment building blocks are key, but this is far beyond our scope here. Clearly, India's software industry is built on a strong and early commitment to higher technical education. Entrepreneurship plays the key role in making the right things happen (a subject we return to in Chapter 5 and again in Chapter 9). And culture, 'the way things get done', is crucial to building the right capabilities (see Chapter 8). Here, we focus on accessing the right technology in the right way, and the subsequent effort put into taking this technology further.

Access: technology transfer to build technological capability

Technological capability in an industrializing country firm generally begins with the import of technology from a more industrialized country. Early theories of technology transfer saw technology as a precise, well-defined body of knowledge, something that could be instantly mastered by accessing the right technology sitting on a shelf. But, as we suggested in myth 5, technology is more complex than that.

Successful technology transfer involves appreciation of several key points, all needing to be learned the hard way:

1   It is almost always sensible to access technology instead of developing it in-house. It may be necessary to pay for it, but the cost is generally far below the cost of developing it afresh. As Dore pointed out for Japan:

> Between 1950 and 1978 during which time the Japanese bought the bulk of the new knowledge produced in the West between 1940 and 1978 (including the big wartime production), they paid out to foreigners – in royalties, outright purchase, returns on equity participation, etc – $9 billion. Putting that sum in constant 1978 dollars would increase it, but would not bring it near the $60 billion-odd which was spent on R&D by the US alone in the single year of 1978.[18]

Japan may well have had the best conditions for successful negotiation of technology transfer of this type, with excellent human capabilities, strong firms and innovative government ministries. But other nations have also found that buying technology is almost always cheaper than building it in-house, even when there are many failures, a relatively weak capability to negotiate terms and restrictive clauses, and the necessity of adapting the technologies to local needs.

2   Technology transfer, as Dore points out, is not 'primarily a matter of whether or not rich country multinationals will hand over hardware or industrial property rights' but a matter of 'getting knowledge which is only in some foreigner's heads into the heads of one's own nationals.'[19] The need to think of technology transfer as more than the transfer of blue-prints and machinery, to include know-how and the need to learn and adapt has been known for at least four decades. In the 1960s and 1970s this realization provoked a major critique of multinational corporations that controlled and sold technology. More recently, with the realization of just how key is tacit knowledge, there has been increased effort to build the capability to transfer the 'softer' elements of technology, especially in East and South-East Asia. It has long been well known that technology transfer is costly. Niosi *et al.*[20] in their empirical study of 50 major international projects conducted

by the largest Canadian engineering consulting companies, found that the key costs were to build human capabilities, with training costs often much higher than expected. These costs were much higher than costs associated with adapting technologies and with development work.

3 The price of technology cannot be estimated through conventional economic analysis. For the seller, the technology was developed for it to make profit by selling the products of the technology, not the technology itself. 'Neither buyer nor seller of technology seem to have a clear idea of the value of the commodity they are trading ... Royalty rates may simply be a function of the negotiating skills of the parties involved.'[21]

4 A firm can exercise greater control over technology if it 'unpackages' it, or separates the technological component from the associated supply of investment, capital goods, managers, raw materials and intermediates, and so on. At the very least, separating these out allows the firm to choose the best alternatives, and build up knowledge of the package's make-up. Knowing how to unpackage often results in a lower cost, since one need buy only those bits really needed. Unpacking is desirable, but comes at a cost – doing it effectively necessarily involves a high degree of ITC. That is why technological capability and technology transfer are so interwoven.

Technology management as the effective deployment of effort

Technology transfer has mostly been analysed as an issue of negotiating the initial deal, and the initial import of machinery, perhaps also getting it to work for the first time. However, it is day-to-day effort which results in indigenous technology capability, and development of ITC which improves future technology transfer: unpackaging requires effort. How do firms best develop innovative in-house capabilities together with acquiring and assimilating outside technology? Technology management is the effective deployment of effort. It involves building technological, entrepreneurial and learning competences.

1 technological competence: the ability to master the particular technologies relevant to the needs of the enterprise;
2 entrepreneurial competence: the ability to generate and implement strategies for research and development coherently linked to the enterprise strategy, taking account of long-term trends in the evolution of technology, markets and competition;

3 learning ability: the ability to adapt organizationally and culturally in order to accommodate technological change.[22]

More recently, the term 'knowledge management' has increased in importance as a part of technology management, partly as a means of opening up the technology management arena to include a more detailed inclusion of intangibles. Nonaka and Takeuchi have argued not only that tacit and explicit knowledge are different, which is obvious, but that they are complementary and that knowledge is created by social interaction between them.[23] They argue further that Japanese companies are successful because they are better than western companies at tacit to tacit conversion – the creation of shared mental models – and therefore at the ability to mobilize tacit knowledge for innovation. This insight is obviously crucial for those who wish to build the innovatory capabilities of follower-firms, which are full of tacit knowledge and contain less of the codified, explicit, formal forms of knowledge.

The effort required to build technological capability can be separated into two categories: learning by doing, and learning by investment. *Learning by doing* is a passive, automatic and costless by-product of production. While it plays a vital role in building industrial competitiveness, the environment in which it takes place is all-important. As Bhagwati points out, in a strong import-substitution environment, learning by doing can easily become learning to do – often at any cost and quality.[24] What matters is learning by doing within an appropriate environment, which results in learning to be internationally competitive, as we shall see in Chapter 3.

Learning by investment is more complex since it involves at least three categories:

1   *Learning by analysing* involves the careful study of what the firm is doing now, such that it can improve it. The first step in improving a process often is to codify it; the best example of learning by analysing is traditional industrial engineering in firms. By breaking a job into its constituent parts, documenting each process and then analysing each step, the firm learns.[25] Learning by analysing also includes reverse engineering, where a competitor's product is taken apart to see how it was made.

2   *Learning by explicit action* covers a variety of actions that are anything but costless, passive and automatic. The best example is training, both within and outside the firm. An outstanding example is the Korean steel firm Posco. Posco sent over 1,300 engineers overseas for training in its initial stages. Other ways of learning by explicit action include importing foreign specialists for local workers to learn from. The distinction is between a foreign specialist brought in to *do* something and brought in to *learn from*.

3   Last is *research and development*. Although R&D is often perceived, as described in myth 6, as the most obvious investment to make for ITC, for it to be productive the context is key. R&D in a technology-follower environment has a distinctive role to play and must be organized appropriately for it to be worthwhile (see Chapter 6).

Innovation management in follower-firms

What being a technology-follower means

We conclude this chapter by setting out the innovation task in technology-followers. Technology-leader *countries* are those which collectively define the technological frontier at any point in time *and move it forward*. In practice it is unlikely that any one country will be pushing forward the technology frontier in all sectors. The US might define and move forward the frontier in aerospace, while Japan does so in automobile manufacturing and Switzerland in food processing. It is probably more accurate to talk of *sub-sectors* – braking systems, or avionics or microcomputers. It is certainly more accurate to talk of technology-leader *firms* that operate in countries within particular innovation systems. Successful innovation in technology-leaders requires two achievements: first, a commercially correct definition of the new frontier, and second, the activities involved in reaching it. There is uncertainty in both these tasks, and the challenges involved will depend on the specific innovation. That contingency is important can easily be exemplified with the rather simplistic difference between innovating the next generation RAM chip, a generic pill against a range of cancers and the manufacture of laser printers for the first time in a particular country, say India.

The technology-follower innovation required in producing laser printers in India for the first time is quite different both in its technological uncertainty and the technical effort required. Technology-follower countries (and firms within them) may be far, near, or even at the technology frontier for particular industries or sub-sectors, but are generally not involved in pushing it forward. For technology-followers *the future is already shaped*. Technology-follower countries and firms usually approach the frontier through the transfer of technology from a technology-leader, avoiding reinventing the wheel. The innovation task in this example is to *learn* how to make laser printers efficiently. The laser printer exists as a product; the future is specified. There is also less uncertainty – it is known that making a laser printer is possible, and that as a product it is commercially successful.

But does this mean, then, that the innovative task for technology-followers is a minor one of adapting imported technology to local conditions? Clearly not so. First, the technology-leader may not be willing to supply all the technology possessed. Second, technology has a large uncodified component. This tacit component means that even in the best case, where the supplier is willing to provide all the technology available, the receiver always ends up with less technology than the supplier has.[26] The follower is thus, by definition, behind the frontier to begin with. Reaching the technological frontier means that the receiver has to make up for this difference locally. Third, as the technology frontier is always moving, and that too at an increasing pace in many industries, if a follower does not progress technologically at more than the speed of the leader, it will not catch up. Indeed, one key mistake made in many developing countries in the 1960s and 1970s was precisely to see technology as static and technical change as a one-off change with technology transfer happening in one move. Fourth, even adaptation to local conditions often involves much more than minor adaptation. Tackling problems thrown up by local materials, labour, market and environment requires a major development effort. Finally, the development of new products to move up the value-chain of international manufacturing directly demands substantial technical effort. The first four innovative tasks make up a large proportion of the follower task – but missing the fifth is to miss an increasingly important task.

To summarize, a technology-follower is not concerned with the generation of new technology. The frontier is defined by the technology-leader. The follower approaches the frontier by transferring technology from a relative leader. Even if the technology-leader is willing to provide all the technology available, the tacit dimension and dynamic nature of technology requires considerable innovation on the part of the receiver to keep up with the technological frontier. The conclusion is that the innovation task in technology-followers is not less difficult, but it is very different.

Overall, the technology-follower might begin by building *process innovation* capability on the ground/shop-floor with the aim of being as efficient as other producers, but must then move beyond competing on price to competing on product features (from *process to product,* from increasing efficiency of *processes* to higher value-added *products*). At its most basic, both types of innovation aim at the addition of value-added per employee. Both product and process require major *cultural change* in the enterprise.

Putting what we have learned from the myths together with our discussion about indigenous technology capability, we are now in a position to identify some key propositions on the innovation task in technology-followers. To those who accept 'new' innovation studies, the propositions may seem uncontroversial. However, together we believe they suggest a basic direction for technology-followers that moves away from traditional linear model practices. The issue is how to break old and develop new practices, by taking up relatively small but essential propositions and avoiding other well-meaning but complicating ideas.

Incremental innovation is key

It is not unusual to note that innovation is more a matter of thousands of small improvements in product and process, and less a matter of radical leaps forward. The radical leaps are seen and noticed, but they are few and far between – and essentially the preserve of technology-leaders pushing out the frontier. But it is simplistic to think of innovation in either incremental or radical terms. Innovation is more a continuum from incremental to radical and a combination of incremental and radical, what Tushman and Nelson call: 'the essential interplay between major and incremental innovation' over the course of the product cycle.'[27] A radical innovation can provide fertile ground for subsequent incremental innovations, often in follower-companies.

The analysis of innovation as a leap process followed by subsequent steps applies both in technology-leaders and followers. In leaders, the leap can be a *new technological paradigm*, often followed by a stream of incremental improvements that 'sets in' the new paradigm and brings major commercial returns. But in followers, smaller innovations can be for that firm just as big a leap, a new technological paradigm of a kind, one that is *new to the firm*. The firm acquires this paradigm by transferring technology from a technology-leader. Thus, for a follower, transferring technology can be just as new and complex as a big innovation in a leader. And just as a radical innovation in a leader requires subsequent incremental improvement, technology transfer also needs constant incremental improvement if the follower is to keep up or catch up. Why? Because the follower is behind the frontier by definition. As the technology-leader continues to improve the technology, even keeping up requires incremental innovation. Catching up requires incremental innovation at a faster pace than in the leader.

Incremental innovation is then, we argue, the primary source of long-run competitiveness in technology-followers.

Process innovation

Process innovation (making things better) will often be more important than *product* innovation (making better things), but both process *and* product innovation matter and are different at different stages in industrial development. Most industries in technology-followers are more mature and established. As an industry matures, the innovation drivers change from technical performance to cost competition. When cost-cutting becomes more important, process innovation matters more. Riggs argued in the mid-1980s that the Japanese industrial 'miracle' until the mid-1970s was built around process innovation and, to a lesser extent, incremental product innovation.[28] More subtly, innovation is a *unity* of product and process. This is the essence of design for manufacturability. As an example, Hewlett-Packard's subsidiary in Singapore reduced manufacturing cost of the HP 41C calculator by 50 per cent by redesigning the product to use fewer components. This case illustrates well that products may be changed to improve the manufacturing process, and vice versa. Chapter 5 takes up the process/product innovation issue in more detail.

Shop-floor innovation

Innovation arising in day-to-day operations, thrown back from 'day-to-day' work problems, is the major source of cost-saving on the shop-floor. A 'bottleneck approach' has been formulated as an explicit means to use shop-floor innovation as manufacturing strategy. By removing all 'fat' from the system (buffer stock, for example, in just-in-time systems), production becomes very sensitive to small problems, which may bring the whole process to a halt. When one bottleneck is removed, the system is further 'tweaked' to force out another one, which can again be solved. In this way, problems are systematically eliminated instead of being concealed in the fat. Chapter 4 takes up these issues of shop-floor innovation.

The organizational, cultural and managerial

Building an environment where innovation happens everywhere is crucial to firm technical capability, in followers as much as leaders. For incremental innovation to be powerful, it has to be widespread and continuous. Quality circles, suggestion schemes, *kaizen* continuous improvement programmes and other techniques, known sometimes as Japanese management techniques,[29] are systematic ways of capturing creativity across the organization.

There are many variables that go into the crucial issue of building an innovation culture. A most important barrier is a subtle combination of 'not invented here' and 'foreign is better', which is quite lethal to technological effort (and quite pervasive in technology-followers). What is this combination? The *not invented here* (NIH) syndrome, where firms cast a supercilious eye on learning from outside the firm, is often combined with a big exception in its gaze – *foreign is better* (FIB) (see Figure 1.2). The result is an attitude and practices against fiddling with imported technology – a feeling that it cannot be improved on locally. Instead, the objective is to be as close as possible to the foreign firm's quality, and to never attempt improvement. International competitiveness requires cultural confidence, which permits a combination of openness to learning from others and pride internally that takes nothing as given, regardless of nationality. We focus on these cultural issues in Chapter 8.

The role of R&D

The role of R&D in a technology-follower will be different. An obvious role is to solve problems that arise in manufacturing which cannot be solved on the shop-floor and need the special collection of skills embodied in an R&D department. Some newly industrializing countries spend, by developing country standards, relatively large amounts on in-firm R&D. In 1998 South Korea spent $5.4 billion on corporate R&D, while India's total corporate R&D, spread over 1,000 firms, came to $450 million. However, General Motors alone spent $7.9 billion. These examples, and there are many more, drive home the point that technology-followers cannot hope to compete with technology-leaders in R&D spending. But they do not need to, because the role

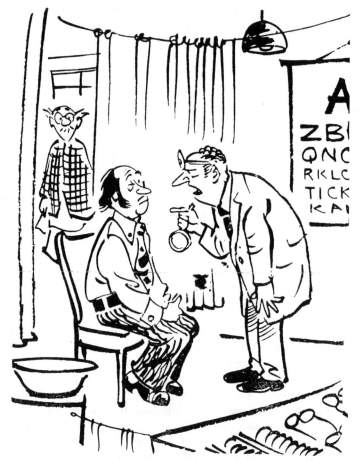

Figure 1.2   Laxman cartoon. 'There is some foreign matter in your eye. Would you like to keep it since it's foreign?'

of R&D in a follower environment is quite different. We said earlier that the future is known for a technology-follower. Briefly, the R&D task in a technology-follower is to build absorptive (learning) capacity so that the firm can effectively access work done elsewhere. The different role of R&D in a follower, in turn, demands that R&D is organized differently, and we devote Chapter 6 to it.

Design

Efforts to build indigenous technological capability have often missed out the need to build indigenous design capability. By design capability, we mean the ability to conceptualize a product to achieve certain design performance characteristics, both aesthetic (form) and performance (function). A new design, a new form and function, is concerned with 'matching techniques and markets'.[30] Design tends to be market driven rather than technology driven, with technology providing the capability to meet new market needs.

We argue, above all, that technology-followers should be concerned with new design. It is design that can provide the means to move from a process to a mixed product–process innovation style in a firm. We further argue that the design and technology frontiers are distinct so that it is quite feasible to push out the design frontier while being a technology-follower. Indeed by focusing on building design capability, a technology-follower can capture a higher value-added market segment. Developing new designs is an intermediate point on the innovation continuum, a jump in capability, within an existing technological paradigm, but beyond incremental innovation. Chapter 7 takes up these issues in detail.

Conclusion: growing value-added in firms is the core objective

Technology has been seen as essential to development at least since the Second World War. Until the late 1970s, developing countries were seen as more or less passive recipients of technology transferred from developed countries. Since then, focus has shifted to the study of technological capability *in* developing countries. Much of the difference between countries that have developed rapidly and those that have developed more slowly is a difference in indigenous technological capability, and how that technological capability has been used. ITC itself is all about continuously growing value-added by innovating. It is easily forgotten, however, that national ITC is the sum of all firm-level ITCs. Industrial innovation happens in firms and the firm must be the centre of all analysis of industrial technology.

Value can be added in different ways. At its simplest, value is added by putting more people to work in a higher value-added activity – that is the story of Mexico's maquiladoras, the Indian software industry and China's export manufacturers. But value can also be added through innovation, through the deployment of local effort to manage technology in firms. Some exceptional follower-firms have been very successful at growing value-added, and have almost closed the gap with leaders. For the bulk of others, the potential still remains, with firms spread out along a spectrum ranged from barely moving to almost there. In Chapter 2, we study some prominent successes, including some of the firms that have just about closed the gap. Also in Chapter 2, and in smaller cases throughout the book, we cover the lesser successes, and draw some comparisons with those barely moving. These cases provide a mine of illustration for us to draw on in subsequent more analytically focused chapters. In Chapter 4, we show how value can be added, indeed *must* be added, in every firm by innovating on the shop-floor. In Chapter 5, we introduce the need for a move to more proprietary innovation, and the move up the value-chain to products. In Chapters 6 and 7, we discuss how product innovation can be organized in R&D, and focused on building design capabilities. And in Chapter 8, we discuss the components of an effective innovation culture in follower-firms. Finally, in Chapter 9, we pull together action for firms that seek to implement constant value-added growth. Although our focus is the firm, the firm itself operates within a specific national policy environment. Some great successes, as we will see, have grown in the most surprising and inhospitable of policy environments. But an effective policy environment can play the key role in enabling the great bulk of firms to make the move up the value-chain. How the policy environment has been effective or disastrous in the past is the subject of Chapter 3. In Chapter 9, with action points for firms, we will return also to the implications of policy for states seeking to enable the bulk of their firms to go from followers to leaders.

2 Innovation success in follower-firms

Introduction

In this chapter we present a range of relatively successful firms from three countries on three continents, from five different sectors – brewing, bicycles, glass, cement and software. One firm, Cemex, is a world leader in the cement industry and in one decade has closed the gap to become the world's third largest and, of these top three, the most profitable. The others have not achieved Cemex's success but have made significant advances in production, growing value and improving competitiveness, nationally and sometimes internationally. Three were set up in strongly protected environments and have recently had to become more efficient and innovative. One is in a highly export-oriented and competitive industry but is still well behind the world leaders. The chapter illustrates, then, a variety of success in moving up the value-chain in a range of firms and industries.

To what extent have the firms succeeded by following patterns set out in Chapter 1? We look particularly at: How important has shop-floor innovation been? What is the importance of process and product innovation? Has R&D played a role in the firm's success? Has design been key? How important have firm culture and management been? And how have firms responded to international competition?

Each case will examine the criteria for innovation success, introducing some key questions affecting where these firms go from here. These will be taken up in Chapter 9.

Tanzania Breweries Ltd*

Company background

Tanzania Breweries Ltd (TBL) represents an attempt to rehabilitate an important national producer, via privatization. As a case of rehabilitation and privatization it is a success story. As a case of local capability building it is less successful.

---

* The material for this case is based on Economic and Social Research Foundation (ESRF), *Tanzania Breweries Limited Before and After Privatization,* mimeo, Dar Es Salaam, 1996 and H.H. Semboja and J. Kweka, 'Divesture impact and privatization process in Tanzania', paper presented at the International Conference, Manchester University, July 1997. Collected by the Economic and Social Research Foundation, Dar Es Salaam. Many thanks to them, and Professor Sam Wangwe for these data.

TBL was set up in Tanzania in the 1920s. It was nationalized in 1976, and merged with a second nationalized brewery. It was privatized in 1993, with South African Breweries as main owner and the government with a share of 15 per cent in 2000.

In the decade before privatization, it suffered from lack of investment and weak management. A significant US$6 million investment in Czech technology in the late 1980s and early 1990s failed dismally. There was a lack of internal innovative capacity to deal with rehabilitation, a general decline in the Tanzanian economy and little capacity in the state-owned industrial sector to cope with global liberalization.

TBL initiated its own denationalization, unlike most state companies in Tanzania. The process was very open, involving all employees and the board in decision-making on how to privatize. South African Breweries (SAB), the fourth biggest brewing company in the world, was keen for TBL to increase its competitiveness relative to neighbouring countries. The change of management to a South African Breweries team has been associated with 'dramatic improvements in firm performance' – production increases, rehabilitation, marketing, technological capabilities and improved supplier links.

The TBL mission and vision statement was ambitious: 'to be a successful brewer and marketer of quality beers being recognized as a good corporate citizen by stakeholders' and to be recognized 'as the most successful and best run Tanzanian enterprise by the year 2000'. The statement then focused on six key values: product quality, continuous improvement, wealth creation for all stakeholders, employee development (of individuals and teams), health and safety and customer service.

TBL owns three breweries, barley farms and a malting company. It owns the major beer brand in Tanzania, Safari, which dominates production. TBL has decided to concentrate on Safari, which implies that it has decided to focus on the internal market, and not attempt to build up export markets.

Process/shop-floor issues and innovations

Overall

Production increased by 320 per cent from 1993 to 1999 by which time TBL had over 80 per cent of the domestic market, breaking the hold of imported beer, mostly from Kenya. Capacity utilization increased from below 20 per cent in 1992 to more than 65 per cent in 1996. Productivity increased from 180 hectolitres per employee in 1993 to 600 in 1995, and 1,066 in 1999. However, highest international levels are around 3,000.

Employment has dropped significantly, from 2,800 in 1993 to 1,750 in 1996. Employee recompense increased by almost 500 per cent in seven years, not including medical assistance for families, free tea and lunch. Minimum pay increased six times. The goal is to ensure 8 days training per employee per year, with 5.6 days achieved by 1999. TBL invested half a million dollars in a training centre and has set up an annual training budget of $1.5 million.

Product quality improved dramatically – from 1.5 to 5.1 in international measures (Independent Rating System out of 10). Profits also improved from negative in 1993, to US$14 million profit in 1995 to $32 million in 1999. First dividends of $8 million were paid in 1995, including $3.2 millon to government to add to the $42 million tax revenue – itself a massive increase.

Technological capability

Rehabilitation costs between 1993 and 1996 were US$18 million. Major redesign of plant layout was necessary to facilitate the effective operation of the existing Czech equipment. Rehabilitation involved not only repair of equipment but establishing new changing rooms, dining rooms, transport, etc. Other key changes have been made to the production process to enable it to use more local ingredients and to save energy.

Quality control systems have been improved, with 49 staff. TBL introduced sophisticated quality control systems, initiated the ISO 9000 system in 1995, and worked with the Tanzania Bureau of Standards to ensure ISO 9000 was fully implemented.

Energy-saving efforts have paid off handsomely. Electricity per hectolitre was halved between 1993 and 1995, water consumption dropped to one-third, and boiler oil to around one-quarter. This is now at global standards for best energy efficiency. TBL has also invested around $23m in waste treatment of materials from plant.

Linkages

TBL has emphasized supplier linkage with the aim of improving the quality of local suppliers and of lowering import costs, an initiative called 'partnership in profit'. Innovative initiatives include support for national R&D institutes to assist with the improvement of barley production. TBL is also examining the possibility of producing one-use bottles to facilitate exports. It has spent time assisting with quality improvement of the glass bottle, bottle top crown corks and sugar production. In one case, paper label production, it was unable to get the quality it needed and is now producing its own labels.

Distribution warehouses have been cut from twenty-four to twelve, and those remaining have been improved. In other locations, local private distributors are now trained and used.

Product innovation, R&D and design

Product innovation has so far been weak. The emphasis has been on improving quality and productivity of the local Safari beer. Castle canned lager has been imported for sale from South Africa, but there do not seem to be plans to produce it locally, for local consumption or export.

TBL has invested in barley growing R&D to test new hybrid varieties, together with a government agricultural station and the Agricultural University, and has supported three senior research staff to work with these institutions.

Design is also rather weak. Brewing is a strongly brand intensive business and TBL has begun market research, consultations with employees and customers to get feedback, has increased advertising to 0.5 per cent of budget and is, for example, sponsoring soccer sports leagues. It has taken care to improve its labelling systems – Safari Beer was famous for having labels with glue so poor that it allowed the labels to crumble or to fall off altogether. Safari was often the beer with no label.

Conclusions and questions

The key issues in the immediate future concern: the building of local managerial capabilities and export capabilities; and improvement of public policy on industrial competitiveness.

Local management capability

TBL has dramatically improved processes but it is not clear how robust process-innovation capabilities are in the longer term. Local management capability needs to be improved.

Export competitiveness

TBL remains a nationally oriented firm. TBL argues that it is too early to export – they need to improve quality first. It is also true that the government taxation system does not reward export. Finally, before export can begin, there is also the technical need to begin production of non-returnable beer bottles for export. One means of improving competitiveness would be to aim at gaining export markets, beginning in Kenya. TBL is almost certainly being bench-marked against other companies in the South African Breweries group. A good means of assessing TBL then is to compare its position with other companies in the group.

Public policy

Infrastructure is still very weak and firms often have to set up their own infrastructure at high cost. For example, they drill for their own water, buy electricity generators, and use cellnet rather than landline phones.

Government services have not improved either. Government bureaucracy is a major constraint. In the case of TBL, there is weak government support for inward investment and export promotion. One example was when the Investment Promotion Centre responsible for assisting new investors could not clear new equipment through customs, even after direct links with the Treasury. A convoluted tax structure places a higher tax on locally produced beer than on imports. And TBL has been unable to change government policy to lower taxes on beer destined for export.

Overall, the case of TBL illustrates what can be done quickly in very unpromising circumstances. It suggests that a lot more can be done, and that this depends on local institution building.

Questions

For TBL to move further up the value-ladder:

- Can the government, given its share in the enterprise, negotiate with SAB to build local technological capabilities, beginning with shop-floor innovation (see Chapter 4)?
- To what extent is TBL's recent success based on a protected local market? To what extent does TBL need protection? And can a gradual lowering of tariffs help build local competitiveness and also export competitiveness?

- Will TBL be able to expand internationally? Can the government increase incentives to export and build international competitiveness? Does SAB impose restrictions on export which the government can use its share holding to change?

Hero Cycles: success through flexible specialization

Company background

Light-engineering industry in Ludhiana, an industrial town in Punjab, India, has been the focus of much research since the mid-1990s on the role of history in transition to industrial clusters[1] and the dynamic patterns of small-firm growth in an industrial district.[2] A noteworthy case is the bicycle industry and particularly Hero Cycles (HC). What started off as a modest business of bicycle spare parts in Amritsar in 1944, in 2000 produced over 16,000 cycles a day. Hero Cycles claims to have been the world's largest manufacturer of bicycles since 1987.

The shift to Ludhiana after Partition in 1947 provided the initial impetus to the business. Kattuman hypothesizes that: 'The post-partition influx of refugees brought into Punjab considerable entrepreneurial energy and fed it with a wealth of skills [giving rise to] a flexible skilled labour market in towns like Ludhiana.'[3] Hero Cycles benefited from Ludhiana developing as a centre for engineering goods production.

In 1956, Hero began manufacturing complete bicycles. Production began on a relatively small scale – 639 bicycles in 1956. Nevertheless, Hero was better able to capitalize on the buoyant demand of the period than the leading Indian bicycle firms at that time.

O.P. Munjal, one of the founder directors, recalls how Hind Cycles of Bombay, the then dominant player, fell behind through its cost structure. Their practice of paying piece rates to workers translated into a cost disadvantage when smaller groups such as Hero and Avon were able to produce higher volume bicycles at much cheaper rates. Hero operated with fixed wage rates from inception.

HC's success shows in its performance in both domestic and export markets. Domestic sales increased to nearly 5 million in 1999 with a 52 per cent share of the domestic market. HC started exporting bicycles to neighbouring countries and East Africa in the early 1960s. Today, it exports bicycles and cycle parts to over 85 countries including the USA, Germany, France and the UK. Exports accounted for 9 per cent of total output in 1999 and the major share of exports in the 1990s went to France, Sri Lanka and Uganda. Hero ancillaries also command a significant presence in the export market. Rockman Cycles produces 25,000 chains a day, exporting 25 per cent of its output.

Table 2.1   Some data on Hero Cycles

	1990	1995	1999	2000
Turnover (Rs Million)	2,050	4,626	6,970	8,269
Profit (Rs Million)	76	205	381	406
Sales (000's)	2,920	4,049	4,948	

Process/shop-floor issues and innovations

Starting as a low-cost manufacturer, Hero emphasized efficiency from its foundation. Hero's founder explains:

> I would sit with workers during production hours and observe each one carefully. After the workday was over I would hold back the best worker and see the maximum he could produce of a given part in a given time. The next day each worker would be told to achieve the same rate of produce (productivity). Following this, a time-rate target was laid down for each bicycle part – x pieces in an hour; the workers were expected to achieve this target. I in turn attended the courses offered at the National Productivity Council.[4]

Hero followed a policy of deliberate increases in production and wages each year. So what led a small firm such as Hero, operating in a vertically disintegrated production organization, to surpass the established, integrated and sophisticated manufacturers of its time and go on to achieve a dominant share of the world's second largest bicycle market?

Just-in-time

Hero Cycles has a striking just-in-time (JIT) arrangement. JIT at Hero Cycles has existed almost as long as the company, much before the concept itself came to be formally known as JIT. The arrangement evolved as a natural response to the lack of working capital – a direct parallel to Toyota.

> Until 1983, the company operated solely through its own finance. As a result, continuous expansion required a constant need to minimize costs especially in the beginning when the company was still in its fledgling state. The direct onslaught of this fell on inventory, giving rise to the JIT arrangement.[5]

JIT required local sourcing of most raw materials and the company benefited from its location in Ludhiana with its strong engineering base. Most parts were sourced from local vendors who had mushroomed in and around Ludhiana by the early 1950s. 'By 1953, there were at least 400 small manufacturers of bicycle components.'[6]

Over time, Hero Cycles has internalized the production of some capital-intensive parts in wholly owned ancillaries. The requirements for these parts were high enough to sustain their independent production and this has helped Hero cut costs, providing it with greater control over the production process. In 1990, it integrated backwards to set up its own steel cold rolling division in Ludhiana.

As a result, apart from generic raw materials like paints, chemicals and leather, all other raw materials, semi-finished and finished components are sourced locally in Ludhiana.

Suppliers

Hero Cycles has 340 permanent suppliers, two-thirds captive to HC alone. Most suppliers started out as small manufacturers operating from workshops. Most are still family-owned enterprises with some family members now professionally qualified. They have grown considerably, such that there now exists a near equal mix of small, medium and large suppliers. HC's largest vendor supplies it with handles and handle assemblies employing around 700 people. HC's ancillaries, Rockman Cycles and Highway Cycles, supply chains, hubs and freewheels, employing more than a thousand people; and Rockman Cycles exports 25 per cent of its output. The smallest ones are individual households or cottage industries supplying items like cotton bags and fasteners employing under 30 people. The average number of suppliers for any item is four. The maximum number of vendors for any item is six, as in the case of tube liners. Most vendors are located within a radius of 10 km, with the nearest ones less than 2 km away. Vendors ship by truck and inspection of material is HC's responsibility.

The JIT arrangement ensures deliveries into the factory from 10 a.m. to 8 p.m. Frequency of supply varies. Some deliveries of bulky items such as tyres occur every two hours. Other more specialized parts are supplied once every five or six days. Hero's in-house subsidiaries, Rockman Cycles and Highway Cycles, are also part of this JIT arrangement. Stock at Hero Cycles is continually replenished during the day.

Operating in a vertically disintegrated production organization, HC maintains close links with all suppliers. Every component is completely specified from drawings to gauges. Hero's tool room produces the gauges used by suppliers. Every six months the gauges are re-calibrated by Hero. There is thus complete standardization and interchangeability between HC and the supplier. Control over the process is ensured and consistency in quality maintained. As such, quality remains Hero's responsibility.

Hero Cycles maintains a 'Vendor Development Section' that has been in place since inception. Engineers conduct daily visits to suppliers to sort out immediate problems with focus on process control. In the case of new products or modifications in existing products, the relevant technology is diffused to suppliers. Hero exposes vendor management to skill development programmes either at Hero or external organizations like the local National Productivity Council and the Institute of Autoparts Technology. Once a year Hero holds a workshop for all vendors.

Working in a cluster environment obviates dependence on a single supplier. If a supplier supplies poor quality materials or delivers late, there is a built-in penalty, as unfulfilled demand is immediately split among the balance suppliers. Suppliers thus must have the capacity to respond flexibly to fluctuations in demand.

Hero routinely invests in process improvements. For instance, vacuum-moulded polyurethane saddles are made in a fully automated plant, the only one of its kind in India. Other technical improvements include robotic welding and electro-static painting.

Since 1990, Hero Cycles has used several external consultancy services. McKinsey was hired in 1997 to conduct a one-year study on performance improvement. In 1998, IBM Global Service did a one-year study on layout and material handling.

Product, R&D and design issues

Until the early 1990s, Hero's growth was based on one model, the Roadster, which was its only product. Since then, Hero has moved into more specialized product segments. The cluster arrangement in Ludhiana made it easy to source specialized parts from local vendors – a prime feature of flexible production (a subject of Chapter 4). Today, about 25 per cent of output is specialized bicycles. The specialized segment of the domestic market is projected to grow at 15 to 18 per cent while the mass market grows at just 3 per cent. The company targets 50 per cent specialized output by 2010. As profit margins for specialized bicycles are twice that of standard bicycles, Hero is consciously moving up the value-chain.

HC established an in-house R&D department in 1994 which employs 22 people with an annual R&D expenditure of Rs10 million (0.12 per cent of turnover). The department introduces 8–10 new models into the domestic market and about 15–20 models into the international market each year. Exports are often original equipment manufacturer (OEM) requirements* where finished bicycles are developed by Hero R&D against the particular OEM specifications of a foreign brand.

Models introduced into the domestic market are generally product adaptations of their export cousins, adapted to Indian conditions. New design features include both cosmetic and functional improvements. For instance, a rear mudguard for women's bicycles was provided following customer suggestions and a polyurethane saddle was introduced in the 'Ranger' model, which provides better cushioning.

Questions

Hero Cycles has grown to become the dominant producer in the world's second largest bicycle market, with some very successful diversifications – its joint venture with Honda for the manufacture of motorcycles, Hero Honda, has a 45 per cent share of the motorcycle market, and in late 2000 overtook Bajaj Auto to become the country's largest two-wheeler manufacturer. What questions can one raise about so successful a company? There are two key areas of concern: first, manufacturing cost. Hero is by far India's most efficient bicycle manufacturer and its success in exporting to Europe and Africa shows that it is internationally efficient. In recent years, though, it has seen its exports to some markets (like the US) replaced by Chinese exports, and it finds that it cannot match Chinese costs. In 2000, China exported 20 million bicycles, four times more than Hero's total production. Although Hero produces standard bicycles at prices competitive with China, at the specialist, high-quality end Chinese bicycles are cheaper. Given that Hero has the necessary global scale of production as the world's largest manufacturer, how will it compete with China?

Second, Hero has moved rapidly up the product value-chain in recent years, with a growing share of output from higher value-added specialized bicycles in place of the generic black Roadster. Producing specialized bicycles involves building design skills and Hero has recently set up a design institute in Ludhiana in collaboration with the Italian design firm IDEA. As we will see in Chapter 7, design can play a key role in moving up the value-chain. Hero's ability to keep growing and to build export success may well depend on how effectively it builds design capability. How will it do that?

Grupo Vitro[†]

Company background

Mexico's economic opening continues. This case explores the effect of the increasing export orientation of the Mexican economy on the acquisition of technological

---

* OEM, original equipment manufacturer, is a specific form of sub-contracting where a follower-firm produces a finished product to the precise specification of an international firm which then sells it under its own brand name (see Chapter 5).

[†] The Vitro case has been very kindly provided to us by Cristina Casanueve.

learning and the development of technological capabilities by Vitro, a Mexican firm in the glass industry. We include a brief analysis of Vitro's competition in the glass market, Vitro's innovation strategy prior to the opening of markets and the evolution of this strategy. We compare the technological innovation embodied in the processes of glass manufacturing before and after market liberalization.

The Vitro group produces glass containers, flat glass, automotive glass, fibreglass, glassware and plastic containers, aluminium cans and household appliances for commercial, industrial and consumer use. Vitro supplies numerous industries, including food and beverage, construction and automotive.

Founded in 1909, Vitro comprises over 50 companies and subsidiaries (with its main facility in Monterrey, Mexico) and employs 33,400 people in more than 100 facilities in seven countries. Vitro has strategic alliances with a dozen large corporations around the world, and exports products to more than 60 countries world-wide.

The integration of all of Vitro's product lines has allowed it to grow as an international business group. Vitro is now organized into: glass containers, flat glass, diverse industries, glassware and household products.

Competitiveness

Vitro flourished for several decades in a protected market. Vitro's success was based on effective operational management and relatively easy access to the Mexican market, and to technology. Vitro depended on licensed technology.

The market has changed for Vitro since Mexico joined the WTO and NAFTA. Tariffs have been reduced from 16 per cent *ad valorem* in 1994 to zero in 2001.

The liberalization of the Mexican economy has represented a major challenge to Vitro's business strategy. Originally oriented to the domestic market, today Vitro faces large, technologically advanced competitors: Pilkington from Britain, Saint Gobain from France, Owens-Corning and others from the US and Asahi Glass, Nippon Glass and Central Glass from Japan.

Faced with intense competition, Vitro has reoriented to compete globally. This has shaped both Vitro's business strategy and its innovation strategy. As a result, Vitro's export sales have grown at an annual rate of 11 per cent between 1993 and 1997.

Innovation strategy before market opening

Vitro's innovation strategy was mainly focused on maintaining efficient operation of manufacturing processes by strengthening both process and product engineering capabilities. Technology was transferred through licensing and partnership with foreign glass producers and technology world leaders. In flat glass, Vitro's technology partners were Pilkington, Monsanto and Ford; in the container business, the technology suppliers were Owens-Brockway and Vetro Pack; in glass machine manufacturing, Vitro's technology partner was Owens Illinois; and in glassware, the partners were Libbey and Ishizuka.

Before market opening, Vitro's business strategy was based on economies of scale and vertical integration of production. Although the business was successful and margins high, this came from market protection more than international competitiveness. Little attention was paid to the selection of suppliers, operating costs, quality control, customer satisfaction or environmental concerns. There were long product and process cycles. Maintaining operations was the priority, and innovation and global competitiveness were not major concerns.

Evolution of innovation strategy resulting from market opening

In the late 1970s senior managers at Vitro anticipated globalization and aimed at achieving competitiveness in the glass industry with world-class standards and technology. This led to the creation of 'Vitrotec' in 1978, the first formal corporate R&D unit. Shortly after, Vitro created technology management centres at each operational unit.

Vitro faced pressures that prompted orientation to the global market before the opening up of the national market. For example, in flat glass, Vitro had to supply US auto assembly plants in Mexico which had a global mindset. The 1980s witnessed a changing pattern of integrating production operations across national boundaries. This globalization of industry, especially involving the car industry, was based on complementarity in production between developing and developed countries. The opportunity to participate in the global car industry compelled Vitro to enhance the value of its products and upgrade technology to meet new technical specifications and quality standards.

The containers division also faced incentives for greater internationalization of production. Environmental concerns of some US states opened up a niche for returnable glass containers. Vitro identified this need and upgraded and adapted the production of returnable bottles to take advantage of this new business opportunity. Orientation to new markets represented the challenge and opportunity to strengthen technological capabilities.

Current innovation strategy

The opening of the Mexican economy saw major world competitors, including the French glass manufacturing company Saint Gobain, start flat glass operations in Mexico, to take advantage of the North American car market.

The new innovation strategy resulted in better selection of strategic suppliers, and a strict programme of total quality management in all operations. The strategy emphasized more careful identification, selection, negotiation and acquisition of technology from external sources and more conscientious focus of R&D activities on areas where technology was not yet available in international markets.

Vitro's technological capabilities are evolving, from the acquisition of technology licenses and partnerships, to acquisition of a higher level of mastery of these technologies. This technological assimilation has resulted in more efficient operations, paving the way for fundamental innovations in glass manufacturing.

Vitro's technology effort and acquisition of firm technological capabilities

Lall distinguishes different levels of complexity and depth of technological capability, including *basic* (experience based), *adaptive* (search based) and *innovative* (research based) to illustrate the nature and range of skills involved (Table 2.2).[7]

- The basic level is related to 'technology mastery', building up the skills and capabilities needed to operate a technology efficiently. In Vitro's technology strategy, this level of technological capability is defined as 'operational maintenance' or 'technical performance'.
- The adaptive level refers to adaptations and improvements which raise the productivity of a given technology. In Vitro's technology strategy, this level of technological capability is defined as 'operational improvement'.[8] 'Incremental innovation' is the key issue; process innovation is more important than product innovation, but both product and process innovation matter.
- The innovative level refers to activities leading to the introduction of new products and processes. For Vitro's technology strategy this level of technological capability is called 'operational innovation'.

To assess the evolution of Vitro's technological capabilities, in response to new Mexican economic conditions, Casanueve's study identifies the main technologies embodied in the processes of glass manufacturing: (1) batch preparation; (2) glass melting/refining/conditioning; (3) glass forming; (4) processing and postforming; (5) finishing; and (6) design, distribution and commercialization.

Briefly, *batch preparation* consists of measuring and blending raw materials and delivering them to the glass furnace. *Glass melting/refining/conditioning* refers to the processes of decomposing, reacting, melting, homogenizing and refining raw materials, and preparing the melt to feed the forming machine. *Glass forming* consists of shaping the final glass product. *Processing and postforming* refers to the processes of stress relief and treatment for enhancing final glass product characteristics. *Finishing* refers to the activities of decoration, encapsulation and packaging of final products. Finally, *design, distribution and commercialization* consists of the information and communication infrastructure that supports design and support activities. *Design* consists of computer product design systems that allow the integration of market and client information and specifications of the product. In addition, computer ordering systems process orders, such as electronic data interchange to support all the in-bound and out-bound logistics handling and follow up (stock control, materials handling, dispatch, distribution, marketing and selling activities).

Table 2.2 Definitions and different levels of complexity and depth of technological capabilities

Levels of complexity and depth	Definitions	
	Lall's firm technological capabilities	*Vitro's definition of core competencies*
First level	Technology mastery (basic)	Maintenance of operation level
Second level	Minor innovation or incremental innovation (adaptive)	Improvement of operations
Third level	Major innovation (innovative)	Operational innovation

Sources: S. Lall, *Building Industrial Competitiveness in Developing Countries*, Paris: Organization for Economic Co-operation and Development, 1990; A. Pita, *Competencias Medulares Taller de Liderazgo en Tecnología*, mimeo, Monterrey: Vitro, 1998; SRI-International, *Key Terms in Indentifying Technical Core Competences*, Menlo Park, CA, 1994.

The list of glass technologies was reviewed by senior personnel in Vitro's R&D at both corporate and division levels. Some of the processes and their embodied technologies cut across the manufacturing process of flat glass, containers and glassware, while some are specific to each. Each technology was ranked according to complexity and depth in Vitro, based on the conceptual framework in Table 2.2. The level of technological development accomplished before and after the opening of the Mexican economy is compared in Table 2.3.

Table 2.3 shows that before market opening, Vitro emphasized mastery of production engineering and adaptation. With initiation of open markets, skills and capabilities were built in order to operate technologies more efficiently. Finally, as the market opened up, major innovation efforts began. By 1998, 42 per cent of technological effort was in technology mastery, 38 per cent in minor innovation and 16 per cent in major innovation. Innovative efforts tend to be more specialized; there is an attempt to master production engineering faster, and to make adaptations when this is required in order to increase exports. Exporting itself feeds back free information that promotes minor innovations and strengthens Vitro's technological capabilities.

Conclusions and questions

Despite its achievements, Vitro suffered a decline in market share along with a drop in operating margin from 17 per cent in 1996 to 13 per cent in the first half of 2000. While it remained one of the top three glass producers in the world there was a visible decline in the company's performance over 1998–2000. The main reason cited for this was the heavy competition from manufacturers of plastic and aluminium bottles in its core business of glass containers. Over 1998–99 the market for glass containers contracted by 10 per cent resulting in a like fall. The company was also hit by over half a dozen high level resignations in 2000.

Table 2.3 Technological capability improvements at Vitro, 1985–98 (no. of innovations)

Process	Technology not in use			Technology mastery			Minor innovation			Major innovation		
	1985	1985–94	1994–98	1985	1985–94	1994–98	1985	1985–94	1994–98	1985	1985–94	1994–98
Batch preparation/ blending	1	1	1	7	4	3	0	3	3	0	0	1
Glass melting/ refining/conditioning	1	1	0	6	5	4	1	2	3	0	0	1
Forming	1	1	0	4	3	5	6	5	3	0	2	3
Processing/ postforming	0	0	0	6	5	2	0	1	4	0	0	0
Finishing	0	0	0	7	6	3	0	1	2	0	0	2
Design/distribution/ commercialization	4	1	0	0	3	3	1	1	1	0	0	0
Total	7	4	1	30	26	20	8	13	16	0	2	7
Share (%)	16	9	4	67	57	42	17	29	38	0	5	16

A number of stabilization initiatives were taken by the company that included an austerity plan for the glass containers division. As part of the plan, Vitro closed down its glass bottle plant in Mexico City in 1999 and planned to reduce its labour force by 15 per cent (4,000) over 2000–01. In the meantime, the company was shifting focus to other areas. In 2000, Vitro invested $23m in the vehicle glass segment where it hoped to maintain competitiveness through implementation of new technology. The company also identified the environmental market in Latin America as a new growth opportunity.

How should Vitro respond further to increased liberalization of the economy? How can it become more internationally competitive and globally oriented? Can it pass the global leaders in selected markets?

The Indian software industry: miracle in the making or a high-technology 'sweat-shop'?

International competitiveness based on low wage is normally associated with low-skill occupations such as assembly and low-wage industries such as garments. However, higher technology industries and more sophisticated services are increasingly characterized by an international division of labour. The global software industry is such a case. Over the past two decades the industry has grown rapidly, reaching revenues worth $300–500 billion in 1999–2000. An explosion in the demand for software services in the late 1980s, growing at 14 per cent annually, resulted in a world-wide shortage of software professionals whose supply was expected to grow by only 4 per cent every year.[9] This led to outsourcing software development to Ireland, Israel and – especially – India.

The Indian IT industry was dominated by public research organizations in the 1960s and early 1970s. Software development in those days consisted of writing applications for imported hardware from IBM and others that came with systems software. Software exports from India started in the early 1970s when Tata Consultancy Services began providing contract programming services. However, with an import ban on computers, except for those producing export software, very few systems were imported, resulting in outdated software knowledge.

The mid-1980s saw a change in government policy with the establishment of export processing zones allowing duty free imports of hardware for software development firms along with tax breaks. In the late 1990s the software industry grew an average of 50 per cent per year and increased in size from $243 million in 1991 to $8.3 billion in 2000. Employment increased from 71,000 to 400,000 over 1992–2000, making India the second largest software and services industry employer in the world after the US. Software dominates India's IT industry, accounting for 65 per cent of total IT revenues.

Indian software firms can be broadly categorized into three types. First, firms that provide solutions based on the acquisition of user-sector specialization and the accumulation of domain knowledge. Second, firms that develop software including the tools that provide these solutions in a cost effective and timely fashion. Finally, there are firms, albeit very few, that are involved in product development.[10] Uniquely in India, the industry is overwhelmingly export-oriented, with an export share of 70 per cent in 1999–2000 (see Table 2.4).

Table 2.4   Domestic and export turnover of Indian software industry ($ billion)

Year	Industry turnover	Domestic	Export
1998–99	3.9	1.25	2.65
1999–2000	5.7	1.7	4
2000–01[a]	9	3	6

Note: [a] Estimate.

The Indian software industry has attracted increasing international attention in recent years. Cover stories in various issues of *Fortune* and *Time* in the late 1990s describe India's Silicon Valley in Bangalore and television specials argue the merit of permitting Indian software programmers to occupy high-wage jobs in the US or Germany. The US specifically passed immigration legislation in 1990, in response to the employment of low-cost Indian programmers by leading American firms through 'body-shopping' contracts. In 1999–2000, over 200 of the US Fortune 500 companies outsourced software requirements to India.

Lower technology process production

What is less commonly recognized is the structure of the industry, and the concentration of Indian firms at the lowest value-added end of the market. Indian software exports consist primarily of low-level design, coding, and maintenance services. In 1998–99, of total export revenues of $2.65 billion, 44 per cent came from body-shopping, 37 per cent from turnkey projects and 8 per cent from the development of finished products (Table 2.5). Much of the turnkey project work done in India has itself been in relatively routine and low value-added areas: Y2K* solutions accounted for almost half the share (46 per cent) of total software exports over 1996–99. In a

Table 2.5   The Indian software industry by activity, 1998–99

Software activity	Domestic software		Software exports	
	(Rs million)	*(%)*	*(Rs million)*	*(%)*
Projects	14,100	29	39,950	37
Professional services (body-shopping)	2,500	5	48,300	44
Products and packages	23,900	48	8,650	8
Training	2,300	4	1,880	2
Support and maintenance	2,000	4	4,650	4
IT enabled services	4,700	10	5,970	5
Total	49,500	100	109,400	100

Source: www.nasscom.org

* Software to correct possible millennial glitches in computer systems.

survey of US firms in 1998, Arora *et al.* report that, 'the type of work outsourced was neither technologically very sophisticated nor critical to their business'.[11] The reliance on low value-added activities illustrates the dependence of the Indian industry on wage differentials. Indeed, one could argue that as an economic phenomenon, the Indian software industry can be better compared with the garment industry in Sri Lanka or China than with the software industry in the US.

Indian software industry spokespersons have argued otherwise, saying that the industry competes more on quality of skills provided and less on labour cost. If there were no cost difference, however, much of the industry would disappear. An entry-level programmer, for instance, earns $3,500 per annum in India while a US counterpart earns $40,000. When all costs are factored in, the cost of software development is only half that in the US. Even when compared with other countries, barring China and Russia, India turns out to be the cheapest (Table 2.6).

India can be usefully compared with Israel and Ireland, two countries with which India's software industry bears a close resemblance. Table 2.7 shows that of the three, India had the highest employment and growth in revenues. However, while the industry has grown at a remarkable pace, it has not witnessed a concomitant rise in productivity. Revenue per employee in Indian firms was about $20,000 as against $150,000 in Israel and $112,800 in Ireland in 1997.* Given that the industry in both Israel and Ireland is similar to the Indian industry in terms of revenues and exports, the difference may be explained by the kind of work done. Firms in Israel are primarily engaged in product development in areas like security and anti-virus

Table 2.6 Software industry cost comparisons, 1994 (indexed)

	USA	Japan	Germany	France	Britian	Mexico	India	Russia	China
Programmer cost	1,164	1,293	1,351	1,135	781	652	100	80	75

Source: W. Kuemmerle and W. Coughlin, 'Infosys: financing an Indian software start-up', Case Study, Boston: Harvard Business School, 2000.

Table 2.7 Comparison of national software industries, 1997

	India	Ireland	Israel
Total revenue ($m)	2,700	6,283	1,300
Export revenue ($m)	1,800	5,940	540
Export share (%)	67	95	42
Employment	180,000	18,300	10,000
Growth[a] (1991–97 %)	57	14	13
Revenue/employee ($)	20,000	112,800[+]	150,000

Source: Arora *et al.*, 'The Indian software services industry', *Research Policy*, 2001, and [+]www.tiu.ie
Note: [a] Compounded annual growth rate.

* Note that a more correct comparison, were comparative data available, would use value-added per employee to factor out differences in software imports. Indian export revenue is almost all value-added so the gap with Israel and Ireland is over-stated.

technology while over half of Irish software firms are into new product development. Indian firms, by contrast, are overwhelmingly service oriented. Very few Indian firms have ventured into product development and the number of successful attempts is even smaller. The reluctance to go into products comes from the higher profitability of service exports. Even product-focused firms have added software services and consulting to fund product development. Large Indian companies like Tata Consultancy Services and Wipro invested in a few products – some of which found acceptance in the domestic market – but none made any significant impact internationally. Narayana Murthy, Infosys chairman, and the Indian software industry's most articulate and visible spokesman, says that 'products are not an issue we have to get worried about – because there is a tremendous opportunity in services itself. We can create a service brand.'[12] This is reflected in Infosys' corporate vision: 'We will be a globally respected corporation that provides best-of-breed software solutions delivered by best-in-class people' and the company's breakdown of total revenues (Table 2.8).

In the first three-quarters of 2001, Infosys increased the number of employees by over 4,000 to reach a total of 8,910. Revenue per employee in Infosys was $38,000 in 1998 rising to $49,700 in 2000. The personpower-centred nature of the industry means a continued shortage of skilled personnel. This is leading many companies to look beyond engineers and convert fresh science graduates into software professionals after giving them some initial training. This is exactly what is done at Wipro Academy of Software Excellence (WASE), one of many such initiatives of Wipro. As Sudip Banerjee, of Wipro Technologies, says, 'The output of engineering colleges and university is far less than what industry requires, which is why we have taken many steps to augment the talent pool'.[13] Infosys realized this need in 1992 when it set up a dedicated education and research department, which in 2000 had 56 full-time staff.

Product innovation

Some firms have realized the importance of products and are making a strategic shift away from services. According to Nirmal Jain, MD Tata Infotech, 'Human capital can easily move out. So you cannot base your entire strategy on human capital . . . it is very important to develop our own product . . . the services business today is thriving on the cost advantage that may be mitigated by competition from countries such as China and Russia.'[14] The company plans to get 40 per cent of its revenues from products by 2005 as against a present share of 5 per cent. A few smaller companies have already made the transition to products but this has not been easy. Ramco's own software product had Rs650 million in revenues with Rs1 billion in development and promotion costs and led the company into losses (see Chapter 5). The imperative to shift to products is recognized by Nasscom, the Indian software industry association, which lists it as one of the challenges facing Indian software and services companies: 'Changes in the

Table 2.8   Infosys' breakdown of total revenues

	Development	*Maintenance*	*Package implementation*	*Re-engineering*	*Consulting*	*Products*	*Others*
%	42	25	7	9	4	3	10

Source: www.inf.com

(global) IT landscape are creating exciting new opportunities for Indian software and services companies . . . however, they also pose challenges for their current service delivery model, for instance, raising the importance of "productionisation".'[15]

The particular challenge is building sales and marketing competence to penetrate global markets. A Deutsche Bank report attributes the limited success of Indian companies in products to lack of funds and resources for sales and marketing and lack of professionals with a product mindset.[16]

Market valuations of Indian software firms rocketed at the end of the 1990s, creating hundreds of dollar millionaires through stock options, an entirely new phenomenon in India. The heads of Infosys and Wipro are the most sought-after representatives of this new India. The IT boom saw many companies add a software suffix to their name to improve their valuations: the collective price of 15 finance companies that changed their names – such as to ABC Infocoms and the like – appreciated by 30 per cent over 1998–99.

IT firms have been on a roller-coaster in the past two years, reflecting (uniquely for India) global trends. Market capitalization of IT firms shot up from $4 billion in January 1999 to $95 billion in February 2000 followed by a fall to $55 billion five months later and a further halving by May 2001. Between January and December 2000, valuations fell between 40 and 90 per cent.

The majority of IT companies that experienced a downslide were, as globally, dotcoms. Venture capital has been available in abundance – according to one estimate there is around $5 billion waiting to be absorbed.[17] However, venture capitalists have become more risk-averse, shifting their focus from early stages to the expansion stage of investment.

Nasscom predicts continual 50 per cent annual growth to 2008. Total revenues are expected to grow to $87 billion with exports of $50 billion. The sector is expected to reach 7.5 per cent of GDP and the share in India's total exports is projected to rise to 35 per cent by 2008 from the current level of 11 per cent.* IT-enabled services and e-business are expected to contribute nearly $30 billion out of the total of $87 billion of 2008 revenues. According to Nasscom, IT-enabled services offers higher growth potential than software development. Future revenues are projected to rise to $19 billion and employment to one million by 2008. Here again the opportunity mainly stems from the cost advantage of India's large pool of skilled personnel.

Table 2.9   Revenue prediction for the Indian software industry in 2008

	Total revenue ($ billion)	*Export revenue ($ billion)*
IT services	39	23
Software products	19	8
IT-enabled services	19	15
E-business	10	4
Total	87	50

Source: Nasscom-McKinsey, *The Indian IT strategy*, National Association of Software and Service Companies and McKinsey, New Delhi, 1999.

* At $50 billion, Nasscom's projection of software exports in 2008 will exceed India's total exports of US$39 billion in 2000.

Table 2.10   Cost analysis for service centre making outgoing calls

| Cost | (US$ per person per year) | | |
	US	Ireland	India
Labour	30,000	20,000	5,000
Telecom	–	2,500	3,600
Others	25,000	21,500	16,400
Total	55,000	44,000	25,000

Source: Nasscom-McKinsey, *The Indian IT Strategy*, National Association of Software and Service companies and McKinsey, New Delhi, 1999.

Table 2.10 shows that low labour costs more than make up for the poor infrastructure facilities reflected in the comparatively higher telecom costs. The savings can even justify investment in captive power and telecoms facilities: GE Capital International Service (GECIS) created its own four-level power back-up and an earth station for its call-processing centre at Gurgaon near Delhi.

Conclusions and questions

There is no question that the Indian software industry is a great success story. With revenues growing at 50 per cent annually, the industry is India's one great export success story. The gap with international business practice that characterizes many industries in India is simply missing in software, with firms in Bangalore having cultures that are more similar to Silicon Valley than to Calcutta (as we will see in Chapter 8). The industry is, however, totally dependent on employing enough people. Growth in revenues has mirrored growth in employment, representing little growth in value-added per employee. Nasscom's ambitious projection for the industry in 2008 reflects this same dependence. The industry is expected to grow 11 times (from $6 billion in 2000 to $68 billion) in revenue terms – this is truly dramatic. Employment is expected to grow an equally dramatic nine times (from 240,000 to 2.2 million) reflecting a marginal increase in value-added per employee.

Perhaps a move to products is not the only way out, but other ways of growing value-added must be found. Firms such as Infosys have grown value-added by moving into turnkey projects where they take on a larger management responsibility. As we will see in later chapters, perhaps the software industry's greatest contribution remains to be made through serving the domestic market, a focus that is largely missing today. The key questions for the industry relate to moving away from the low-cost model of providing low-skill programming.

Cemex

Company background

Founded in 1906, in Monterrey, Mexico, Cemex has become one of the three largest cement companies in the world with approximately 65 million tonnes of production capacity. Cemex has operations in 30 countries and trade relations with over 60.

Cemex produces and sells cement, ready-mix concrete, aggregates and clinker through operating subsidiaries in four continents. In addition, Cemex is the world's leading producer of white cement and the world's largest trader of cement and clinker. Over the course of the 1990s, it has gone from a mostly Mexican concern to the world's number-three cement maker, after France's Lafarge and Switzerland's Holderbank (Table 2.11). A 1993 ranking based on foreign assets placed Cemex first amongst the top 50 transnational companies from developing economies.[18] Indeed, Cemex has over half its assets outside Mexico. Almost all of recent growth has been due to overseas acquisitions. A 1999 *Economist* article on consolidation in the world cement industry reported that 'multinational giants [like] Switzerland's Holderbank, France's Lafarge, Britain's Blue Circle [and] Mexico's Cemex . . . are jockeying to divide up the world's markets'.[19] In an industry that is prone to pronounced cycles of bust and boom, such geographical diversification provides Cemex with financial stability.

Table 2.11   History of Cemex

1906	Cemex founded with the opening of the Cementos Hidalgo plant
1920	Cementos Portland Monterrey initiates operations with 20,000 tons of annual capacity
1931	Cementos Hidalgo and Cementos Portland Monterrey merge to form Cemex
1966	Cemex acquires Cementos Maya's Merida plant and builds two new plants
1970	Acquires a plant in central Mexico
1976	Makes an IPO, listing on the Mexican stock exchange, acquires three more plants
1985	Shifts focus to cement, divests non-core interests in mining, petrochemicals and tourism
1987	Acquires Cementos Anahuac, gains access to Mexico's dynamic central market
1988	Installation of satellite dishes facilitating voice and data transmission among Cemex's eleven Mexican plants
1989	Acquires Cementos Tolteca to become Mexico's largest and one of the world's ten largest cement firms
1992	Acquires Spain's two largest cement firms, demonstrates ability to turn around inefficient operations
1994	Acquires Venezuela's largest cement firm, Balcones plant in Texas and Cemento Bayano in Panama
1996	Acquires majority stake in two firms in Colombia, becomes world's third largest cement company
1998	Acquires strategic stake in Indonesia's largest cement producer, PT Semen Gresik
1999	Becomes Philippines' second largest firm, acquires majority stakes in Costa Rica's and Egypt's largest firms
	Lists a new American Depository Share on the NYSE, forms Cemex Asia Holdings
2000	CxNetworks created to implement the company's e-business strategy, acquires Southdown (US's second largest cement producer)

Industry background

Cement is a cyclical business. Markets depend on population, economic growth and construction expenditures. In developing countries, cement expenditures grow at about one and a half to two times the rate of growth in GDP. China is the world's largest cement market followed by the US.

Cement is costly to transport over land, being relatively heavy and with a low value to weight ratio; it is uncompetitive to move cement more than 300 km from production sites. Because of Mexico's coastal ranges and large inland cities, cement factories must be spread out over Mexico in order to be competitive in serving its main cities. Mexico's three largest markets are all inland: Guadalajara 220 km, Monterrey 300 km and Mexico City 300 km from the sea, which means expensive inland transportation across mountains in a country with relatively few highways.

However, cement can be economically transported by sea. Cement produced in plants in foreign port cities can compete effectively with cement produced in domestic port cities.

Cemex's success

Cement is very much a commodity business, where low margins and cyclical demand traditionally threaten survival. Cemex was able to change this by: (1) building market share and improving margins and (2) ensuring the highest level of customer service possible. Cemex's CEO, Lorenzo Zambrano, made continuous changes in Cemex's operating procedures, focusing on these two objectives, and in the decade to 2001 Cemex grew from being 28th to 3rd in the global cement industry. Changes included the sale of non-core businesses, acquisition and rapid turnaround of leading cement producers in overseas market with high growth potential, and widespread adoption of information technology systems to improve customer service.

Acquisition as process innovation

Cemex concentrates its acquisition dollars on companies that are inefficiently run and markets that offer long-term potential for growth. Virtually every acquisition thus far has strong growth and turnaround potential.

Together with this acquisition strategy, Cemex management has repeatedly ripped up legacy systems within the acquired company, trimmed operating stocks relative to sales revenue and shown profitability. New companies are integrated into Cemex's existing operations and management retrained, so as to prevent the company from spreading itself too thin. When Valenciana and Sanson, Spain's two largest cement companies, were acquired they were reorganized from top to bottom. Top management was scrapped, purchasing operations merged into Cemex's central system, accounting systems computerized and operations linked via satellite and telephone lines to Mexico. Within twelve months Cemex had reduced the Spanish plants' work-force by 25 per cent. These moves translated into an enormous improvement in operating margin: 7 per cent to 21 per cent in two years. Charles Gepp, Cemex-watcher at Morgan Stanley Dean Witter, says: 'They [Cemex executives] are very good at going to a country, buying a cement operation, turning it around and squeezing enormous efficiencies out of it. And the expertise managing, say, the

Venezuelan operation becomes transferable to turning around an operation elsewhere.'

In 2000, Cemex acquired Southdown, the US's second largest cement producer, for
$2.6 billion, the largest acquisition ever by a Mexican company. Lorenzo Zambrano
argued that 'Southdown has very healthy cash flow, and also, it is an operation that . . .
increases our cash flow from the moment of the purchase'. He added that Southdown
was attractive because it was efficient and said they would make it even more so by
melding it into Cemex's highly technological global system for procurement,
production and distribution.[20] The combined company had over $6.3 billion in annual
sales and 77 million tonnes in installed capacity, up 18 per cent on Cemex's 65 million
tonnes, of which only 1.2 million tonnes were in the US.

Adoption of information technology systems

Over the years Cemex has developed a data network that uses a combination of local
and international carriers, plus Cemex's own satellite system. The system hooks up
every plant and office, providing streams of real-time data on everything from daily
sales and output to truck oil-change schedules. Technical flying squads get newly
acquired subsidiaries online in only a few months. The result is three integrated
systems: one for taking orders, another for checking a customer's financial profile and
the last for tracking despatches. The whole system is accessible from any computer in
the Guadalajara headquarters.

Because Cemex's strong global cash flow depends upon local sales, the company
continuously works to improve the service it provides to its customers. An interactive
customer service system takes orders quickly (2 to $2^1/_2$ minutes upon credit approval)
and fills and ships the orders within 24 hours of receiving them. In 2001, 98 per cent of
all cement orders placed in Mexico City were shipped within 24 hours of receipt. The
company aims to raise that to 100 per cent.

Delivering ready-mix concrete is not an easy business anywhere, especially in developing markets. In 1995, because of traffic gridlock, capricious weather and labour
disruptions at the construction site, Cemex could promise delivery no more precisely
than within three hours of the scheduled delivery time. Such conditions often forced
customers to cancel, reschedule or change their orders.

At its largest operations in Mexico and Venezuela, Cemex is committed to
delivering ready-mix shipments within 20 minutes of the scheduled time. The reason
for this dramatic improvement in Cemex's customer service is its Dynamic Synchron-
ization of Operations programme. Once CemexNet, the company's private communications network was in place, it was well positioned to introduce a sophisticated
navigational system in its delivery trucks. Cemex learned about central dispatching
in 1994 and applied it to cement delivery. Since its implementation, there has been a
35 per cent increase in the productivity of company trucks. The results are significant
savings and a considerable increase in customer goodwill.

Organizationally, the company brought in executives from outside the company to
join the top ranks, thus constantly infusing it with an external worldview. The
'conversations' where new ideas were invented and actions hatched worked extremely
well because the company supported an internal culture of progressive change.
Employees of Cemex, it is said, 'radiate the sort of intellectual energy and engagement
that one expects from scientists or university professors or political activists'.

R&D and product innovation

The construction of the Öresund Bridge, linking Denmark and Sweden, is testament to Cemex's commitment to solving its customers' challenging problems with new and innovative products. Technologists and engineers in Cemex Spain's Buñol laboratory designed a special kind of cement that can withstand the extreme weather of the Baltic Sea. The lab also offered technical assistance to ensure that this important project was successfully completed.

Questions

Cemex has demonstrated the ability of a firm from a developing country in a mature industry to grow into one of the world's three leading companies. It has a global presence, investments in many of the world's most rapidly growing markets, and a reputation for responding innovatively to customer needs. Where does it go from here? How can value-added grow further when you are already at the top? What role will process and product innovation play in its future success?

Conclusions

The firms in this chapter have all been relatively successful at climbing up the value-added chain. They have all improved competitiveness in their own way – and each way is different. TBL instituted a radical managerial revolution that dramatically improved processes. Hero made constant and continuous innovations through JIT arrangements for its standard Roadster, together with a recent entry into the specialist bike market. Vitro has focused on product innovation to enter more attractive glass markets. The Indian software industry has prospered by entering a rapidly growing field based on low cost but highly skilled labour. Cemex has become a leader with a radical acquisitions strategy strongly linked to process and IT innovation.

In a real sense these firms illustrate that there are many (small and large) leading edges, many ways of climbing up the value-added chain. Each company has tried to move up the chain but each faces different competitive pressures.

Each industry is different. The bicycle industry has a huge mass sector, where Chinese competition could be devastating. However, there is a high value-added specialist niche sector that Hero is tentatively entering. The brewing industry is large scale but with significant national market differentiation where brands are key. The industry is process intensive and TBL has worked hard to improve processes. The glass industry is also process intensive and has both a commodity and high tech side. Vitro has been attempting to advance in both but still has some way to go before it is an equal player with the world's leaders. The Indian software industry is extremely cost competitive, but any attempt at advance to the leading edge has to reckon with US dominance of software product development. Cemex has made it in the cement industry by turning acquisition into a vehicle for building competitiveness and by tight integration of systems so that its just-in-time delivery systems are global leaders. Particular industry conditions, of course, affect the possibilities for follower-firms to advance, but each firm has grown value-added better than its peers.

Table 2.12 presents a summary of how the companies fare along the range of patterns set up in Chapter 1. The five firms chosen, although they do not cover the whole value spectrum, allow some general conclusions.

Table 2.12   Innovation in the five firms

	Shop-floor, process innovation (Chap. 4)	Management cultural change (Chap. 8)	Product innovation (Chap. 5)	R&D (Chap. 6)	Design (Chap. 7)	International competitiveness (Chap. 3)	Weaknesses
TBL	Yes	Yes	No	No, but some small R&D funding	No	No	Local management capabilities, R&D design, public policy
Hero	Yes	Yes, strong culture from the beginning	Yes, recent	Yes, recent	Yes, some, but needs more to improve international competitiveness	Some	Design for specialist market
Vitro	Yes	Yes	Yes	Yes, increasing	Yes increasing	Yes, but uneven results	Competition from international technologically sophisticated firms
Software	Yes	Yes	Little	A bit	Weak in product development	Yes	Low value added
Cemex	Yes	Yes	Yes	Yes	Yes, increasing	Yes	

First, it is possible to see how the firms perform in shop-floor innovation and process innovation. For example, TBLs rehabilitation focused on process/shop-floor change. Hero Cycles has historically taken shop-floor innovation seriously and has long-standing just-in-time systems and suppliers. Indian software firms compete based on 'production' efficiency and technical effort is focused on making software development more efficient. Vitro and Cemex have both shown dramatic gains in operational efficiency. As such, in all five cases success has been grounded on getting better at producing, at making things. Shop-floor innovation is the subject of Chapter 4.

Second, on firm management and culture TBL underwent a major cultural change with privatization. Cemex specializes in turning round ailing cement companies. The Indian software industry operates with at least some of the culture of Silicon Valley. We look more carefully at firm culture in Chapter 8.

Third, on R&D there are more differences. R&D is non-existent in TBL, a potential weakness, and has not been core to the success of any of these firms in the past.

However, there is evidence of increasing R&D effort: Hero has been trying to build design capability as it moves into specialized bicycles; Infosys has its education and research department with 56 staff; Cemex has its IT systems network and the Spanish Buñol Laboratory that developed the bridge cement to withstand Baltic Sea temperatures; and Vitro is increasing emphasis on major innovations and R&D. Chapter 6 deals in detail with forms of R&D that are key for follower-firms.

Fourth, efforts in product development and design are also uneven. Hero has recently strengthened its capabilities in up-market designer bicycles, on top of their shop-floor, process-oriented competitiveness. Cemex and Vitro have increased investment in new products and added-value products. Indian software firms have focused on lower value software process development and less on software product development. We examine the importance of product innovation in Chapter 5 and design in Chapter 7.

Fifth, the firms vary in relative international competitiveness. TBL is right at one end of the scale, since it appears to be increasing in national rather than international competitiveness. However, its figures for sales per employee are higher than the average for its parent group ($110,800 vs. $80,100). At the other end of the scale on international competitiveness is Cemex, which has internationally competitive units all over the world and is the world's most cost efficient producer of cement. Compared with Holderbank, it has both higher sales per employee and a better trajectory of growth. The Indian software industry is also extremely competitive; and competitiveness comes from labour cost more than technical capability. Hero is a dominant producer in a huge domestic market, but exports are still small, although growing. For Vitro, the technical demands of competing in a business like glass, dominated by a few global giants, are probably the greatest of our five cases. Vitro has built international strategic alliances with producers to increase exports but is having problems holding its market share. However, compared with its big rival, Owens-Corning, it increased its sales per employee by four times between 1991 and 2000 as against two for Owens-Corning.

These five cases demonstrate our point from Chapter 1 that the focus of attention in studying innovation must be the firm. Mexico does not obviously spring to mind when one thinks of the home of the world's leading firms in global businesses like cement and glass. 'India' and 'strong export competitiveness' can rarely be used positively in the same sentence. And Tanzania would not be in the top ten of anyone's list of efficient beer producers.

These firms have been successful regardless of their location. But although in every nation some firms have succeeded against the odds, the national policy environment is a key factor in the overall success of firms. The right policy environment can play a key role in determining whether such successful cases are rare exceptions or more representative of overall industry. That is the subject of Chapter 3.

3 Changing policies for science and technology

Governments and markets

Introduction

Make the choice: if you were to start a firm, which national policy environment would you choose? The US in 2001, or the USSR in 1981? That is an obvious set-up but it illustrates that national environments matter. Exceptional firms – such as Cemex and Vitro – can transcend their national environment, or bypass it – like the Indian software industry. But all firms are constrained or facilitated by the policy environment. And for most firms, growing value-added is determined by the policy environment.

So if the environment matters, it follows that it is possible to shape effective policy to move firms up the value-chain. Over the last fifty years, there have been two distinct models for thinking about the policy environment for industry. In the first 'development decade' after the Second World War, thinking about technology and development was dominated by the view that the transfer of technology from rich to poor countries would enable developing countries to *leap-frog* (the term was everywhere) intermediate development stages. The objective was to get as much technology as quickly as possible, and to attract those who had industrial technology – foreign firms – into the country.

By the mid-1960s, it was apparent that the objective of development in general and industrial and technological development in particular was just not happening quickly enough for most countries, and a search for answers led to a new orthodoxy. Free markets were suspect, and the protection of industry and of technology became the dominant means to achieving desirable development goals. Export pessimism led to import substitution being the dominant development paradigm. This period of import substitution had solid economic backing – several development economists (Myrdal and Lewis, for example) were awarded Nobel Prizes and others were considered leaders of their generation.

By the early 1980s two things were clear: first, the great bulk of countries that had followed an import-substitution path were languishing with low economic growth rates in general and industrial growth rates in particular. Second, a few countries (especially the Asian gang of four – South Korea, Taiwan, Hong Kong and Singapore) were now well on their way to richness, and attention turned to what they did. As Jagdish Bhagwati pointed out, economic miracles are a public good: every economist sees in a miracle the vindication of his own theories.[1] The East Asian miracle was seen by one group of economists as a clear vindication of free market policies, and by another as demonstrating the need for intervention and state direction of the economy. As is usually the case, the truth is more balanced, and it is our objective in this chapter to harvest fact from theory on the role of policy in fostering technical progress. We will argue that what happened technologically in East Asia is critical to understanding the miracle.

Between 1980 and 1990 the dominant paradigm of policy for industry almost reversed, as we can see from Table 3.1. Pre-1980, the chances were that if you picked up any article on development for Latin America or South Asia or Africa the right policies would consist of the list in the first column. Post-1990, pick up any article in the same journals (occasionally written by the same authors!)* and the right policies would tend to be the list in the second column.

While this comparison shows dramatic paradigm shift, the pre-1980 paradigm included an explicit role for innovation. The crucial policy mistake was that this role for industrial innovation was not focused on the firm, where it happens. The post-1990 list does not target innovation, and essentially says 'don't' – don't protect local industry, don't control direct foreign investment (DFI) or technology, don't invest in science and technology (S&T), and don't try and pick industrial winners. So is the right role for the state in fostering technical progress *don't*? Is this enough to move most of the firms up the value-chain as rapidly as possible? We believe there are much more constructive roles for the state in building technical capability in firms, and identifying them involves distinguishing between reality and armchair theorizing on which policies worked and which did not. Before we begin, two points make our own position explicit. First, countries like Brazil, Mexico and India did relatively poorly as a result of following the pre-1980 paradigm. These policies in many cases led to lower industrial development and economic growth, and ultimately kept hundreds of millions of people in poverty. But second, we must ask whether 'don't intervene' is enough to build technical capability in most of the firms in a country. The East Asian experience is often cited to show how intervention can foster industrial development. In several later chapters, we show how building useful technical capability in particular enterprises was at the heart of East Asian industrial development.

If we contrast the experience of just which policies worked to build firm technical capability in East Asia and which did not almost everywhere else, we can gain a richer

Table 3.1 Dominant industrial technology-in-development paradigm

Pre-1980	*Post-1990*
Import-substitution	Export-orientation
Regulate technology imports	Free technology imports
Invest at home in science and technology	State should not invest in science and technology
Discourage direct foreign investment	Encourage direct foreign investment
Select strategic sectors	Open up markets to free competition. Don't try to pick winners

* There is no better illustration of this shift in paradigms than Fernando Henrique Cardoso. As a leading sociologist of the 1970s and 1980s, he was the lead author of *Dependency and Development in Latin America*, Berkeley: University of California Press, 1979, which became the standard textbook around the world espousing the pre-1980 paradigm. As President of Brazil from 1994 to 2002 (and as Finance Minister before that) he practised many elements of the post-1990 paradigm.

understanding of effective policy environments. We will construct myths to gain this richer understanding, and use this understanding in the following section to see what policy environments were effective in building firm technical capability. In particular, we focus on two policy measures with the strongest historical economic pedigrees: infant industry protection and export-orientation. We provide an overview in Table 3.4 of industrial policy instruments used by six newly industrializing countries over the past forty years. Finally, we pull this together into an overall picture of effective policy for building firm technical capability.

Understanding technology and industrial development

Looking at Table 3.1, the message that comes across is either one package *or* the other. Asked to line up countries with these columns, one could apply India, Brazil and Mexico to the first list and Taiwan, Korea and Singapore to the second list. This would be easy; it would also be dangerously simplistic.

Policy making in most countries usually involves compromise and adjustment, which is not reflected in the two columns in Table 3.1. A less polar understanding of just what policies different countries followed would lead to better policy making. To achieve this, we construct six statements that on the face of it are propositions, even obvious propositions. By calling them myths we wish to provoke a closer look at just what happened as these policy instruments were played out in particular countries.

Myth 1: export-orientation means free markets

Export-orientation does not necessarily mean reliance on the market. Indeed, in both Korea and Taiwan significant subsidies were provided to industry that met export obligations (indeed, that met export targets set by the government). Export-orientation does not even mean free *trade.* It is entirely possible to promote exports while being relatively closed to imports. Most of the US's conditions for China joining the World Trade Organization were around market access – requirements that China open its market to US goods and services such as telecoms, computers and banking, with the compulsion coming from China's huge trade surplus with the US.*

Myth 2: import-substitution (IS) is the opposite of export-orientation (EO)

At first look, this statement seems unobjectionable. However, normal understanding of IS and EO as policy instruments not only sees them as different (they are) but as either/or: one either follows an IS strategy or an EO strategy. That has not been true everywhere. Korea followed a policy of IS simultaneously with policies of EO. Textile

---

* US trade policy for most of the past thirty years is premised on myth 1 indeed being a myth. Most of the noise in the trade wars between the US and Japan centred around opening supposedly protected Japanese markets to US goods given strong export of Japanese goods to the US. The most visible example was cars, where Japan had a huge surplus – and where the US kept insisting the Japanese market was closed. Indeed no cars were exported from the US into Japan until Japanese firms built their own plants in the US and started exporting back to Japan! The US saw Japanese insistence on right-hand drive cars as a trade barrier (its own insistence on left-hand drive cars was, of course, a safety measure). So was the market closed?

exports were promoted through state subsidies in the 1960s while electronics was protected via import substitution. In the 1970s, electronics shifted from being protected from imports (IS) to subsidising exports (EO), while cars were protected through IS. In the 1980s, cars were promoted as an export industry. This policy of an IS period followed by a EO period for particular industries is credited with enhancing Korea's technological learning and industrial deepening. Korea's success in building a range of internationally competitive industries is thus a success for both export promotion (which is widely recognized) and import-substitution (which is not). What mattered was that an initial period of protecting industry serving the local market from imports gave way to promoting exports from those same industries, and this only gave way subsequently to opening up to imports.

Myth 3: export-orientation moves firms up the value-chain

The export-orientation school has clearly won the debate on trade orientation, but the picture still requires qualification: it is wrong to see export-orientation as *always* successful. The Philippines followed an export-oriented trade strategy for most of the 1970s and 1980s; they were hardly successful in industrial growth. More importantly for our focus, export-orientation has not in itself been uniformly successful in pushing firms up the value-chain. As we will see in Chapter 5, no industry has been more export-oriented than the maquiladoras in Mexico. Their success in generating employment has been considerable. Value-added per person has tended to lag, though, and this reflects a lack of technological deepening – which one sees in the same export-oriented industries in East Asia. The Indian software industry we saw in Chapter 2 has also been strongly – uniquely – export-oriented. Again, the push up the value-chain has to date been limited. Indeed, buyers in richer countries have a strong motive to keep developing country exporters as reliable providers of lower value-added items.

Myth 4: state-owned enterprises are an inefficient use of national resources

This hardly seems like a myth. Mexico had, and China and India still have, hundreds of state-owned firms whose return on investment has been negative, representing a squandering of national investment on a grand scale. There are, however, some major exceptions. The Korean state-founded steel firm Posco was started in 1968 explicitly against the advice of the World Bank. From its initial record-breaking construction time to today when it is the world's most efficient producer of steel (a position it has held for twenty years), Posco has always set international records. Usiminas of Brazil was also set up as a state-owned steel producer: it too has long been among the most efficient producers world-wide and was the first company to be privatized by the Brazilian government in 1991. Finally, consider that supposed bastion of free-market policies, Singapore. Singapore Telecom, Singapore Airlines, Port of Singapore Authority and the Public Works Department all have two things in common: first, they are all considered international bench-marks for effective performance in their industries, particularly being among the most innovative service providers. Second, they all started life as state-owned firms. So it is not the fact that firms are state-owned that makes them inefficient, but that state-owned firms can deteriorate into serving special interests.

Myth 5: state R&D institutes can help local firms build technical capability

Each of Mexico, Korea, Taiwan, Brazil, South Africa and India invested in state R&D institutes that were meant to foster industrial development. As we saw in Chapter 1, this came from the linear model of innovation which saw scientific advance leading automatically to technical progress. Each of these same six countries have at various times bemoaned the lack of interaction between these institutes and local industry. Taiwan's leading industrial research institute ITRI (the Industrial Technology Research Institute) is considered to be the most successful in its impact on industry, with KAIS (the Korea Advanced Institute of Science) in Korea seen as partially successful. Most autonomous R&D institutes world-wide, however, are properly seen as having had little impact on local industry, certainly not enough to justify the investment that has gone into them. Reform always seems to take the route of attempting to tie institutes more tightly to local industry through various mechanisms – the most prominent being to require each institute to get an increasing share of its funding from private industry. This may be the right solution, but to the wrong problem.*

Myth 6: regulation of technology limits the import of technology

In a well-documented study, Ashok Desai shows how India's policies regulating the transfer of technology led to less technology coming in than should have, less use made of the technology that did come in than should have, and less done subsequently with the imported technology.[2] In India, Brazil and Mexico the regulation of technology imports certainly limited the import of technology and did not work – it led to industries that multiplied obsolescence in the domestic economy. In Japan in the 1950s, and Korea and Taiwan to some extent in the 1960s and 1970s, the picture was different. Far from limiting technology imports by firms, state regulation actually encouraged it. Japan in the 1950s and 1960s and Korea in the 1960s and 1970s were the largest importers of technology among newly industrializing countries. State regulation of technology imports is considered to have helped the country get more technology more cheaply and make more of it than it would have if left to the market. The difference did not lie in the laws themselves: indeed, the provisions and restrictions in Korea or India or Mexico were remarkably similar. What mattered was how these policies were implemented. In Mexico and India, the local firm and foreign firm negotiated with the government. In Korea, the local firm and the government negotiated with the foreign firm. The difference lies much more in the context of culture and politics than in the policies themselves.

What worked

Infant industry protection

Infant industry protection has a fine historical pedigree, going back over a hundred years. Indeed, one can go back even further, to the first industrial nation, and how it became so.

---

* As one of us has argued elsewhere (N. Forbes,'Should developing countries do science?', mimeo, Stanford University, 2001), there is no broad industrial development role for autonomous R&D institutes. Instead, one solution is to transfer state R&D funding from autonomous institutes to university departments, even if that involves physically transferring the entire institute.

In the seventeenth and eighteenth centuries, Indian textiles were known world-wide for their quality and competitiveness. In the early 1700s, Great Britain, that later paragon of *laissez-faire*, passed the Calico Arts Bill, so called because the objective was to protect the domestic (wool) textile industry from cheaper and better Indian imports. Textiles, and in particular cotton textiles or calicos, were later the driving force of the first industrial revolution in Britain, driven forward by a series of innovations in textile manufacturing that provided leaps in productivity in spinning, weaving and dyeing. By 1850, British textile firms had long been so competitive that exports from Britain drove much of traditional textile manufacturing in India out of business. But could the cotton textile industry have got off the ground in the early eighteenth century without protection?

The father of liberal economics, John Stuart Mill, wrote:

> The only case in which, on mere principles of political economy, protecting duties can be defensible, is when they are imposed temporarily (especially in a young and rising nation) in the hopes of naturalizing a foreign industry, in itself perfectly suitable to the circumstances of a country. The superiority of one country over another in a branch of production often arises only from having begun it sooner. There may be no inherent advantage on one part, or disadvantage in another, but only a present superiority of acquired skill and experience. . . . But it cannot be expected that individuals should, at their own loss, introduce a new manufacture, and bear the burden of carrying on until the producers have been educated to the level of those with whom the processes are traditional. A protective duty, continued for a reasonable time, might sometimes be the least inconvenient mode in which the nation can tax in itself for the support of such an experiment. But it is essential that the protection be confined to cases in which there is good ground for assurance that the industry which it fosters will after a time be able to dispense with it; nor should the domestic producers ever be allowed to expect that it will be continued to them beyond the time necessary for a fair trial of what they are capable of accomplishing'.[3]

This argument, that the state *could* intervene to protect infants in newly industrializing countries, became *should* intervene in every industrializing country since Great Britain. Alexander Hamilton articulated this for the US and Friedrich List for Germany in the first decade of the nineteenth century. Meiji Japan had its own passionate advocates of protection at the end of the nineteenth century.

List's arguments in favour of intervention to support new (infant) industries are the result of his critique of the theory of comparative advantage that all nations benefit if they concentrate on what they do best. Originally, the argument was illustrated by wine from Portugal and wool from Britain, that the two countries should trade rather than try to produce both. The theory of comparative advantage has been used constantly, repetitively, to argue against protection in the developing world. But every state since Great Britain has industrialized behind protectionist barriers to protect infant industry (Table 3.2). A future of producing agricultural products for the rich world was, and is, hardly attractive. As Oscar Wilde said: 'there is this world, and then there is the next, and then there is New Zealand.' This tradition continued into the twentieth century, with much of Europe industrializing behind protectionist barriers,

Table 3.2   Average rates of protection of manufacturing,
              1913 and 1982

Developing countries of the 1910s	
United Kingdom	0
United States	44
Japan	25–30
Canada	26
Australia	16

Developing countries of the 1980s	
South Korea	28
Malaysia	23
Thailand	52
India	40
Brazil	44

Source: P. Bairoch, *Economics and World History: Myths and Paradoxes*, University of Chicago Press, 1993, and S. Lall, *Building Industrial Competitiveness in Developing Countries*, Paris: Organization for Economic Co-operation and Development, 1990.

and with the state playing a bigger and bigger part. The objective, in each case, was to create comparative advantage for local industry.

In spite of its honourable pedigree, there is no question that protectionism in the name of infant industry has much to answer for. Infant industry protection in many cases – in India, in Brazil, in Mexico, in Tanzania, and even in Australia and New Zealand – led to the fostering of permanent infants. However, infant industry protection could also work, as the following three examples illustrate.

The Korean steel firm Posco, which we met in myth 3, is one such case. As is Hyundai Motors, which we will see again in Chapter 5. Hyundai Motors built Korea's first locally designed car, the Pony, in 1975 within a protected home market. Hyundai is today the world's ninth largest car-maker, and Korea the world's fourth largest. Hyundai Motors is representative of a hundred other Korean firms, initially protected and subsidized by the state but quickly meeting stringent performance goals of international competitiveness. This is state and industry colluding, with all that that entails. It is also comparative advantage created through infant-industry protection.

Singapore is a city which was well served by airlines, including Malaysian Airlines, when the government formed independent Singapore Airlines in 1972. Singapore Airlines has long been one of the world's most profitable airlines, setting standards for service and innovative offerings. Singapore is a perfect example of a government 'protecting' infants by simply making it cheaper to do business. Singapore is among the cheapest places world-wide to make a phone call (using the service provided by state-founded SingTel), to ship and tranship goods (using port facilities provided by state-founded Singapore Ports Authority, with record transhipment times), or to connect with the internet (with free internet kiosks on the streets provided by state-funded S-One). All of these ventures are highly successful, internationally competitive, privatized and would not exist if the state had not given birth to these infants.

Finally, the Indian pharmaceutical industry featured in our introductory list of Chapter 1 (and to which we return in Chapter 6) is considered a success story in the making. The industry is founded on the Indian Patent Act of 1970, which did not recognize product patents for pharmaceuticals. India has over a thousand home-grown pharmaceutical manufacturers. Drug prices which were among the world's highest in the 1960s are in the early 2000s the world's lowest. Several Indian pharmaceutical companies are themselves investing in the creation of their own intellectual property, have established manufacturing subsidiaries in China, the US, Ireland, Malaysia and Germany and have among the highest earnings multiples on the stock-market.* We may baulk today at patents being invented around, but US patent policy in the late nineteenth century explicitly targeted protecting patents by US firms and protecting US firms from foreign patents – a distinction that would today be a major violation of WTO norms of non-discrimination.

It is not our intention to make heroes of patent busting, or state-founded enterprise, or cosy state–industry relationships. Each of our examples is meant to question an increasingly dominant paradigm of 'don't protect' that is just as simplistic as the earlier knee-jerk 'protect'. So while we should constantly keep in mind the great human cost of protectionism for millions in many countries, we should recognize too the merit of protecting infants that become world-beaters. Of course, the key question is what would have happened in the absence of this protection? Would these firms have emerged anyway, even sooner and stronger? Would other firms of equal or greater strength have emerged in other sectors? These are 'what if' questions no one can answer, but the historical record suggests for countries everywhere that infant-industry *can* work. This is not to say it will *always* work, and we turn next to the role of import-substitution in making infants grow up.

Making infants grow up

A key means of implementing an infant industry policy has been through import-substitution. Much of the Japanese industrialization from around the turn of the twentieth century was via import-substitution industrialization (ISI) policies, with growth depending on expansion of the domestic market, rather than exports (Box 3.1). Johnson shows that exports in the early 1960s were only about two-thirds of what they had been in the mid-1930s.[4] What was key for Japan, after the Second World War, was a huge and integrated raft of policies for industrial catch-up, co-ordinated industry promotion and international trade measures.

One question emerges, invited by the very word 'infant', and that is: When does an industry grow up and become independent? The linked industrial policy question is: What is the ideal length of infant industry protection beyond which the industry should be able to stand on its own feet and be internationally competitive?

Like many important questions the answer is not straightforward, since 'it all depends'. Wade suggests that protection requires to be integrated into a coherent industrial policy:

> There are indeed many cases where protection has not had any noticeable innovation – or investment-enhancing effect (e.g. India). This reflects the failure to integrate protection with a wider industrial policy, or link it to

---

* Dr Reddys Laboratories was listed on the New York Stock Exchange in May 2001. It was the first Indian pharmaceutical company to be listed there.

> **Box 3.1   What import-substitution industrialization involves**
>
> Import-substitution industrialization (ISI) simply means substituting local industrial production for those goods that a nation has hitherto imported. It is an inward looking strategy aiming to set up domestic industry to supply local markets previously served by imports. Since such goods have been previously imported, it is clear that the local markets already exist, suggesting that establishing new industries should be less risky.
>
> A series of measures can be used to support such ISI, including the use of relatively high import tariffs, quota restrictions on imports, offering financial incentives to those who will invest in new production, controlled access to foreign exchange for machinery and inputs needed for the new factories, export incentives, and so on. But for the successful transformation of a nation's economy implied in the overall project to industrialize, obviously much more is required, such as massive investment in technological learning and incentives for this (for example, insistence on gradual increases in domestic content in local manufacture, incentives to develop technology and technology transfer incentives).
>
> The term primary import-substitution is sometimes used to mean import-substituting for light and consumer industrial products, such as textiles and food processing. The term secondary import-substitution is used to describe the (harder) establishment of industries to produce intermediate and capital goods that have previously been imported, such as chemicals and machinery.

export performance, or make the quid pro quo conditions credible, or to maintain macroeconomic stability. If protected producers know that in the foreseeable future protection will be much reduced or that government will pressure them to enter export markets, then protection may give them breathing space in which to undertake the necessary investment and innovation.[5]

However, he goes on:

> Import protectionism is, as neoclassical theory says, a powerful tool. Like any powerful tool it can be badly used producing a trade regime full of inconsistencies. . . . But that is not the end of the story. The East Asian evidence . . . suggests that protection can also be used in combination with other measures to foster the creation of internationally competitive industries.[6]

Infant industry goes beyond ISI

Infant industry establishment is more than import-substituting industrialization, since the aim is the development of internationally competitive industries, not the substitution of local for foreign production. Infant industries should 'grow up' and be competitive. One way of forcing the pace of industrial and technological learning is to nurture comprehensively for a set period but then open up local industry to international competition. This approach is well illustrated by Korean and Taiwanese industrialization. The Taiwanese government operated an import-substitution policy through the 1950s then gradually opened up from 1958 by lowering tariffs on imports, offering a range of financial incentives to those who exported and by changing the exchange rate to give a stronger incentive to export.

Between 1955 and 1960 in Taiwan and between 1960 and 1966 in Korea, import-substitution contributed as much as one-third of manufactured growth. In both cases import-substitution industrialization preceded export expansion. As early as the beginning of the 1960s the Taiwanese government began planning for the establishment of heavy industries, including automobile and chemical production. Figure 3.1 shows the phasing of government intervention for different industries from textiles and consumer electronics in the 1950s to semi-conductors in the 1980s. It also gives an idea of the length of the infant industry period in this national economy, from eight years to two decades.

If some states have successfully shaped an industrial transformation in the last half century, why have others been less successful and some abject failures? Wade describes how in the Taiwanese textiles example, after three years of extraordinary support even in comparison to some Latin American countries, the regime gradually exposed the entrepreneurs to the market, making export quotas dependent on the quality and price of goods and diminishing protection over time.

What import-substitution does for firms

Import-substitution encourages firms to invest in deepening production to learn by doing. Protection subsidizes the local sourcing of components, leading to the growth of local firms producing raw material, castings and printed-circuit boards, for example. If these upstream industries become highly efficient, as in Taiwan, they directly help the efficiency of downstream manufacturers.

IS also provides time – time to invest in learning by a firm's production engineers, to build product development teams and R&D departments. What is key is that all this should be dynamic and a stage in development, not an end-point. Taken to extremes, as in India, IS meant that R&D departments saw indigenization as their only rationale (see Chapter 6) and time-horizons for product development ignored customers. Learning by doing is indeed crucial to every firm, but as Bhagwati points out, what matters is learning by doing within an appropriate environment.[7]

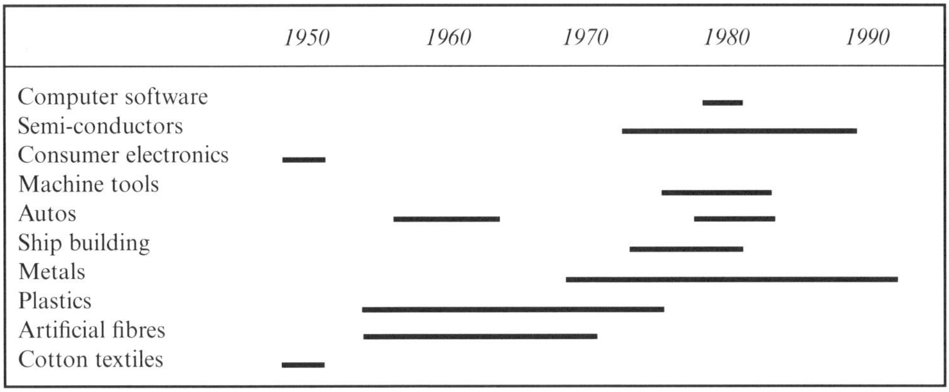

Figure 3.1 Periods of 'state leadership' in various industries, Taiwan, 1959–90.

Source: R. Wade, *Governing the Market*, Princeton University Press, 1990.
Note: The dates should be taken as rough approximations. The diagram does not show all industries, nor is it necessarily complete for the industies shown.

Export-orientation

The theory of comparative advantage, which we mentioned in the last section, has an even stronger foundation and pedigree in economic thought than infant-industry protection. It has been part of the mainstream of economic thought for two hundred years, and is the corner-stone of institutions from the World Trade Organization, and the World Bank to *The Economist*.*

Table 3.3 shows exports as a percentage of GDP in many countries over time. Many countries saw export growth that far outstripped GDP growth. The argument is that both exporter and importer are richer through trade, with local consumers benefiting from cheaper products wherever made.

Since the 1970s, outward-oriented development strategies have been put forward as more effective than inward-oriented ones. Outward orientation generally (myth 1 qualifies this) involves low impediments to imports and incentives for export sales so that the economy will focus on producing those commodities in which it has comparative advantage.

In South Korea from the 1960s, high industrialization rates have been associated with 'high discipline' exerted by the state, where:

> The sternest discipline imposed by the Korean government on virtually all large size firms – no matter how politically well connected – related to export targets. There was constant pressure from government bureaucrats on corporate leaders to sell more abroad – with obvious implications for efficiency. Pressure to meet ambitious export targets gave the Big Push into heavy industry its frenetic character.[8]

Table 3.3   Exports as percentage of GDP

	1960	1980	1990	1999
Korea	3	37	29	42
Singapore	163	196[a]	202	–
Hong Kong	82	111	134	132
Indonesia	13	31	26	54
Malaysia	54	60	76	124
Thailand	17	25	34	57
Mexico	10	14	19	31
Brazil	5	9	8	10
China	4	6	18	22
India	5	6[a]	7	11
United States	5	10	10	12
United Kingdom	21	28	24	29
Japan	11	14	11	11

Source: World Bank World Development Report, various years.
Note: [a] Figures for 1982.

* *The Economist*'s full name when it was founded in 1843 was 'The Economist, or the Journal of the Anti-Corn Law League'. Indeed, the era of free trade, at least for Britain, is said to have begun in 1846, the year when Britain repealed the Corn Laws (which restricted wheat imports) and List committed suicide!

The institutionalization of an export-led system came very early and it came from the top, President Park, who said in his state of the nation message of 1965: 'To go with increased production, the government has set another target – increased exports. . . . in a country which depends heavily on imported raw materials for its industries, export is the economic lifeline.'[9]

What export-orientation does for firms

Exporting has several benefits. Competing with international best practice forces firms to provide value for money. Serving larger markets allows firms to operate at international scale. The key benefit for East Asian firms was *learning by exporting*. Selling in export markets was an essential disciplining tool that focused local technological effort on making firms internationally efficient and pushing them up the product value-chain as local wages rose.

> purchasers, having discovered a reliable source of low-cost, high-quality products, were anxious to enhance the quality of local production. Thus, the very act of exporting became a source of improved technical knowledge substituting for expensive domestic research institutes.[10]

> [exporting became] a training school for technological learning . . . Trans-nationals and other buyers sought to ensure that production was of the highest quality at the lowest possible price . . . utilise exports to force the pace of learning, innovation and industrial development.[11]

By exporting, firms learnt at several levels:

- Firms received feedback on product reliability – the product had to work first time. Particularly when a country has a reputation for cheap products (Japan in the 1950s, Korea in the 1960s and 1970s, China in the 1990s), quality has to be more stringent. As an Indian manufacturer of a technology-intensive product, Forbes Marshall, for example, needs to achieve a higher quality standard than a German or British manufacturer of the same product.
- Product finish and packaging were much more important than in the local market. A pump sold in Japan has to be clean enough to hold against a white shirt, and the product literature has to be printed perfectly on glossy paper. A pump with oil smudges and a shabby manual may work just as well, but a Japanese customer will not then pay twice what his Chinese counterpart pays.
- A firm learns a new definition of time – for such mundane things as responding to requests for quotations, and replying to faxes.

Infant industry and export-orientation

It is today simplistic to think of either infant-industry protection or export-orientation. Infant-industry policies increasingly require export-orientation as a test of international competitiveness. Japan, Korea and Taiwan set up this approach in a series of explicit and detailed policies for rapid sectoral development. The lesson of these economies, as we saw in myth 2, seems to be not inward versus outward or ISI versus EO, but *both*, with the balance changing over time, always associated with building international competitiveness and gradually increasing export-orientation.

Korea is a good example, perhaps *the* example of a strongly outward economy, but its outward orientation went hand in hand with protection for its (still infant) industry. The rate of effective protection of manufacturing was 49 per cent through to the early 1980s.[12] ISI was quickly followed by EO: in the 1960s and 1970s export growth was 40 per cent *per annum* and GNP growth 9 per cent per annum.

Taiwan also moved strongly from an ISI to a EO-dominated strategy, but not to a fully liberalized economy. Protection of industry remained a major priority though there were changes to new sectors as industries 'grew up'. More important than relaxation of import restriction was encouragement of export competitiveness. Export promotion schemes were introduced and strengthened in favour of export sales. Fiscal incentives were introduced for a wide range of industrial goods, provided that exports equalled 50 per cent or more of production. 'These measures resulted from . . . a preoccupation with import substitution toward a preoccupation with both import substitution and exporting'.[13]

Both South Korea and Taiwan had examples of infant industries that grew fast. Both had policies of short-term ISI protection, then opening up to international competition. Both had the power and discipline to implement such opening up – others have not been so successful. The Park regime in Korea was able to discipline companies, to intervene directly to break up or bankrupt inefficient ones. To summarize, as Wade says of Japan, Korea and Taiwan: 'all three countries combined their "outward orientation" on the export side with an "inward orientation" on the import side. They carried through import liberalization very gradually, placing the emphasis on export promotion.'[14]

Comparing national policy environments: what matters for firms?

Table 3.4 compares several policy measures in six newly industrializing countries – Korea, Taiwan, India, Brazil, Mexico and Singapore – over time. What worked for each, using firm technical capabilities as the yardstick?

Infant industry protection and export-orientation

As we saw in the last section, the potent combination of infant industry protection with export-orientation was key to successful East Asian industrialization. This combination played a particularly key role for innovation in firms. While initial protection provided the market entry opportunity, export obligations forced firms to be competitive, and especially provided a strong continuous learning mechanism. What is distinctive about the Korean and Taiwanese pattern is not either IS or EO, but the use of both simultaneously, and the dynamic effect this had on firm technical capability.

Regulating technology imports

When countries used regulations to limit the import of technology by local firms, as in India, Brazil and Mexico through the early 1980s, this policy combined with import restrictions on products to create permanent infants: local firms that made obsolete products inefficiently. Although Korea officially regulated the import of foreign technology, actual import of technology by firms was encouraged. In every country fears that technology import would replace local technical effort were misplaced.

Table 3.4 Industrial development in six countries

	Korea 1960s	1970s	1980s	1990s	Taiwan 1960s	1970s	1980s	1990s
Import substitution (IS) vs export promotion (EO)	EO textiles (subsidies) IS electronics	EO electronics (subsidies) IS cars and steel	EO cars and steel (subsidies) IS Semiconductors	EO semiconductors (subsidies)	EO electronics IS autos, heavy and chemical industries	EO cars (lower tariffs and domestic content requirement) and informatics IS machine tools		Free except in a few industries
Regulation of technology imports	Regulated and 'Picked' but freely permitted, even encouraged. 1971 Law		Regulations relaxed	Free				
State investment in S&T research	Little	State sets up a few leading autonomous R&D institutes e.g. KIST, KAIS	Better reforms to integrate with industry – ambiguous results	R&D mainly in industry so little impact, some continuing initiatives	State R&D institutes set up for nearly all industrial sectors	R&D efforts intensified with focus on strategic areas (ITRI, III, HSIP, ERSO)		
Policies on foreign investment	Regulated, even discouraged in all except a few selective JVs		Gradually relaxed but still regulated	Free only post the 1997 crisis	DFI encouraged (tax holidays, 100% foreign ownership)	Regulation in favour of export production (stringent export and local content requirements)	EO maximized 100% foreign ownership, local content requirements eased	
Selection of strategic sectors	*Autos* Local assembly by chaebols *Informatics* IS strict control on DFI *Steel* Lead in establishing steel mill but foreign tech and loans refused	*Autos* IS *Informatics* EO DFI allowed local content requirements. State R&D support (KIET KIST) ban on entry	EO subsidies for expansion and product development IS in computers increase in in-house R&D. Industry–university R&D tie-ups. Rapid export growth	1994: Korea no. 5 in world. In 1997 Kia and in 2000 Daewoo went bankrupt World no. 4 in IT and no. 2 in consumer electronics	*Autos* IS, local content requirement and ban on investment in simple assembly *Informatics* EO, incentives and support for marketing and training	EO, limit on foreign ownership, local content requirements EO state R&D institutes provide technical support to industry		

Table 3.4 (continued)

	India 1960s	1970s	1980s	1990s	Brazil 1960s	1970s	1980s	1990s
Import substitution (IS) vs export promotion (EO)	IS in everything till 1991			Progressive opening up few export subsidies	IS through a 'triple alliance' between SOEs, private firms and TNCs with increasing intensity over the period		Deepening of IS as a response to the debt crisis	IS continues, a few unsuccessful efforts to ease trade barriers
Regulation of technology imports	Increasingly severe regulations discouraging technology imports		Gradually relaxed but still regulated	Free except in a few sectors	Arms-length technology transfer with strict controls (limited on technology payments, fulfilment of criteria for approval)			Relaxed but not free
State investment in S&T research	Major share of national R&D spent in autonomous state R&D institutes, little industrial impact				Heavy state-led investment in S&T (S&T plans S&T financing institutions) public sector share nearly 90%, weak linkage with industry			Reduction in state share of R&D but still high
Policies on foreign investment	Restricted	Restricted further – MNCs forced to divest	Continued restriction	Freed up	DFI encouraged, focus on specific industries, new entrants kept out, strong local content requirements, export commitments (post-1972)		Strong local content requirement	Free, no local content requirement
Selection of strategic sectors	**Autos** DFI not permitted, entry of new domestic firms not permitted		Public sector JV with Japanese firm in 1982. SOE JV in 1982	DFI and domestic firm entry permitted but local content requirement	**Autos** IS incentives to attract DFI + local content requirements, export commitments (post 1972)	EO led to rapid growth of exports	Debt crisis causes slowdown, renewed IS efforts	Government initiative on growth, huge investments by MNCs, world no. 9
		Pharmaceuticals Non-recognition of product patents, pricing control – growth of an industry churning out reverse-engineered drugs		Local firms equal MNC market share. Local firms begin drug discovery research. Recognition of WTO product patents by 2005	**Pharmaceuticals** 1971 product patents not recognised			
	Steel Private firms prevented from entering or expanding		Firms free to enter and expand but regulated					

Table 3.4 (continued)

	Mexico 1960s	1970s	1980s	1990s	Singapore 1960s	1970s	1980s	1990s
Import substitution (IS) vs export promotion (EO)	IS in all industries till early 1980s (including TNCs), maquila programme an exception		Abandoned IS following the debt crisis	Trade reforms continued, NAFTA	Free imports			
Regulation of technology imports	Strict regulation of technology transfer up to 1991 (controls, arbitrariness, few protection mechanisms)			Free (no limits on royalty payments)	No regulation on technology imports			
State investment in S&T research	Major share of national R&D spent in autonomous R&D institutes (university campuses) funded by state; little industrial impact			Drop in state share but still high	Very little investment by state except in SOEs			State established R&D institutes in selective areas, state R&D spending rises significantly
Policies on foreign investment	Strict regulation of DFI		Some efforts at liberalization following the debt crisis	Free except in some areas. No 'performance requirements'	Encouraged throughout			
Selection of strategic sectors	*Autos* IS, DFI encouraged for domestic vehicle manufacturing		Fall in domestic demand leads to EO, incentives for DFI	Strongly export-orientated and internationally competitive	*Informatics* DFI encouraged (state provides training infrastructure, duty-free imports)			State sets up research and training institutes, focus on higher technical activities

Every study – in India, in Brazil, in Korea – has shown that imports of technology complemented local technical effort, rather than replacing it. In East Asia 'firms did not choose between imported and local technology as sources of technical change. They chose both!'[15]

> Firms in the East Asian NICs have used international transfer as a channel for actively investing in learning . . . but having learned (often with pressure and/or support from government) they ensured that future doing was localised in order to strengthen and further develop the initially acquired stock of capabilities.[16]

When the focus was on building technical capability in the firm, it worked. When the focus was on something else – restricting multinational profits for example – firm technical capabilities suffered.

R&D policy

Every country has seen investment by the state in R&D. With rare exceptions, this approach has not significantly improved the technical capability of local firms. In Korea and Taiwan, the industry share of national R&D mounted early and steadily – as Table 3.4 shows. In Korea this changed from around 20 per cent in firms and 80 per cent in state R&D institutions in the 1970s, to the opposite by the early 1990s. The differences between Mexico, India, Brazil, Argentina and Korea, Taiwan, Singapore are dramatic. In India and Mexico, and to some extent Brazil, the state share has dominated national R&D spending through the early 1990s, and is still over half. Firm technical capabilities require firm R&D, not R&D in national institutes. Indeed, strong firm R&D is required to take whatever limited advantage is possible from R&D done in national institutes, so needs to come first.

Foreign investment

Each of Taiwan, Korea, Brazil, Mexico and India have restricted direct foreign investment (DFI) at different times in different sectors. Korea and India limited it most. In both countries industry is dominated by locally owned firms as a result. In Korea firms are (financial crisis notwithstanding) internationally competitive because of the rest of the policy regime. In India they are inward-looking and internationally weak, because of the rest of the policy regime. In Brazil and Mexico, foreign firms were attracted to invest by protecting the market from imports, a similar policy that China followed in the 1990s.

Selecting strategic sectors

If there were ever a policy that can be guaranteed to attract the wrath of liberalizers it is that of the state picking winners! For good reason: in most countries, at most times, the state has demonstrated much greater competence in picking losers. There are exceptions: Japan, Korea and Taiwan seem to constantly display so much foresight for so many industries in all studies, that one almost suspects the studies! Singapore picked its winners by establishing state-owned firms in key infrastructural areas, as we saw earlier. Brazil and Mexico's local content regulations for the car industry did not particularly lead to internationally competitive car firms but – perhaps not the intended policy – it led to internationally competitive auto-component firms, as we will see in Chapter 5. India's Patent Act of 1970 was intended to reduce multinational company pharma profits, and ended up doing just that, though by growing a vibrant local industry.

Conclusions

Putting all this together, we have four conclusions. First, as we argued earlier, the policy picture is more complex than suggesting that countries which relied on free markets built firm technical capabilities, while those that relied on the state did not. Instead, one can conclude that most countries which relied on heavy state intervention did not succeed in fostering sustainable technological development and industrial progress. However, those that relied largely on the market mechanism did not either. Instead, the most rapid progress seems to have been in those countries that intervened where necessary to foster local effort and learning in infant industries but with some key conditions:

*   The protection provided was for a limited period, and the state worked hard to make this limited period credible. In Taiwan, the state opened up the car market after the period of protection promised in spite of local industry protest that it would be wiped out (it was, but subsequently every other industry believed more strongly in the period of protection).
*   The protection was selective, with decreasing protection rates over time, and with gradually more sophisticated industries protected as local firms mastered less sophisticated ones.
*   Most of all, they used exports as a disciplining mechanism to ensure learning was effectively focused and fully utilized.
*   A guiding principle seems to have been to provide firms with no soft options. If firms choose to become internationally competitive through mixing carrot with stick, fine. If not, simply forcing competition on them through a progressive opening up (and the opening up will always be too soon for firms!) is the surest option.

Second, context is vital and applies at very different levels, including:

*   Culture – policies of intervention that worked in culturally homogeneous Korea or tiny Singapore were ineffective in heterogeneous Brazil or India. The cultural context matters, as we will see in Chapter 8. A future orientation, that expects life to be better for one's grandchildren, enables the balance to shift from consumption to investment, from jam today to jam tomorrow.
*   Politics – studies of industrial policy in Latin America bemoan the capture of the state by industry, which then continued for its own protection. But if the state is prone to capture (and Latin America is certainly not alone), then the option, surely, is not to rely solely on a policy that requires an honest state.
*   Ideology – if policies were implemented pragmatically, and were not rooted in ideology, they permitted a flexible response to ongoing situations. We are reminded of a conversation with Lee Kuan Yew, the architect of Singapore, when asked

about his ideology: 'I have a very simple ideology. I tried something. If it worked, I kept it. If it did not, I changed it.'[17] How the policy was implemented was as important as the policy itself.

- Education – much of our discussion on growing value-added depends on having qualified people. This is a wholly separate issue, but the seriousness and priority of education in every East Asian country, and the focus on technical fields, is surely important to the move by firms up the value-chain.

Third, the package of policies pursued is as critical as each individual policy. It was the combination of subsidies and import protection with exports that helped build world-beating industry in Korea. It was the combination of strong investment in education with pushing industry up the value-chain which worked in Singapore. It was setting up ITRI together with attracting leading Taiwanese technocrats to start firms in Hsinchu, combined with a strong local entrepreneurial tradition that was so productive in Taiwan.

Fourth, some of the success of policies in East Asia has to be put down to luck. It helped Japan greatly in the 1950s that the world's richest country was fighting a war nearby in Korea and sourcing materials locally (it is striking that the record for a day's drop in the Japanese stock market index was the day the Korean war ended). It helped Korea greatly in the 1960s that the nearby war was in Vietnam. Luck also determines which development thinking dominates. It helps greatly if one is influenced by pragmatism rather than by an ideology that sees colonialism as the source of all evil.

Ultimately, the national policy environment determines the rate of growth of value-added for the normal firm. The goal of policy must be to help push firms to build technical capability. However, as we saw in Chapter 2, it is entirely possible for firms to choose to transcend their environment and close the gap with leaders. Cemex and Vitro grew out of just the same policy environment as hundreds of other firms that remained infants. India's export-oriented software industry has grown in just the same environment as thousands of inward-looking firms. Overall, what determines firm success is what happens within the firm. The firm must start from where it is, and close the gap with international best practice. Growing up is much more a matter of hard slog than leap-frog, and the place to begin is on the shop-floor.

4   Innovation on the shop-floor

In 1983, it cost GE $218 to make a typical microwave oven. It cost Korea's Samsung only $155. Then we broke the costs down: assembly labor cost GE $8 per oven; Samsung only 63 cents. The differences in overhead labor – supervision, maintenance, setup – were even more astounding: for GE it was $30 per oven, for Samsung, 73 cents. GE was spending $4 on materials handling for each oven; Samsung 12 cents. The biggest area of difference was in GE's line and central management – that came to $10 per oven. At Samsung it was 2 cents.[1]

Nummi, a Toyota–GM joint venture, occupied an old GM factory in California with terrible indicators of quality, productivity and labour disputes. Nummi hired most of the same workers and managers, and within a few years was a model for US industry on those same indicators of quality, productivity and labour relations. At Nummi, work is broken up into very short cycles (of a minute or two each) but the times are set by the work groups themselves. They do so following a strict work-study process. Best practices are swiftly spread around the plant. Although the work groups set their own practices, Nummi is no flat 'new' organization: the management hierarchy is very much in place as before. So is a speeded-up assembly-line, with each operation just as routine as before.[2]

The JIT arrangement ensures deliveries into the factory from 10 a.m. to 8 p.m. Frequency of supply varies. Some deliveries of bulky items such as tyres occur every two hours. Other more specialized parts such as unfinished handles for powder coating are supplied once every five or six days. Hero's in-house subsidiaries . . . are also part of this just-in-time arrangement.[3]

Introduction: why is shop-floor innovation key in technology-followers?

This chapter proposes that innovation on the shop-floor is especially important in technology-followers. For them, the source of market entry is not, by definition, technological. Instead, firms begin either by serving the local market or by establishing a lower cost manufacturing base for foreign markets, or both. These all require the shop-floor to be the source of competitiveness.

However, while the shop-floor can be the source of competitiveness today, on the basis of a protected home market or low-wage cost, more is required for it to become an *enduring* source of competitiveness. What is needed is *technical capability* from manufacturing – innovation on the shop-floor.* That is the lesson of changes in

* This chapter uses the terms 'shop-floor', 'production' and 'manufacturing'. We regard each term broadly, covering a range of services as well. The 'production shop' for an airline's ticket accounting function is a different place from a car assembly factory, but the concepts we cover are just as relevant. We treat all three terms as related to where the output of the firm is made.

industrial organization as, for example, Japanese manufacturing techniques produced a new wave of manufacturing innovation. Innovation on the shop-floor brought new life to tired manufacturing in the West, and new ways of moving up the value-chain in developing countries.

As tariff protection declines, low wages increasingly become the dominant source of market entry by NICs into internationally competitive manufacturing. In the long term, however, competing on the basis of wage cost is problematic. As a country develops, wages tend to rise. This compels firms to increase productivity, or value-added per person.

Value can be added in several ways. First, by moving to more sophisticated products within the skill levels of local labour. Second, value-added growth can also come from absorbing slack. Simply working harder (producing more per person in a given time) increases efficiency. This is obvious, but often forgotten. It introduces the whole issue of work culture. Explanations for why people work harder range from the cultural (the protestant work ethic and so on) to the economic (if you pay peanuts, you get monkeys). Third, value can be added through new ways of organizing production – by manufacturing differently. One can continuously improve production within the firm – using a set of techniques called 'new manufacturing'. Together, these methods constitute a search for long-run manufacturing competitiveness – a road-map for firms to go beyond wages as a source of competitiveness. Finally, value can be added by organizing outside the firm. One can be part of a dynamic network, often local, which harnesses what economists like to call externalities: efficiency improvements in one group of firms lead to efficiency improvements in other firms, which feed back into efficiency improvements in the first group of firms. In this chapter, since our focus is the firm, we examine the issue of improving efficiency within the firm. We will briefly discuss regional clusters of dynamic small firms as an alternative production system that can spawn continuous improvement.

The key requirement is that innovation on the shop-floor becomes the objective of the firm. But what kind of innovation? And how can one organize for innovation on the shop-floor? These issues are the focus of the chapter.

Wages as a source of competitiveness

Walking through a store in any richer country in 1980, a sweater most likely would have been made in Korea or Hong Kong, a toy in Taiwan, a calculator in Singapore, while a printer would be American. In 2000, the sweater would be from Mauritius, China or Indonesia, the toy from China, the calculator from Thailand and the printer from Singapore (Table 4.1). Cheaper garments are increasingly made in places like Bangladesh (half of all T-shirts in Europe now come from there). In a seminal article thirty years ago, Raymond Vernon argued that as products matured, their manufacture would move increasingly to lower wage areas.[4] This product cycle theory, as in our shopping example, now plays out in an increasingly global production system.

But firms at either end of the product cycle have succeeded through manufacturing by standing the theory on its head. Technology-leaders have sought to use new manufacturing technologies to continue to be competitive in 'mature' markets. Technology-followers have sought to move up the product cycle to higher value-added segments often simultaneously introducing new manufacturing practices. These firms are

Table 4.1 Wages as a source of competitiveness

Products	Typical country of origin	
	1980	*2000*
Sweaters	Korea or Hong Kong	Mauritius, Indonesia or China
Toys	Taiwan	China
Calculators	Japan or Singapore	Malaysia or Thailand
Printers	US	Singapore
T-shirts	Thailand	Bangladesh
Software	US	India

exceptions, although it is the most interesting kind of exceptions that fill this book. For most production in NICs, wages remain the primary source of market entry.

Wages and productivity

Understanding wages as a source of competitiveness means understanding how wages interplay with productivity. As *The Economist* put it, 'If low wages automatically meant low costs, the world's poorest country would dominate world trade. It does not, because differences in wages reflect differences in productivity. Low wages in emerging economies go hand-in-hand with low productivity.'[5] As a result, as Table 4.2 shows, in 1990 average labour costs per unit of output in India and the Philippines were above those in the US while Mexico was well below.

What matters, though, is not the differences between wages and productivity for the whole economy, but for particular industries and firms. As Table 4.2 shows, in 1990 Malaysia was no cheaper than the US in the aggregate, and India was more expensive. However, firms such as Seagate and IBM found it very attractive to manufacture hard-disk drives in Malaysia. Similarly, firms found – and increasingly find – it very attractive to undertake software development in India.

Table 4.2 Productivity, labour compensation and unit labour costs, relative to the United States, 1990

	Wages	*Productivity*	*Labour costs per unit of output*
US	100	100	100
Korea	32	45	70
Mexico	22	31	70
Thailand	15	17	86
Malaysia	15	15	100
India	15	14	104
Philippines	15	14	114

Source: S. Golub, 'Comparative and absolute advantage in the Asia Pacific region',Working Paper No. PB95-09, Federal Reserve Bank of San Francisco, 1995.

Table 4.3 Location of hard-disk drive final assembly (%)

US	South East Asia	Japan	Other Asia	Europe	Total
5	64	15	6	10	100

Source: Gourevitch *et al.*, 'Globalization of production: insights from the hard disk drive industry', *World Development*, 28, 2: 2000, pp. 301–17.

In the hard-disk drive industry, final assembly – a relatively low-skilled job – is mainly concentrated in South East Asia, which accounts for two-thirds of hard-disk drive assembly. While South East Asia provides 44 per cent of world employment in hard-disk drives (HDD), its share in wages is 13 per cent. The numbers for the US are 19 per cent and 40 per cent. When Seagate set up its head suspension factory in Penang, Malaysia, chips were manufactured in the US, with head subassembly in Malaysia, fully manually with row after row of hundreds of workers. Over time, thin film equipment began to be shipped to Malaysia and local engineers started to work on it. Assembly lines also came to be automated requiring fewer workers. This move up the value-chain meant a shift from semi-skilled to skilled workers. The old bread-and-butter semi-skilled manual assembly shifted to lower wage countries such as China.*

While Malaysian productivity is on average one-seventh of the US figure for all manufacturing, in hard-disk manufacture Malaysian productivity is higher, providing a definite cost advantage if one manufactures in Malaysia.

How important are wages anyway?

Firms have two choices if they are to stay internationally competitive: either make low-wage cost production more competitive than others or move into high-wage cost and more sophisticated production where wages become less important. The former often involves relocation. For example, Swissair established its global accounting operations in Bombay in 1991. This meant centralization of all accounting operations in Bombay and Zurich. For a Swissair ticket from Zurich to Atlanta, with a connecting Delta flight to Portland, the accounting that told Swissair it owed *x* dollars to Delta was done in Bombay.

The US textile and garment industry is a good example of the trend. Protected by tariffs and quotas for much of its existence, implementing the trade liberalization agreements of the WTO in 2005 means exposure to full international competition for the first time. The US still makes 50 per cent of its own clothes but that is expected to fall to 25 per cent and then stabilize. However, the industry is not expected to disappear. The reason is technology, not necessarily high technology, but rapid

---

* 'China, with the lowest wages at \$0.39 per hour, is used almost entirely for head subassembly, the lowest skilled and most labour-intensive activity in HDD production. Thailand and Malaysia, with average wages \$1.61 and \$1.53 do some disk drive assembly as well. Singapore (average wage \$6.29) has employment predominantly in disk drive assembly.' Gourevitch *et al.*, 'Globalization of production: insights from the hard disk drive industry', *World Development*, 28, 2, 2000, p. 309. In contrast, a typical assembler of hard-disks in the US would earn \$17 per hour.

product change and just-in-time manufacturing. The US is expected to keep its higher value-added high fashion niche and to switch production to mainstream style, which changes by the week and where speed to market often matters more than price – areas that offshore competitors cannot match.[6]

Going beyond wage competitiveness: the new manufacturing as road-map

In the long term, competing on the basis of wage cost is simply not feasible: economic growth is generally accompanied by wage increases.

Many countries worry about keeping wage costs down. In the 1980s and early 1990s, Indonesia tried to keep wages down, and was apparently prepared to use force to do so.[7] Giving in to international pressure, the Suharto government in January 1994 repealed a law that permitted the army to intervene in labour disputes (there were several incidents of the army shooting workers striking for higher wages), calling instead on companies to pay a new minimum wage.

Uniquely, Singapore tried to push up wages, as a conscious policy to force industry to move to higher value-added areas. Following a recession in 1975, the Singapore government tried to keep wages down to attract foreign investment. Investment happened but primarily in low-paying jobs. In the words of the then Education Minister, 'Industry was not doing justice to the skill level of our population'.[8] In 1979, Singapore launched a three-year wage correction policy with the government 'recommending' annual wage increases of 20 per cent. The policy worked – for two extra years. After five years of 20+ per cent increases, by 1984 so much labour-intensive manufacturing had been forced out of Singapore that there was a recession in 1985! A wage restraint policy for two years followed until the recession ended. Complemented by decades of strong investment in education – primary, secondary and by the 1980s also higher – Singapore had a work-force well-prepared for the higher value-added activities that replaced low-wage manufacturing.

But there is an alternative to either holding down wages in traditional industries or abandoning them in favour of higher technology. The alternative is to add value in existing and new industries. The success of Japanese firms in an increasing number of industries (e.g. consumer electronics, cars, steel, ship-building, semi-conductors) in the 1980s and early 1990s was based on manufacturing excellence. And manufacturing prowess is precisely what American industry was accused of losing by the 1980s. As Hayes *et al.* pointed out, in a passage typical of management books of the late 1980s: 'It was as if, having apparently mastered manufacturing, Americans could go on to worry about other things, safe in the assumption that production would continue as vigorous and robust as before.'[9] Getting trounced by the Japanese drove a renewed interest in manufacturing in the West, and led to the formulation of a set of concepts that are generally referred to as the 'new manufacturing' (or Japanese manufacturing). New manufacturing techniques enable firms in rich countries to retain or improve manufacturing competitiveness, often in these same traditional industries. For lower wage countries, new manufacturing is a way to move up the value-chain by making more sophisticated products. It provides a road-map to move beyond wage competition to long-run competitiveness, by innovating on the shop-floor. But what *is* the new manufacturing? Many know something about the Japanese systems but not so much about how they fit together. The term tends to cover all manner of things, but at its heart are five components:

1   The new quality paradigm.
2   A new perspective on the trade-off between flexibility and unit cost.
3   An attempt to *involve* every member of the organization in innovation, using specific techniques.
4   A combination of different specific manufacturing techniques that add up to a new manufacturing system.
5   Organizing to force innovation on the shop-floor.

The new manufacturing: competing through quality

In a study done a few years ago, *The Economist* reported that there were quality initiatives underway in three-quarters of US and UK companies.[10] Such initiatives were enthusiastically supported by 90 per cent of chief executives, and regarded as 'critical' for their organizations. Much enthusiasm was dictated by the success of Japanese firms in a variety of industries, success properly seen as based on excellence in manufacturing in general, and quality in particular. Cole argues that the Japanese example made quality a fad in the US in the 1980s, but a fad that ultimately led to many useful self-sustaining processes. Three-quarters of Fortune 1,000 companies in the early 1990s reported having a total quality management (TQM) initiative. There was also a dramatic increase in the number of consultants offering information and advice on the quality front: 'By 1991 . . . American companies were paying out $750 million a year to 1,500 third-party providers of advice and materials on quality improvement.'[11]*

The quality function – from inspection to total quality management

Through the 1950s, quality meant inspection and the employment of specialized individuals whose job it was to catch defects. From the 1950s onwards, quality increasingly became quality control. Quality inspectors started using systematic techniques to catch defects. The realization that quality had to be built into the product, not inspected into it, led the quality function towards quality assurance – to control the process and predict when a process was in or out of control, and avoid defects instead of catching them later. Finally, from the mid-1980s onwards, organizations world-wide talked of total quality management, which has become so pervasive that even popular newspapers do not bother to explain the acronym TQM. At its broadest, TQM means good management! Applied to quality, TQM involves using the same systematic process control techniques as before, but with a major change in responsibility for quality and inspection. Every individual becomes responsible for inspecting his or her own work, using anything from systematic statistical techniques to pre-inspection era *ad hoc* techniques. Taking responsibility and authority for the quality of one's own output not only does away with the separate function, but also improves quality through inclusion and ownership.

Perhaps the most widespread expression of TQM is the ISO 9000 Quality System. At its heart, ISO 9000 has two components: first, companies must do what they say they are going to do, and second, there should be a documented system to show that they are doing what they say. As of 1999, there were around 340,000 ISO 9000 approved companies in 150 countries world-wide, and the number is growing all the time. The UK has the largest number of ISO 9000 approved companies, with the US

*So perhaps quality is not, after all, free.

Table 4.4 ISO 9000 approved companies, 1999

	ISO 9000
Total	343,643
UK	60,000
USA	30,000
Germany	30,000
Australia	20,000
China	15,000
Japan	10,000
Republic of Korea	10,000
India, Brazil	5,000
Mexico	1,000

Source: Ninth Cycle of the ISO Survey, 1999 (www.iso.ch).

and Germany second, and with an increasing number of certified companies from China to Brazil to India (Table 4.4).

Quality and manufacturing competitiveness

TQM uses a powerful concept – the cost of poor quality – which involves producing a periodic quality expense statement:

> If your company doesn't have a poor-quality cost system, you can estimate that between 15 and 30 per cent of your annual revenue is lost in poor-quality cost [PQC] and an additional 30 per cent of your white-collar cost is the result of errors or the cost of checking their output to ensure they are not delivering errors to the next person in the company.
>
> Poor-quality cost reporting is a strong tool to gain management attention and to pinpoint problem areas that will provide maximum financial return when the problems are defined and solved.[12]

The focus of improvement effort within an organization should not be to increase the productivity of direct labour (typically 5–10 per cent of turnover), but to reduce poor quality cost (typically 30–50 per cent). The ideal level of quality is zero defects, as Japanese firms showed.

The source of much high-wage manufacturing competitiveness – from Nissan to Motorola – is seen as quality. But there are three caveats. First, there are many failed quality initiatives. Florida Light and Power (FPL) is one case in point: 'In 1985, it became the first large American company (15,000 employees) that threw itself whole-heartedly into comprehensively and systematically learning directly from the Japanese.'[13] In 1989, it was the first non-Japanese company to win the Deming Prize (the leading international quality award). By the early 1990s, though, a backlash developed in the company against the documentation requirements that had been set up. In a much-publicized decision, the staff of the quality department was reduced from 46 to 6. As Cole points out, 'for the mainstream business media, in the short period between 1984 and 1994, FPL moved from being a positive to a negative role model.'[14] The gains from quality depend on implementing the rest of the management package.

Second, most organizations approached ISO 9000 as a documentation exercise more than a change exercise – their customers saw little improvement in the product/ service package they received. Forbes Marshall, in Pune, India, was one of the first Indian engineering companies to be certified to ISO 9001 in 1994. Re-certifications also happened smoothly. But there was much soul-searching on just what improvement customers had seen in product and service *as a result of the quality system*. The entire quality programme is now much more strongly result-focused, with the measure of a good quality system being key indicators of defects and after-sales support, not the ISO 9000 certificate.

Third, even if implemented perfectly, quality has become an entry ticket, not the sole source of competitive edge. In the 1980s it was a competitive edge, with Japanese cars most visibly beating American and British cars on every indicator of quality and customer satisfaction. By the mid-1990s, however, US and British car companies had learnt to play the quality game. This pattern was repeated in other industries, if less prominently. Today, operating at international quality levels provides access to the game, but won't win it.

The new manufacturing as no trade-off: from craftwork to flexible specialization

The move from craft to mass production revolutionized manufacturing. 'New manufacturing' has meant another revolution, this time in lower volume production.

Craft production involves a skilled craftsperson producing one-offs. Craftspeople learn their skills through apprenticeship with a master. Quality depends on the skill of craftspeople. Mass production* has been massively criticized in the past fifteen years, but achieved much from economies of scale and scope. First, as Chandler says, 'the two decisive figures in determining costs and profits were (and still are) rated capacity and throughput, or the amount actually processed within a specified time period'.[†] These economies could be sensational. In Chandler's late nineteenth-century examples, the cost of producing a gallon of kerosene dropped by two-fifths in five years by investment in economies of scale. The price of synthetic dyes dropped to 3 per cent of the price twenty years before, first by investment in economies of scale (large-scale plants) and second by economies of scope (using those plants to process chemicals into hundreds of different dyes and pharmaceuticals). Thirty years after German synthetic dye production began, on the eve of the First World War, eight German firms produced 140,000 tonnes of the 160,000 tonnes of dyes produced world-wide, 80 per cent for export.[15]

Second, it achieved quality gains by working to gauge and interchangeable parts. The use of interchangeable parts allows for investment in specialized tooling to produce and check output. Henry Ford is remembered for the assembly line he set up at his Baton

---

* The three aspects of mass-production – throughput, interchangeable parts and 'scientifically' designed work – developed at different times, and spread unevenly in different industries.
[†] A.D. Chandler, *Scale and Scope: The Dynamics of Industrial Capitalism*, Cambridge: Harvard University Press, 1990, p. 24, for examples of economies of scale and scope. Large-scale refineries permitted by Rockefeller's Standard Oil Trust reduced the cost of producing kerosene from 2.5 cents per gallon in 1880 to 1.5 cents per gallon by 1885 (p. 25). Bayer, Hoechst and BASF 'were able to reduce the price of the new synthetic dye, red alizarin, from 270 marks per kilogram in 1869 to 9 marks in 1886, and to make comparable price reductions in their other dyes' (p. 26).

Rouge plant in the 1920s. The assembly line rigidly sequenced and paced work. However, Ford's productivity gains from using interchangeable parts were much greater than from the assembly line – which in itself depended on interchangeable parts to function. This sounds obvious, but the importance of working to gauge is fundamental to modern manufacturing. In lower volume markets, this transition remains to be made across the organization (particularly in service functions) and has the same potential to add value as it did in Henry Ford's day.

Third, is scientific management, or Taylorism, which involves breaking work up into its component parts, analysing, optimizing and timing each part of work, and then codifying the new method as a standard process of repetitive simple tasks to be followed by every individual who does the job. This has two implications on work organization: the work analysis is done by technical specialists, industrial engineers, and the work itself usually requires much less skill to perform, attracting much criticism for its impact on the worker who becomes a cog in the machine.*

Flexible specialization: the end of the trade-off between flexibility and unit cost

The changes in industrial organization in the 1980s and 1990s towards flexible specialization shook many mass production industries. Craft production represents flexibility while mass-production represents cost efficiency from throughput. Flexible specialization attempts to end the flexibility/cost trade-off either within the firm (the Japanese 'model') or through networks of firms in industrial districts (the Italian 'model'). While thinking about *the* Japanese model and *the* Italian model provides a convenient conceptual focus, there are in reality almost as many Japanese and Italian models as there are firms or industrial districts adopting such practices. Seeing one model provides strong prescriptive power (this is what you must do); but is also dangerously simplistic.

John Humphrey provides a thorough and insightful overview of these two forms of industrial organization in developing countries. He describes the main elements of the Japanese model:

> A set of core principles aimed at eliminating waste in production, summed up in the terms:
>
> - just-in-time (produce only what is required when it is required);
> - total quality management (quality is produced at source and all sources of poor quality should be rectified);
> - continual improvement (the restless search for improved performance at all levels of the company, including the shop floor) . . . ;
> - a system which is more decentralized, with less hierarchy and less departmental specialization . . . ;
> - team working, quality circles or other means of mobilizing workers input into the improvement of process . . . ;
> - designed to involve motivate and control workers . . . ;
> - changes in supplier relations.

* The classic comedy film *Modern Times,* released in 1936, began with Chaplin playing an assembly line worker that defines 'cog in machine'.

The Italian model has four key factors:

- a cluster of mainly small and medium enterprises spatially concentrated and sectorally specialized;

- a set of forward and backward linkages among economic agents, based both on market and non-market exchanges of goods, information and people;

- a common cultural and social background linking the economic agents and creating a behavioural code, sometimes explicit but often implicit; and

- public and private local institutions acting to support the cluster.[16]

Take the example of Panasonic, which entered the highly competitive US bicycle market. The mass-market was dominated by 'made-in-China' bicycles selling for around $150. At the other end were $3,000 bicycles handmade in Palo Alto, California, where adjustments would be made for the difference in length between left and right leg! In the late 1980s, Panasonic started a programme to supply semi-custom bikes using JIT production methods where the frame was stock, but the bicycles could be painted to order with a custom-length handlebar stem. This was followed by a $500–1,000 bicycle, made from 3,000 components that could be chosen on a computer, with the bicycle made up to order and shipped in a few days. Value-addition went up greatly. Organizing efficient production of one-off bicycles required fundamental change in shop-floor layout, worker multi-skilling, inventory policies and supplier relations. The requirement is for a whole new manufacturing system, not just the application of a new manufacturing technique.

Box 4.1   Flexible specialization in Japanese Zimbabwe and Italian Brazil

'Japan' in Zimbabwe

Kaplinsky shows how the Japanese model was implemented in the Zimbabwean firm Autoco. When it began restructuring, Autoco produced automotive components in a protected market with long customer waiting lists. Restructuring was more a response to pressure from its British parent firm (which was restructuring its global operations) than to competition pressure. The exercise began with the observation that 'manufacturing time and space-utilisation were significantly higher than that which was intrinsically required to manufacture the product . . . mainly due to excessive levels of work in process (WIP). For example, in one division . . . a product spent nine hours on the shop floor of which only 48 minutes involved value-adding processing.'[17]   This translated into high working capital costs. The hired team of consultants began by immediately reducing the batch sizes and lot sizes. Stock levels were reduced to 2–3 days. Coloured *kanban* cards were introduced for stock handling, providing greater control over WIP. Handling of fast- and slow-moving items was separated to achieve smoother production. The team also introduced purpose-designed pallets to ensure both production smoothing and control of WIP. This meant that 'there was no longer any requirement for WIP to be stored in another building', reducing carriage costs as well as in-plant damage.[18]

Next the team focused attention on the assembly process itself. The earlier system of workers undertaking their tasks on a pile of WIP, completing and passing them on to the next stage was replaced by a single-unit flow procedure. This meant that, 'the previous worker was only expected to continue producing if the *kanban* square in front of him . . . was empty.'[19] Assembly in large lot sizes needed large space requirements, which automatically became unnecessary once the single-unit system was put in place. The restructuring team then went on to establish a pilot cell. 'In moving to this cell, 13 meters of the 20 meters of conveyor previously utilised. . .were physically removed . . . impressed by the benefits arising from the pilot cell,' the Autoco management decided to introduce a second cell.[20]

The results were impressive. Output increased by 50 per cent in the three years following the restructuring programme, with no extra investment in plant and equipment. There was significant reduction in WIP. Operating efficiency also increased. Labour productivity increased by 50 per cent, workspace was cut by two-thirds and cycle time and throughput time both fell. Finally, there was substantial reduction in waste.

'Italy' in Brazil

Schmitz documents the case of Sinos Valley, Brazil, as an example of an industrial district. Within a radius of 50 kilometres are located almost 500 shoe manufacturers subcontracting work to over 700 workshops that produce most of the inputs, 'all of them made to many different technical specifications'.[21] In addition, the cluster has nearly 500 firms engaged in producing raw materials and machinery for the footwear industry.

The cluster is aided by a wide range of specialized producer services. Besides 70 export agents, 'who fulfill more than a mere trading function', there are freelance designers, technical and financial consultants and specialized transport services. 'The industry is also served by two weekly papers (which specialize in the shoe trade) and four bimonthly technical magazines (of good quality and in competition with each other) . . . adding to the enormous concentration of specialized know-how.'[22] Institutional arrangements include three centres that provide technical and training services, six specialized industrial associations and two professional associations.

Schmitz notes that while shoes are produced in many parts of Brazil, 'the capacity to export exists only in a few places, notably where the industry has clustered and the cluster has depth.'[23] The Valley accounted for 30 per cent of total footwear production in Brazil but 80 per cent of total exports in 1991. Seventy per cent of total output was exported. He further notes that 'The sectoral and geographical concentration laid the basis for the . . . export boom in two ways . . . importers recognized the advantages of buying from an established cluster which included some specialized suppliers . . . [and] manufacturers took collective action' in attracting export orders. The national shoe fair was promoted overseas, foreign buyers and journalists invited – airfares paid – and advertisements placed in foreign newspapers, all in an effort to gain greater recognition for the Brazilian shoe industry.[24]

The new manufacturing as people involvement: mobilizing the work-force

Incremental innovation, like quality, must be widespread and continuous if firms are to succeed. And turning incremental innovation into a concern of everyone requires systems, just like quality. We introduce two systematic approaches to involving people in innovation: suggestion schemes and small group activity. Both these Japanese manufacturing techniques have spread widely around the world, including to developing countries.

Suggestion schemes rely on the voluntary proposals of all members of the organization for improvement within or outside their own work area. Employees make suggestions through a formal mechanism. Different organizations motivate suggestions differently: at some, the employee is given a share of the resulting savings, and monetary awards can be substantial. At others, motivation relies on corporate recognition provided by a publicly presented certificate or a token monetary award. The Indian lorry maker Telco has one of the most active suggestion programmes in any developing country (see Table 4.5). Kawasaki Heavy Engineering reports receiving nearly 7 million suggestions in a year, about two suggestions per employee per day (Table 4.6).

Suggestion schemes typically rely on individual innovation, though group suggestions and improvements are usually encouraged. *Small Group Activity* (SGA), as the name implies, relies on a group of individuals. Quality circles are a special form of SGA, by far the most widespread and organized, and the most studied. Quality circles can be defined as a group of people who voluntarily come together to solve problems using systematic problem-solving tools. See Box 4.2 for quality circles at Bajaj Auto and Alfa Laval India.

Table 4.5   Suggestion schemes in three countries

Parameter	US[a]	Japan[a]	Telco[b], Jamshedpur, India (Average 1993–99)
Suggestions per worker per year	11	3,235	4
Acceptance ratio (%)	32	87	16
Savings per accepted suggestion ($)	–	–	232
Reward per accepted suggestion ($)	492	2.5	7.7
Savings per employee ($)	–	–	134
Worker participation (%)	9	72	64

Sources: [a] US and Japan data from R. Kaplinsky, *Easternisation: The Spread of Japanese Management Techniques to Developing Countries*, Ilford: Frank Cass, 1994. Data are for 1990. [b] Telco, Jamshedpur.

Table 4.6   The ten most active suggestion programmes in Japan, 1990

Company	Total suggestions	Ideas per worker per year
Kawasaki Heavy Engineering	6,980,870	427
Nissan	6,043,344	127
Toshiba	4,166,864	77
Matsushita	4,114,398	44
Mazda	2,417,264	113
Toyota	2,003,646	35
Olu Tyre	1,475,707	83
Nihon Victor	1,247,523	227
Nissan Diesel	1,169,745	88
Fuji Heavy Industry	998,359	–

Source: R. Kaplinsky, *Easternisation: The Spread of Japanese Management Techniques to Developing Countries*, Ilford: Frank Cass, 1994.

Box 4.2   Quality circles at Bajaj Auto (BAL) and Alfa Laval India

Two leading engineering firms in India, Bajaj Auto and Alfa Laval, demonstrate divergence in implementation of quality circle (QC) activity. At Bajaj Auto, QCs continue to expand, fifteen years after they began. At Alfa Laval India, QCs grew rapidly in the early years, but died within a decade. The first quality circle in Bajaj was formed in 1984, in its Akurdi plant in Pune (Table 4.7).

In July 2000, BAL had 646 circles, with over 400 at its newer plant in Waluj, Aurangabad, where quality circles began later but have since grown faster. In Alfa Laval, numbers stagnated, then in 1997 collapsed.

QCs are well integrated into Bajaj's shop-floor management. Although QCs are entirely voluntary, they are seen as a vehicle for communicating with top management. Motivational appeal largely stems from the annual conventions, both in-house and national, where QCs make presentations on the improvements they have made throughout the year. The number of problems solved annually has grown steadily to 313 in Pune and 646 in Waluj. QCs at Bajaj have been driven by operational management since inception.

At Alfa Laval, by contrast, QCs were seen primarily as a people-building activity, with little or no direct emphasis on improvements. Problem-solving remained peripheral to people-building. QC activity was driven largely through the personal leadership of an inspirational Chief Executive, but once she moved to the parent organization the activity was seen as consuming more time and effort than it returned by way of results, and was allowed to lapse.

BAL has a high penetration rate for QCs at both plants (a 40 per cent rate in Akurdi and 70 per cent in Walju). Although QC activity is fully integrated into the management structure of the company, it is still seen as only a 'useful' activity, not an activity 'essential' to the future success of the company. Current focus is to aim QC problem-solving more directly at corporate goals.

Table 4.7   Quality circes in Bajaj Auto and Alfa Laval

Year	Bajaj (Pune)	Bajaj (Waluj)	Alfa Laval (Pune)
1984	21	–	–
1985	41	–	–
1986	52	–	–
1987	96	–	–
1988	117	11	n/a
1989	120	14	n/a
1990	122	16	n/a
1991	130	22	n/a
1992	137	29	n/a
1993	140	15	34
1994	149	40	34
1995	158	55	34
1996	177	117	34
1998	198	288	–
1999	218	404	–
July 2000	235	411	–

Small group activities can make organizations more responsive by transferring responsibility for implementation to the people who have to make it happen. They can even improve decision-making by relying on accurate and comprehensive information that has not been filtered through layers of management. SGAs can rapidly disseminate generic problem-solving techniques and solutions and thus can be an important learning tool.[25] And finally, they are a human resource activity that 'builds people'.

Thus, small group activity has great potential. However, in countless organizations in India, the UK and USA groups have tended to wither away. The problem lies with the way SGA has been implemented in different environments. Robert Cole provides an insightful analysis of how small group activity has been differently implemented in Sweden, the US and Japan – in Sweden SGA was an attempt to *democratize* the workplace and in the US a way of fostering *participation*. Cole argues that the Japanese approach was quite different: QCs were formed in the late 1950s and early 1960s initially to study the Deming and Juran quality control materials then being promoted by the Japan Union of Scientists and Engineers. Further, the circles, consciously called quality *control* circles, were expected to use this knowledge: they picked up problems in their own work areas to practise what they had just learnt. Seeing QCs as voluntary misses reality: a survey of Japanese employers in 1973 found that 56 per cent of SGA leaders reported starting circles on orders from superiors. Further circles were often subject to quotas for suggestions and problem-solving in their initial years. Cole reports of one company that 'by 1980, however, the company reported that the monthly quotas had been dropped because the activity had become so well institutionalized'.[26]

This discussion matters to NICs because it seems as if these lessons are not being learnt. The Quality Circle Forum of India (QCFI) reports around 1,000 institutional members in 2000. Of these, under 200 have several circles operating and could make a claim that the movement was alive and well in their organizations. Even the most active QC organizations have QCs covering a small fraction of their work-force. As an example, the five most active QC organizations in the most active QC chapter of the QCFI report coverage of under 20 per cent of total employees in QCs. In organization after organization, QCs have started with tremendous enthusiasm but then interest flags once top management stops driving them forward: as at Alfa Laval India, they never become self-sustaining. Too often QCs are seen as nothing more than a people-building activity. They *are* a people-building activity but unless their problem-solving is focused on matters of first priority to the organization, managers see them as nice but peripheral. It is no coincidence that one of India's most active QC companies (they claim employee participation of 100 per cent), Sundaram Clayton, has been the only Indian company to have won the Deming award.

Japanese manufacturing as techniques or system

So far we have described two key techniques of Japanese/new manufacturing. But Japanese manufacturing is both a series of techniques and a total system. Capturing the full benefits of new manufacturing involves knock-on from one technique to another, all the way to a new system of manufacturing. Kaplinsky illustrates this for a British firm:

> It supplanted its previous production system aimed at 'efficiency' with a new system focusing on 'effectiveness'. It had formally laid out its plant in a functional configuration, with like machinery being grouped together. The

emphasis had been on maximizing machine utilization and therefore large batches had been manufactured. This meant that production was insensitive to the market, and because lead times were long, forecasts were made of customer orders. This in turn required the holding of high stocks and required complex production controls with a large number of specialized supervisory workers, including end-of-line quality inspectors. In the new production system, the emphasis was placed on rapid response and only making to customer orders. This enabled the plant to work with low inventories, but required a different approach to machine layout . . . But the transition to flexibility also required new quality procedures, that the workers be trained in a variety of skills and perform a number of tasks, and that relationships with suppliers be restructured. Among other things this reduced the number of indirect workers and required significant changes in social relations.[27]

A major concern regarding the spread of Japanese manufacturing techniques (JMTs) to developing countries is the skill requirements of the work-force. As Kaplinsky argues, though, training in basic quality system and people involvement techniques can compensate effectively for a lack of formal education. In Zimbabwe and India, firms with a large proportion of barely literate shop-floor members were still able to successfully implement several JMTs. Indeed, it is a truly inspiring experience to watch a presentation by a Quality Circle where members with just five or six years of schooling analyse a problem through fishbone diagrams and Pareto Charts. But, as Kaplinsky indicates: 'as a range of techniques are introduced, however, the requirements of formal education tend to grow. . . . In the long run, therefore, as the Japanese clearly believe, formal education is an important adjunct to the systemic utilization of JMTs even though in the short run continual progress can be made with low levels of literacy on the shop-floor.'[28]

Organizing for innovation on the shop-floor

Achieving the systemic benefits of Japanese manufacturing requires change in how the shop-floor is organized. Even more broadly, fostering innovation everywhere requires organizational changes for the firm generally.

Just-in-time manufacturing

Perhaps the most powerful vision of JMTs as system is just-in-time manufacturing. It was spawned by Toyota's success in establishing a manufacturing system that minimized inventory, thus triggering a virtuous chain of events that forces innovation through the system. Although Toyota's system was initiated by poverty – it simply did not have the resources to finance high inventory levels – firms around the world have chosen to reduce inventory as a way of driving change through the manufacturing process (see Table 4.8). Inventory is a buffer against variability – raw material inventory protects the firm against unreliable suppliers. Work-in-process inventory protects the firm against machine breakdowns or absenteeism or simply to balance lines. These buffers, though, can lead to waste: raw material inventory means large stocks of raw materials, often unmatched with expensive materials awaiting cheaper balancing items.

Table 4.8   How JIT drives organizational change

Type of inventory	Rationale	Inventory as waste	JIT implication
Raw material inventory	Unreliable supplies	Large stocks of raw materials.	EOQ – Daily or hourly deliveries from suppliers.
	Economic Order Quantities (EOQ)	Unmatched materials – expensive materials can await cheap balancing items.	⇨ Change within supplier's factory or stock will just shift to the supplier.
		Stock obsolescence. Large area for raw materials stores, several stock-keepers.	⇨ New closeness/ relationship with suppliers. No buffer means everything comes to a halt if one item is not received ⇨ New closeness/reliability of suppliers.
			⇨ New organization of relations between purchase and production planning.
Work-in-process inventory	Machine breakdowns	Large buffer stock sitting between machines.	No buffer so a break-down of one machine means all output stops.
	Absenteeism	Much of the shop-floor area occupied by materials.	⇨ Eliminate break-downs of critical machines through Total Planned Maintenance.
	Line-balancing to maximise output from each machine		
		Materials often move from machine to holding area to machine to holding area to machine – requiring much labour for material movement.	Put machines close together so the operator ideally picks up raw material and puts down a finished part.
			Process parts one at a time.
			Avoid long runs of the same operation ➡ reduce set-up times (SMED).
			Multi-skill workers so absenteeism does not mean the function cannot be carried out.

Table 4.8 (*continued*)

Type of inventory	Rationale	Inventory as waste	JIT implication
Finished goods inventory	Meet demand from finished stock as orders come in, instead of as it is produced.	Sophisticated mechanism to predict demand.	Pull material through the factory with rapid demand fulfilment instead of pushing material through by planning based on projected demand.
		Large finished stocks, often several weeks of sales.	
		Problems with obsolescence.	Make-to-order as throughput times should match committed order fulfilment times.

JIT turns all this on its head: eliminating raw material stock requires that materials arrive as they are needed, daily or even hourly – Japanese firms often have hourly deliveries of materials in small delivery vans plying across Tokyo traffic. Not only does this require a new relationship with suppliers, it requires a new organization of relations between purchase and production planning functions in the firm. Eliminating work-in-process inventory means removing the buffer against breakdowns and absenteeism. Absenteeism can be compensated by multi-skilling, and eliminating breakdowns require preventive maintenance as opposed to 'if-it-ain't-broke-don't-fix-it'. The focus becomes workflow. Instead of laying out the shop by type of machine, the shop is laid out by type of job, so that one worker can carry one job from machine to machine to get one unit out at a time. This in turn requires, again, that workers be multi-skilled and able to operate several different machines.

JIT is also known as the Toyota Production System, after the organization most prominently associated with it, and which took it furthest. However, as we saw in the Hero Cycles case in Chapter 2 and in one of the quotes that began this chapter, JIT can arise in a very different culture, though fed by the same drives. Limited finance and a similar need to reduce cost led to the Hero Cycles JIT arrangement.

However, not all manufacturing lends itself to zero inventory and lot sizes of one. Instead, product complexity and volume should dictate the level of inventory. With low-volume high-variety manufacturing, it may make economic sense to provide *some* buffer stocks. Small buffer stocks of some, preferably cheaper, items can have the effect of reducing system variability and so increasing throughput. Balance, as always, is key: too much inventory bring the same problems that JIT so effectively targets, providing such a large cushion that there is no need to fix the system. The focus has to be on throughput, and increasing value-added per person.

Organizing for innovation everywhere

The need to tap the creativity of the entire work-force attracts two approaches. The first is systematic people-involvement techniques; but it also needs a change in the

Table 4.9 Old and new organization

The 'old' organization	The 'new' organization
Top-down management	Decentralization
Coercion	Volunteerism
Order	Chaos
Hierarchy	The virtual workplace
Bureaucracy (in particular, a large middle-management group)	Flexibility (drastically slimmed-down middle management)
Functional specialists	Generalists for project teams
Big firms	Small firms, even virtual firms

overall organization of the firm. The old hierarchical structure is supposed to give way to a new structure, where each employee innovates out of choice (Table 4.9).

Clearly, much scepticism is called for when looking at any such generalized list. An easy acceptance of the organizational changes needed to tap the creativity of the work-force would imply a non-hierarchical and less authoritarian system. Actual firm experience suggests otherwise. Adler and Cole call Nummi, referred to at the beginning of the chapter, a 'learning bureaucracy' to emphasize that hierarchy can actually foster learning. Similarly, some observers have characterized the Korean steel firm Posco as having a management style rather similar to the army background of its founding chairman: Posco was simultaneously highly innovative, with much of the innovation springing from the shop-floor.[29] What matters is what the hierarchy does, not its existence. A line manager can foster learning by providing training. A voluntary culture where the norm is to volunteer to improve nothing hardly fosters innovation. What matters is innovation – even if it has to be strongly pushed by senior managers. The experience of Japan in the 1950s and 1960s is more relevant for today's industrializing countries – quality circles often had quotas for the number of problems to be solved each year, and organizations had targets for the number of 'voluntary' suggestions expected. What matters is creating an expectation of and encouragement for widespread innovation until it becomes the norm. Each individual has both something to offer and is expected to offer something. But while innovation is possible within hierarchical and even authoritarian systems, they impose limits.

Making innovation happen on the shop-floor – what do we know? What do we not know?

We began this chapter by arguing that innovation on the shop-floor is especially import-ant in NICs if firms are to compete without protection or low wages. But analysis of new manufacturing often leads to a strongly prescriptive 'to-do' list of measures that require a move from a prevailing mass-production system to a new mantra:

> People should be broadly trained rather than specialized. Staff is 'overhead', and overhead is bad. Rejects are unacceptable. Communications should take

place informally and horizontally among line workers rather than through prescribed hierarchical paths. Equipment should be general purpose, possibly using some form of programmable automation, and organized in cells that produce a group of similar products rather than specialized by process stage. Production throughput time is more important than labour or equipment utilization. Inventory, like rejects, is 'waste'. Supplier relationships should be long-term and cooperative.[30]

Some healthy scepticism is called for. So just what do we know and what do we not know about the new manufacturing? And how can a firm take advantage of it?

Japanese manufacturing – one model or many?

First, Japanese manufacturing is not one model but many. The earlier discussion from Kaplinsky clarified the distinction between techniques and system. But as Humphrey indicates, it is wrong to see firms as being on one trajectory that ranges from no adoption of any new manufacturing techniques to full adoption of all techniques with all the synergistic knock-on benefits. Instead, he illustrates that JMTs can diffuse rapidly, steadily or unevenly and implies that uneven diffusion is most likely:

> If this scenario is correct, then differences in JIT/TQM use will tend to be persistent. The extent and nature of its use will vary according to the general environment in which firms operate, by sector and by firms within sectors. This suggests caution. . . . It implies that studies of leading innovators may be deceptive. While they show the potential for change in any particular country, they may be leaders with very few followers coming behind. It is important to study what the majority of firms with even limited managerial, technical and financial resources can gain from even limited forms of JIT/TQM, and to consider how such firms might be enabled to move beyond their current limitations.[31]

One conclusion, then, is that JMTs are useful in themselves – there are many quick benefits in adopting specific techniques. At the same time, a systemic approach can lead to synergistic knock-on benefits. The key element of such a manufacturing system is the end objective – innovation for competitiveness. Quality systems and people involvement are means, not ends in themselves. The new manufacturing dictum to focus on process must be balanced with a focus on the end. Let us take the example of ISO 9000. It is a sobering fact that the country with the largest proportion of ISO 9000 approved companies is the UK (Table 4.4), and the most distinctive attribute of UK manufacturing in the last fifty years is its long-run decline. The country most associated with quality manufacturing is Japan, with a fraction of the UK's number of ISO 9000 quality-certified companies. ISO 9000 is not useful if the end objective is a certificate to adorn the reception area but it is if it provides a base of codification that captures current practice and so forms the basis for improvement. Ultimately any quality system is only worthwhile if it results in continuous improvement of product and service as perceived by the customer.

So too with people involvement. The UK, the US and India are all rife with organizations that jumped on the quality circle bandwagon of the 1980s. In firm after firm, the 'movement' never became self-sustaining: without constant drive from top management, it simply withered away. One example is the Quality Circle Forum of India where the number of active QCs added each year roughly balance the number that drop out.

Looking beyond the firm

For most of this chapter, we have focused on harnessing innovation within the firm. It is possible, though, to improve productivity beyond the firm via dynamic networks and to look beyond firm-level efficiency to optimize the entire supply chain.

Industrial clusters as an innovating institution

The interplay between various elements of a cluster brings about what Schmitz[32] calls collective efficiency, the competitive advantage that arises from local externalities and joint action. Rabellotti mentions the generation of the following economic effects: external economies that reduce costs for clustered firms; accumulation of know-how and knowledge within the district; reduced transaction costs through easier circulation of information and face-to-face contacts within the district; and overall synergy enhancing the local innovation capability through imitation processes.[33]

She further mentions that clusters are characterized by high flexibility that is 'obtained through "special" relationships in the labour market: intensive use of home-workers and availability to work extra hours, allowing fast and easy adaptations of the labour force . . . to demand changes'. The cluster is also marked by specialization that occurs due to the division of various phases of the production process, allowing for, 'a more efficient exploitation of the different economies of scale and a higher innovation capability than in vertically integrated firms'.[34]

Bell and Albu draw attention to the accumulation of technological capabilities in industrial clusters. They make a careful distinction between production systems as against knowledge systems and emphasize the role of knowledge systems in harnessing the dynamic economies that originate within a cluster. In particular, they emphasize the 'knowledge embedded in people, organizations and social institutions' which is responsible for 'generating and managing changes in the products, processes or organization of production'.[35] This in turn can make for the difference between a 'learning-rich' and 'learning-poor' cluster.

Clusters can act to build learning through the synergy of 'new capital goods' industries such as software. Capital goods industries have strong linkage capabilities, backwards and forwards in the value-chain. The supplier–user relations involved can be used to improve manufacturing and add value locally – creating synergy between local needs and local supply. Today software can play the role of a capital goods industry. Indian firms have not as yet taken advantage of their software capabilities to build local synergies (Box 4.3).

Older firms in developing countries which followed an import-substituting policy have often developed higher levels of vertical integration than in developed countries primarily because of the absence of good local suppliers when production commenced. These higher scales of vertical integration exist alongside lower scales of production; as markets globalize, restructuring means that these firms must focus on the key parts of the manufacturing process. As Humphrey points out, analysing the

---

Box 4.3   Capital goods and industrialization – from machinery to software

Capital goods consist of those products that are used to make things, machine tools being the best-documented example. Capital goods have long been associated with benefits in the process of industrialization. For example, a paper mill working with a paper machine manufacturer may develop an energy-saving technology particularly suitable for local pulp. The paper manufacturer benefits. But when the paper machine-maker includes the new innovation in all paper machines sold, every paper maker benefits too. Such technological dynamism leads to constant growth in value-added.

Almost forty years ago, Nathan Rosenberg argued that one of the key problems of industrializing countries was the lack of a competitive capital goods industry. 'Many of the major innovations in Western technology have emerged in the capital goods sector of the economy. But underdeveloped countries with little or no organized domestic capital goods sector simply have not had the opportunity to make capital-saving innovations because they have not had the capital goods industry necessary for them.'[36] Having to import most of their capital goods requirements has meant lack of any significant development of a technological base so crucial for further technical progress.

Rosenberg also points to another benefit of a local capital goods sector: 'the kinds of skills which are needed to develop a technology more appropriate to their own peculiar factor endowments are, themselves, undeveloped.'[37] This benefit, of local machinery producers being particularly responsive to the peculiar problems of local producers, is a major benefit of clusters. The competitiveness of many regions of the 'new Italy' is built around the close proximity of producers and machinery makers: knitwear firms next to knitwear machinery firms, noodle-makers next to pasta machinery firms, and so on.

Writing in 1963, Rosenberg was most concerned with machine tools. In the 2000s, the software industry has many of the characteristics of a capital goods industry. Software is not, after all, consumed. Instead, it is used to do things – in manufacturing industry to produce other things. Here is where the Indian software industry has both its greatest potential and so far its greatest missed opportunity. By being overwhelmingly export-oriented, the industry has so far contributed (in Percy Barnevik's words) 'to save costs for the competitors of Indian producers'.[38] This is exactly the kind of capital-saving innovation Rosenberg was writing about forty years ago, but for other economies. The same potential exists within the country – but this requires change for both software and Indian producers: the software industry to see the domestic market as important; and local producers to find ways to use local software firms to become more competitive.

---

merits of industrial districts, 'Clusters provide ready-made networks for firms wishing to deverticalize'.[39]

Conclusions

Becoming the best manufacturer is important for every firm. We have covered many approaches used to improve manufacturing, arguing throughout that the final arbiter of what is useful for adding value must be the firm. We have argued that 'new manufacturing' should be seen as many models, not one, and that JMTs are both useful in themselves and have synergistic benefits from implementation in a package.

The end objective of quality systems, or people involvement, or flexible-specialization or any of the other new manufacturing techniques we discussed, is innovation on the shop-floor. There are many ways of innovating and therefore many leading edges. But there are some basic rules and routines. Ultimately, what matters is growth in value-added per employee – systematically and long-term. Innovation on the shop-floor provides the foundation of firm capabilities to deliver on that goal.

5 From process to product and proprietary

We wanted to move beyond advanced manufacturing to do world-class R&D. .... We also wanted to build products for as low cost as anybody on the planet.[1]

Taiwan is today the world's largest manufacturer of lap-tops. However, value-added is low as key technologies – the microprocessor and operating system from Intel and Microsoft in the US, the LCD displays from Japan – have to be bought in.[2]

Reliance has established itself as one of the best process innovators in its field building global-scale manufacturing plants. In the 1980s, Reliance built a polyester plant with an annual capacity of 40,000 tonnes, equivalent to India's entire annual consumption at that time. Again in 1997, Reliance commissioned the world's largest single-stream ethylene cracker. These world-class plants have been built in record time. Reliance's first backward integration project in polyester yarn and fibre was completed in 17 months against a global standard of 26 months. For a PVC plant, Reliance took 24 months for project completion, three months below the global standard.[3]

Introduction

Chapter 4 showed that all firms in NICs must innovate on the shop-floor to grow value-added. At some point competing on manufacturing alone limits the potential to add value. This chapter argues that firms can continue to move up the value-chain in two key ways: by developing their own proprietary technology, and by making the transition to compete through product innovation.

We speculate that there is a learning hierarchy in NICs which progresses from learning to produce, learning to produce efficiently, learning to improve production, learning to improve products and finally culminates in learning to develop new products.

This learning hierarchy of *process to product* raises several questions that we explore in this chapter. First, what is the relationship between process and product innovation? As we shall see, it is not simply a case of one (process) giving way to another (product). Second, especially for process industries, the learning hierarchy involves a move to technology that is proprietary to the firm. What drives movement from one step to the other? Is it government policy (the state), national culture, or indeed the exceptional experience of each individual player (the firm)? We will explore how each of state, culture and firm affect the learning hierarchy and how they relate to one another. Third, we examine why the move to proprietary and product is necessary, and make the argument that both process *and* product are needed. Fourth, we argue that while the move to proprietary and product is attractive, it is also extremely difficult, and we explore some of the challenges firms must face as they move up the hierarchy. This points to the rest of the book where we explore building innovation capabilities. Finally, we discuss the limitations of the learning hierarchy.

To help explore this broad range of issues, we set up three 'ideal types'* of firms: the East Asian Miracle (EAM) Firm, the Maquiladora, and the 'Indian' Firm. We will explore our arguments through these three ideal types.

As we said in Chapters 1 and 4, as firms in technology-followers enter markets by competing through manufacturing, process innovation is key. The drivers of innovation are different at different stages in the development of a particular industry. Riggs argued that the Japanese industrial 'miracle' through the mid-1970s was built around process innovation and incremental product innovation.[4] But it is simplistic to think of *either* product *or* process, rather it is important to think of innovation as a *unity* of product and process. As an example, Hewlett Packard's subsidiary in Singapore reduced manu-facturing cost of the HP 41C calculator by 50 per cent by redesigning the product to use fewer components. In other words, products may be changed to improve the manufacturing process, just as the manufacturing process can be changed to improve the product. In each case, though, the objective is to make stuff better, not to make better stuff. In talking of product innovation, our concern is the acquisition of the capability to make better stuff.

To move beyond product or process, another dimension needs to be considered: proprietary capability. Proprietary capability comes from knowledge that is distinctive to the firm. In some cases, this proprietary capability takes the form of intellectual property formally owned by the firm: patents, trade-marks, designs, copyright. In other cases, the intellectual property may not be formally protected through intellectual property rights (IPR) – much mechanical engineering know-how, for example, is the sum of tacit knowledge spread among the firms' employees and routines. This knowledge is rarely IPR protected but is no less proprietary to the firm: it often forms the core of the firms' competitiveness.[5] Proprietary knowledge can also take the form of management capabilities, or widespread and distinctive knowledge in the heads of a large sales force. The test of proprietary knowledge is whether or not it permits the firm to add value ahead of competitors – as with the three examples that began this chapter. One can, therefore, think of a proprietary dimension to a product-process grid (Figure 5.1). We argue in this chapter that as firms seek to grow value-added they need to move out from the non-proprietary/process box to proprietary and product innovation. We return to this figure and fill it in at the end of this chapter (Figure 5.2).

Three 'ideal types' of firms

The East Asian Miracle Firm: defining a learning hierarchy

To explore the issues of process, product and proprietary we first examine the three ideal types of firm, beginning with the East Asian Miracle Firm (EAM). Recent work by Hobday shows the importance of Original Equipment Manufacture (OEM) arrangements in the industrial development of East Asia. Industrial development in

---

* No particular firm illustrates each and every distinguishing characteristic – hence the construct of an 'ideal type'.

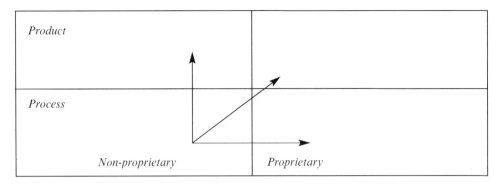

Figure 5.1 Process–product–proprietary grid.

Korea and Taiwan (and also Singapore and Malaysia) was led by exports, and exports were led by electronics, which was the largest export in all four countries by 1990. In Korea and Taiwan, electronics exports were in turn dominated by OEM arrangements, as shown in Table 5.1. In Singapore and Malaysia, electronic exports were dominated by multinational subsidiaries that had lower assembly costs.

Even more importantly, several firms in Taiwan, Singapore, Korea and Hong Kong made a transition from OEM to Original Design Manufacturer (ODM) and then Original Brand Manufacturer (OBM).[6] Table 5.2 defines these terms.

Firms such as Acer in computers and Samsung for microwave ovens began by making products to the specification of technology-leading firms in the US, Japan and Europe. In the late 1980s, for example, Acer was one of the world's three largest PC manufacturers, even though most users of Acer-manufactured PCs had never heard of it. Taiwanese firms dominate the world market for computer peripherals, most sold under US or Japanese brand names. Samsung has been one of the world's two largest microwave oven manufacturers since 1989. In 1985, one would most likely have bought an oven made by Samsung in Korea but with much design input from GE in the US. By 1990, the brand would still be GE but the new design was probably Samsung's. And today, one would most likely buy a Samsung-branded microwave oven (Table 5.3).

Table 5.1   Original equipment manufacture in Taiwan and Korea[a]

	Korea	*Taiwan*	*Singapore*	*Malaysia*
Exports as % of GDP	19	36	168	34
Electronics as % of exports	26	20	40	35
OEM arrangements as % of electronics exports	50	43[b]	–	–

Source: Formulated from M. Hobday, 'East versus South East Asia innovation systems: comparing OEM and TNC-led growth in electonics' and H. Pack, 'Research and development in the industrial development process', in L. Kim and R.R. Nelson (eds) *Technology, Learning and Innovation: Experienses of Newly Industrializing Economies*, Cambridge University Press, 2000.
Notes: [a] Numbers are as close to 1990 as possible.
    [b] This is the OEM/ODM share of computer hardware production in Taiwan in 1989.

Table 5.2   Technological and market transitions

	Technological transition	*Market transition*
1960s/1970s Original equipment manufacture – OEM	Learns assembly process for standard, simple goods	Foreign transnational corporation (TNC)/buyer designs, brands and distributes
1980s Original design manufacture – ODM	Local firm designs (or contributes to design, alone or in partnership with foreign company) and learns product innovation skills	TNC buys, brands and distributes. TNC gains post-production value-added
1990s Original brand manufacture – OBM	Local firm designs and conducts R&D for new products	Local firm organizes, distributes, uses own brand names and captures post-production value-added

Source: Table 5.1 from M. Hobday, 'East versus South East Asia innovation systems', in L. Kim and R.R. Nelson (eds) *Technology, Learning and Innovation*, Cambridge University Press, 2000.

Table 5.3   Samsung's rise to leadership in the microwave market

1979	Started making microwaves
1980	First export order (foreign brand)
1983	OEM contracts with General Electric
1985	All GE microwaves made by Samsung
1987	All GE microwaves designed by Samsung
1990	The world's largest microwave manufacturer – without own brand
1990	Launch own brand outside Korea
1999	Samsung microwaves no. 1 or 2 world-wide, 12 factories in 12 countries (including India, China and the US)

This move demonstrates substantive learning and competence building. So is there a learning hierarchy for technology-following firms?

- *Learning to produce*: the first step in learning is to learn to produce – the learning at this stage is learning by doing. Every firm learns by producing, whether in a protected import-substitution environment or in the face of international competition as an OEM supplier.
- *Learning to produce efficiently*: the next stage is to learn how to produce at internationally competitive levels. The source of competitiveness may simply be low-cost labour, as in the maquiladora industry in Mexico or in the garment industry in countries as far apart as Bangladesh and Puerto Rico.
- The next stage is *learning to improve production*, so that as an economy develops and wages rise, the firm is in a position to improve the whole manufacturing

process. This was our focus in Chapter 4. This stage also includes design for manufacturability, that is, improving the manufacturing process by changing the product.

*   Next comes *learning to improve products,* so that the firm can improve the performance and specification of the product itself. In practice, this step may well precede or overlap the previous stage of improving production. In some industries, improving production may take much more learning than improving products.
*   The last technology-follower stage is *learning to develop new products.* This stage requires the ability independently to conceptualize and develop new product designs.
*   Finally, when a firm has *learned to develop new technology,* it is no longer a technology-follower.

Hewlett Packard's (HP) subsidiary in Singapore illustrates this learning hierarchy well – see Table 5.4.[7] Although HP is hardly a technology-follower internationally, the case of HP Singapore illustrates how a firm in a newly industrializing country can move up the value-chain as wages rise in the economy.

The key points to note from this chronology are the move step by step from simple component assembly based on low labour cost, to developing new products. Some of these steps nested with others – for example, assembly of much more complex printers began after HP Singapore had successfully redesigned calculators.

Table 5.4   Learning hierarchy in HP Singapore

Late 1960s	Singapore identified by HP as a provider of low-cost labour
1970	HP Singapore begins operations with stringing of computer core memories
1973	Move from component manufacture to product manufacture, with assembly of HP 35 calculator
1977	Manufacture of calculators, computer keyboards, solid state displays, ICs, isolators
1981	Manufacture of HP 41C programmable calculator; HP Singapore initiates cost-reduction exercise
1983	HP 41C redesigned to reduce manufacturing cost by 50%; HP Singapore sets up R&D operation (partly to get continued tax breaks from the Singapore government); manufacture of Thinkjet printers begins; sourcing components in Asia reduces cost by 20%
1986	Design of new keyboards; Singapore assumes sole responsibility for design and supply of keyboards to HP world-wide; Thinkjet manufacturing costs reduced by 30% through improvement of production process
1988	Thinkjet redesigned to reduce manufacturing cost by another 30%
1990	Singapore initiates development of new product – a Japanese language inkjet printer
1991	Japanese language printer launched
1992	Singapore designs and introduces a colour Deskjet for Japan; Singapore undertakes the design of a whole new printer, the Deskjet Portable – very successful, and HP Singapore is given full R&D, manufacturing and marketing responsibility for the portable printer product line
1993	Portable printer wins several design awards

Source: Harvard Business School (1994a, b, c) *Hewlett Packard Singapore, Case Study.*

The engineering manager of HP Singapore in 1988 expressed the ambition of this learning hierarchy: 'We wanted to move beyond advanced manufacturing to do world-class R&D. HP wanted to utilize [the Singapore employees] in a better way than any other company, by integrating them closer and closer into the fundamental strategy. We also wanted to build products for as low cost as anybody on the planet.'[8] Today, HP Singapore is considered an equal player with any technology-leading part of the company. Indeed, the best illustration of HP Singapore's arrival was the move of printer manufacturing from increasingly high-wage Singapore to Australia in the late 1990s.

As firms moved up the value-chain, they developed a series of backward linkages with local suppliers. Taiwan is not just the world's largest manufacturer of notebooks (it makes around 40 per cent of the world total); even more it dominates the world market for assemblies such as the computer mouse (with a 60 per cent market share) and motherboards (a 65 per cent market share).[9] While the laptop was initially made to a foreign buyer's design, many key components were sourced from local suppliers. Reading descriptions of these cases gives the striking impression of desire to build technological capability proprietary to the firm.

As EAM firms make the transition to ODM, they also make a transition to higher value-added products in OEM. Both usually involve independent product development capabilities, including R&D. In many of the firms studied by Hobday, R&D rose as technological deepening took place, but it is important to note that R&D expenditure follows excellence in manufacturing.

The Mexican Maquiladora

This ideal type is a classic case of international competitiveness based on low wages (Table 5.5). Consider the following facts:

- From zero in 1966 when the maquiladora programme began, by the year 2000 3,800 maquilas employed 1.4 million people.
- Maquilas account for over 40 per cent of manufacturing employment and 9 per cent of total employment in Mexico.
- Maquila exports are 45 per cent of the national total.
- Against about half of manufacturing employment, maquilas account for just 13 per cent of value-added in manufacturing.
- Domestic value-added within maquilas has fallen in twenty-five years, from 32 to 22 per cent.
- Thirty years into the programme, the share of domestic material content in local production was just 2 per cent in 1998.[10]

Maquiladoras are nothing if not internationally competitive: their existence from inception has been based on duty-free imports and 100 per cent exports. As Chapter 3 showed, an export-oriented policy regime is supposed to drive a more effective kind of industrial development. In their export orientation, the maquiladoras were remarkably similar to the OEM suppliers of East Asia. Firms in the US and Europe sourced very similar products from both East Asia and Mexico. Indeed, the same firms often began sourcing items like toasters and TV sets from a maquiladora and an East Asian firm at

---

*The big names in maquila manufacturing are white goods firms and three auto-components firms (Delphi, Yazaki and Lear).

Table 5.5 Maquiladoras in Mexico

Year	No. of firms	Employment	Average wage ($ per hour)	Value-added (as % of gross production)	Share in national exports (%)
1970	120	20,300	n.a.	–	–
1980	620	119,500	1.1	31	14
1990	1,938	460,300	1.7	25	34
1998	3,130	1,038,800	1.9	22	45
Sept 2000	3,890	1,386,800	2.4	–	–

the same time.* The subsequent development pattern was very different. While both started with low value-added assembly based on low labour costs, the East Asian Miracle Firm moved up the learning hierarchy. Local suppliers were developed, and the proportion of value-added locally increased as the firm itself grew. Maquiladoras started with low-wage assembly and stayed with low-wage assembly. There has been relatively little deepening of local value-added with the bulk of raw materials still imported. Several factors account for this lack of technological deepening:

- The proximity to the US affords no natural protection. Indeed, it is cheaper to ship products from Ciudad Juarez (across the boarder from El Paso, Texas) to Chicago than to Mexico City.
- The policy regime targeted employment – fostering a local supplier base or enhancing learning within the firm was not an objective.
- Firms have long suffered from high rates of labour turnover – over 20 per cent per month in some cases. There is thus little incentive to invest in training.
- Firms themselves have demonstrated little ambition to move up the value-chain. Some investment in JMTs has taken place, but little investment in process or product technology.
- Local management has a limited role in supervising the work-force. Product design or process specifications are the responsibility of foreign personnel and 'decisions about acquisitions of inputs and product mix are the responsibility of corporate headquarters'.[11]

Having learnt to produce efficiently, based on low wage costs, the maquila firm has stayed there. Low wages continue to be the main driver of maquila growth: in 1998 average wages in maquila industries were 62 per cent of average wages in all Mexican manufacturing.*

So has the maquiladora programme been successful? From our perspective of building technical capability to grow value-added, there is little to appreciate. The root cause is ambition: the objective was not to build technical capability but to provide employment. In this, the maquilas have succeeded brilliantly. Analyses of the maquilas, though, leave a sense of untapped potential.

* This is up from their 1994 level of 53 per cent, so the gap is narrowing. As the rest of Mexican manufacturing becomes more export oriented, the contrast with the maquilas is diminishing. See C. Casanueve, 'Globalization and industrial restructuring in Mexico: the cases of the electronics and automotive industries', Working Paper, Instituto Tecnologico y Estudios Superiores de Monterrey, Mexico City Campus, 2000.

The 'Indian' Firm

If the absence of a strong local supplier base characterizes the maquiladoras, the pre-1991 Indian firm ideal type has the opposite characteristics. Four decades of inward-looking protectionist policies fostered capabilities that extend down the learning hierarchy. Firms developed the capabilities to improve products and to develop new products. What they did not learn was to produce efficiently. Indeed, until 1991 for the typical Indian firm, exports were not of *low* concern: they were of *no* concern whatsoever.* The development of a new product meant the development of every component and subassembly locally. Manufacturing volumes just did not matter. Neither did time. The 'Indian firm' buys only in India and sells only in India. R&D means indigenization, often involving complex work and major projects. It does not mean developing products that can be sold internationally. Learning to produce means learning enough to get the product out the door; it does not mean doing so efficiently. Competition means competing with other Indian firms doing the same kind of thing, not international best practice.

Crompton Greaves, one of India's better-known engineering firms, is a good example of an 'Indian Firm' (Box 5.1). The product range is very varied – with the firm making everything from motors to switchgear. Exports are at 1 per cent of sales and almost all raw materials are sourced within India. Overstaffing was rife and in spite of a major total quality management initiative, the firm lagged international standards by a long way. In-house product development was not a priority, with old designs (to take an extreme case, the fan design had changed little since 1937) co-existing alongside new ones which had been licensed.

Box 5.1   Crompton Greaves

Crompton Greaves (CGL) is one of India's bigger and better managed firms. It was the twenty-first largest private company in India in 1995–96 with a turnover of US$416 million, making it one of the larger electrical industry firms in India. However, it was less than one-hundredth the size of the world's electrical industry giants such as Hitachi and Siemens.

A recent book by Humphrey *et al.* traces how CGL has adapted under liberalization in the 1990s. Many, if fewer, features of the import-substitution era remain. As the authors remark, 'the uncompetitive climate . . . had led CGL into a low-growth, low-profitability trajectory'.[12] Its profits averaged just 1.7 per cent of sales over 1983 and 1987.

As was typical with Indian companies before liberalization, CGL 'was used to operating in sellers' markets, in which consumers had little choice but take the product on offer'. Catering almost entirely to domestic demand, there was hardly any incentive to export and indeed '(CGL) exported very little, and much of this at a loss'.[13] Exports remained low throughout the 1980s, averaging roughly 3 per cent of sales.

CGL's product range was highly diversified – ranging from consumer items like fans and toasters to a large variety of motors along with transformers and switchgear. 'Like many Indian companies, it had over-diversified, and its product range was broad for a company its size.'[14]

---

* Much changed in 1991 with the opening up of the Indian economy. For a fuller discussion, see Forbes, 'Doing business in India: what has liberalisation changed?', in A.O. Krueger (ed.) *Economic Policy Reforms and the Indian Economy,* University of Chicago Press, 2002.

Customer service levels were also low by international standards: 'Despite adequate production capacity, customer service performance was poor, with an average response time of around eight weeks; this was despite high levels of managerial input – often as much as 12–16 hours per day.'[15]

'Managements largely accepted low productivity and overstaffing, passing on the costs to the consumer.'[16] Labour laws in India are in general more favourable to labour and 'companies have to seek labour's support and co-operation' to bring about changes.[17] However, overstaffing was prevalent for management as well. After a continuous period of training in JIT and TQM in the 1990s, little change in employment practices was visible. Relations with suppliers were long term but unproductive, 'contributing little towards CGL's capacity to meet increasingly competitive market conditions'.[18] Speaking about the fans plant of the company, the authors note that 'Low prices based on low labour costs were the key to winning orders, even if this entailed a quality penalty for the plant'.[19]

The kind of subcontracting arrangements witnessed in South Korea or Taiwan never gained ground in India. The response of the industrial motors plant to rising demand 'was to invest heavily in raising plant capacity . . . (but) no plans to expand the use of suppliers'.[20] As a result, flexibility was low and the growing demand for customized products in the 1990s led to a fall in CGL's market share.

R&D was a low priority for Crompton Greaves. Since manufacture of fans began in 1937, the authors note that 'little has changed in the basic design of this product'.[21] CGL's relative investment in R&D was weak. It devoted only around 1 per cent of sales to R&D compared with 4 per cent by GEC-Alsthom and nearly 8 per cent by ABB,[22] two of the three MNCs in this industry.

Corporate restructuring that began in the mid-1980s also mainly 'focused on promoting new procedures and forms of organizations rather than in developing technology'.[23] The results of the restructuring were positive but 'there was a pervasive tendency for strong initial gains either to flatten out or for a falling-off of performance'.[24] Consequently the restructuring programme was given a fresh emphasis in 1994–95 and a number of new issues such as supplier development and focus on technology were included.

The second round of restructuring also had mixed results. The company reported losses of Rs1.5 billion in 1999–2000. A recent article[25] reported that CGL has appointed a consultancy firm to evaluate the feasibility of the company's various businesses and suggest a further restructuring. A committee including the owners is to chart Crompton Greaves' future.

As for many Indian firms, the increase in competition under liberalization is subjecting Crompton Greaves to drastic change. It remains to be seen how successful it will be in the long run.

What explains the differences – state, culture or firm?

Each of our three ideal types of firms (East Asian, Maquiladora and 'Indian') represent contrasting experiences in growing value-added. What explains the differences? State policy? National culture? Is the difference simply about firms? Or have we chosen selectively at arbitrary points of three similar distributions?

State policy

As Chapter 3 showed, the 1960s and 1970s debate between the export-orientation and import-substituting schools was definitively won by export-orientation, not least through the striking growth of East Asian exports. The importance of a competitive economic environment, where the yardstick is international efficiency, is critical. Accessing world-class technology is a distinctive feature of East Asian firms: the ratio of technology licensing payments to manufacturing value-added in Korea, Taiwan and Singapore was consistently higher than in Brazil, Mexico and India throughout the 1960s, 1970s and 1980s.[26] Openness to trade and technology would, then, seem to be critical to deepening learning and building useful technological capabilities. So while a competitive environment is key, this is hardly a revolutionary proposition – it is at least 200 years old. But is a competitive environment *enough,* precisely the question we asked in Chapter 3? Maybe not. The maquiladoras have been operating in a fiercely competitive environment right from their beginnings. But there has been relatively little movement up the value-chain or the learning hierarchy. So a competitive economic environment open to trade and technology would seem to be a necessary but insufficient condition for growing value-added over time.

Culture: the crucial importance of wanting to

This brings us to the next factor – culture, the subject of Chapter 8. Reading Hobday's descriptions of firms moving from OEM to ODM and OBM, or reading Kim's many descriptions of Korean chaebol building competence in one industry after another (first textiles, then consumer electronics, then autos, then semi-conductors and computers), leaves no doubt of the strength of East Asian entrepreneurship. There is a pervasive sense of a 'will to develop', to use Dore's phrase, an eagerness to catch up and bridge the gap, that operated on a widespread basis in Korea, Taiwan and Singapore. Take, for example, the earlier quote from HP Singapore's manager that talked of going beyond manufacturing to do 'world-class R&D' and 'to build products for as low cost as anybody on the planet' or Kim writing about Hyundai:

> Hyundai constructed a crisis by setting an ambitious goal to accelerate plant construction in an attempt to minimize production lead time . . . engineers, technicians, and construction workers lived together in makeshift quarters on the plant site, toiling sixteen hours a day, seven days a week. . . . While plant construction was underway, teams rehearsed operations by disassembling and reassembling two passenger cars, a bus, and a truck over and over to routinize procedures, internalizing transferred explicit knowledge . . . into tacit knowledge.[27]

These are all statements of aspiration, of wanting to. They are missing in every description of the maquiladora experience.

But is this really national culture or is it a firm-level phenomenon? Is it simply a matter of each firm 'wanting to'?

Differences in firms

Take the following description. Firm R grew rapidly from the mid-1960s when it was founded right through to the present day. It started as a textile company, but invested rapidly in backward integration, moving through several stages of petrochemicals right through to crude oil refining. While the firm grew on dominance of a local protected home market, investments were made in world-scale plants, licensing the best technology available world-wide. Plant capacities were often a multiple of total local market demand, such as the polyester and PTA plants set up in the 1980s. The firm had close connections with the government and exploited its government connections to the maximum. It never permitted these connections to excuse inefficiency. The world-scale plants were set up in record project execution times, with a per unit expansion cost that set a new record, establishing firm R's international reputation for project execution. This all culminated in commissioning the world's largest grass-roots refinery in 1999, with a project execution time of six months below schedule and cost per tonne 30 per cent below international best practice.

Reading this description one thinks 'Korean chaebol', but the firm is the Indian firm Reliance. No firm, of whatever nationality, better represents the crucial importance of wanting to. A description of the Mexican firm Cemex over the last twenty years would also read like a chaebol success story. Cemex grew from a protected home environment (where it has a market share above 60 per cent) to establish a world-wide presence with operations in 60 countries as one of the world's three leading international cement firms.

These three factors of state policy, culture and firm, though distinct, are not independent. Differences at the firm level can emerge out of culture, policy and firm ambition (Samsung) or in spite of the state (Reliance). Culture can be influenced by firm ambition, a few firms 'wanting to' and 'doing', serving as an example for others, a pattern emerging, and the pattern becoming the culture. State policy can either reinforce the move up the hierarchy or frustrate it.

An example is the auto industry in Korea, Brazil and India (Box 5.2). Kim shows how Hyundai and Daewoo were encouraged by the government to enter the car market, to invest in new models and higher technologies, and to develop new cars for export in record time. Firms were given subsidized credit and government grants, and protected within Korea while they ventured overseas. In Brazil (and in Mexico), a policy of protecting the local market attracted several MNCs in the 1960s who agreed to strict local-content regulations (of 100 per cent!). These regulations went too far and were subsequently relaxed, but a large auto-component industry emerged. This auto-component industry in both countries includes several firms that are today internationally competitive, and which would not exist if it had not been for the earlier local content requirement. The Indian government through to the mid-1980s often frustrated the initiative of firms to move up the learning hierarchy. The Indian truck manufacturer Telco was refused a license to make cars in a joint venture with Mercedes in the 1960s, not permitted to make cars on its own through the 1970s and 1980s, and not permitted to license technology from Honda in the late 1980s. It finally entered the car market with both its own car and a joint venture with Mercedes Benz in 1993 after the industry was finally de-licensed.

Box 5.2   Autos in Korea, Brazil and India

South Korea

In Korea, automobiles was designated a strategic industry in the early 1960s. Hyundai and Daewoo were encouraged by the government to enter the car market and develop capabilities to compete in the world car market. While, 'the average effective rate of protection was atypically high, protection was quickly lifted as firms accomplished a rapid rite of passage from infant to exporter'.[28]

The industry began in 1962 through 'tariff exemptions for imports of parts and components, tax exemptions for assemblers, and local market protection from foreign cars'.[29] The next significant stage came when the government established a domestic content schedule. 'The preferential allocation of foreign exchange was tied to the degree of localization achieved, consequently pushing the domestic content ratio from 21 per cent in 1966 to more than 60 per cent in 1972 and to 92 per cent by 1981.This was implemented through preferential financing and tax concessions making it 'easy for producers to expand production facilities'.[30] Hyundai decided to acquire production capability.

In 1973 the Korean government 'ordered', to use Kim's indicative word, the three passenger car-makers, Hyundai, Daewoo and Kia, to submit plans to develop Korean cars. As Kim notes, 'The government plan was very specific . . . the indigenous model had to be new in the world . . . [having] a local-content ratio of at least 95 per cent, cost less than $2,000 to produce, and it had to be on the market by 1975'.[31] What is noteworthy is the speed with which the Korean government initiated the next higher stage of development. The government took a long-term view requiring that individual plant production capacity had to be more than 50,000 units when the total market for cars in Korea was less than 13,000. The government restricted new entrants and foreign imports and offered various incentives. The year 1975 saw the appearance of two original domestic models on the market – Hyundai's Pony and Kia's Brisa.

The second oil crisis prompted the government to consolidate the car market to bring about greater economies of scale. The rationalization plan involved merging the two largest companies, Hyundai and Daewoo-GM, and suspending production by others. The attempt failed. As Kim put it, 'This failure signaled the waning influence of the state, marking the end of government-directed development and the beginning of industry-initiated growth'.[32] Having directed and supported the industry through the risky initial stages of learning, world-class players like Hyundai went on to develop and produce more new models.

Brazil

The automobile industry in Brazil can be considered 'an example of development based on the local activities of multinational firms'.[33] Production started in the mid-1950s with the government allowing 100 per cent foreign ownership. Special fiscal, financial and foreign exchange incentives were offered along with a requirement to reach 95 per cent local content by 1960. By 1960, eleven firms including Volkswagen, Ford and GM had entered the market and 'by 1962 the nationalization content had reached virtually 100 per cent'.[34] According to Dahlman, VW and others developed their local suppliers providing them with finance, training and technical assistance: 'In 1957, VW had 150 suppliers, increasing to . . . 4330 in 1974 (only 900 of which were foreign) . . . the development of the automobile industry has had great externalities in terms of stimulating the development of the parts, components, and input-supplying industries.'[35]

From the late 1960s car output expanded rapidly, from 168,000 to 708,000 by 1974. The first oil crisis was followed by a rise in exports from 3 per cent in 1972 to 14 per cent in 1980, as the auto industry became the largest exporter of manufactured products in Brazil.

In 1995, the government came up with the Brazilian Automotive Regime. It reduced the 100 per cent domestic content requirement to 60 per cent. This attracted a lot of new automotive investment from many international firms. Brazil was the ninth largest vehicle producer in 1994.

There are approximately 1,000 auto-parts manufacturers in Brazil. Total revenues in 1997 were over US$17 billion, of which 22 per cent was exported. The new regime has led to considerable transformation in the auto-parts industry. In the mid-1990s, local manufacturers supplied over 82 per cent of the market. With increased competition from foreign firms many have since been acquired by MNCs or formed joint ventures with them. As a result, international presence in the auto-parts market has increased from 48 per cent in 1994 to 69 per cent in 1999. Existing domestic manufacturers have been forced to upgrade their standards in order to meet OEM demands for quality, price and delivery and be competitive. The cost reduction programmes, production of global models and global sourcing policy adopted by automobile manufacturers have strongly affected the auto-parts industry. There is greater participation of auto-parts firms in the design and development of new products, limiting the number of suppliers to those with financial strength and technological capabilities. Despite the significant shift of capital ownership from Brazilian-owned to international companies, a number of Brazilian-owned auto-parts manufacturers are also becoming global players. The Brazilian experience shows an initial stage marked by the entry of a large number of MNCs. Localization requirements led to the growth of a large local auto-parts industry, which would have been largely impossible if left only to market forces. Taking localization too far led to a drop in efficiency levels. As a result, relaxation of requirements in the 1990s caused many small auto-components firms to disappear, forcing others to form joint ventures with MNCs in order to survive. Today in a relatively open market, Brazil has a more competitive auto-components industry of international scale. This in turn makes Brazil a good place to make cars. It is a better place to make cars than it would have been if left solely to market forces from inception.

India

The Indian government through to 1991 often frustrated the initiative of firms to move up the learning hierarchy. In 1950, India made more cars than Japan and more than South Korea in 1965. Cars were considered a 'luxury' product (with excise duties over 100 per cent), anathema to socialist values and subject to severe regulatory and discriminatory policies of the licence *raj* – restrictions on capacity, foreign exchange allocations and foreign collaborations limited, as well as price controls, punitive taxes and tariffs.

In 1952, the government decided to keep the number of makes and models to a minimum so as to offer economies of scale for each type. During the 1980s, there were just three car-makers. The government simply did not want too many cars and used policy measures to contain demand. Domestic manufacturers concentrated on import-substitution and indigenization was the main thrust. This in turn had serious effects on quality, which in general was of low or no priority for the manufacturers. Model changes were minimal. Hindustan Motors, one of the three auto companies, licensed the UK Morris for local manufacture. In 1957, the Ambassador was launched and remained unchanged until 1993 (the body still is unchanged as of 2000).* The company enjoyed a 50 per cent market share through the early 1980s. In 1964, PAL, the other main auto firm, began making the Fiat 1100 Delite, which continued in its original form well into the 1990s. Instead of using the auto industry as an engine of economic growth, as Korea did, the policy regime in India directly created a technological gap of over thirty-five years.

Telco was refused a licence to make cars in a joint venture with Mercedes in the 1960s, not permitted to make cars on its own all through the 1970s and 1980s, and not permitted to license technology from Honda in the late 1980s. It was only after the delicensing of the industry in 1993 that the company could go ahead with its plans to enter the domestic car market with its own indigenously designed car. When it finally released its own car, the Indica, in 1998, it did so at a time when it had to face competition from Ford, Hyundai, Daewoo, Suzuki, GM and Mitsubishi, all manufacturing within India. Far from directing (as in Korea) or supporting firm ambitions, the Indian government directly frustrated Telco's, delaying its entry into cars to a much tougher competitive period.

---

* The Ambassador is now exported to the UK – brand-new vintage cars!

Is there one learning hierarchy for all?

A learning hierarchy implies a trajectory applicable to all industries and that all firms should choose to follow. Neither assumption is valid – for two reasons. First, rather than seeing the learning hierarchy as trajectory – going from efficient production *to* improving production *to* developing new products – it is more correct to see the learning 'hierarchy' as a list of competencies the firm should worry about. As the firm seeks to move up the value-chain, each step is what the firm needs to be good at relative to international best practice. The learning hierarchy then becomes a structured way of thinking about opportunities, options and actions at a particular point of time.

Second, product innovation can add more value in industries with more differentiated products – consumer electronics more than steel, for example. However, all industries can add value by going proprietary, in process and in product. What matters is that this proprietary capability is distinctive to the firm.

Capturing innovation rents by going proprietary

Our mantra throughout this book has been that the whole point of innovation is to add value. In Chapter 4, we saw how value can be added incrementally, via process innovation. This matters even if a firm has no proprietary technology. But acquiring proprietary technology allows a firm to move a step up in value. The importance of proprietary technology can be seen from Table 5.6 that compares industrial exports from ten countries.

Table 5.6 shows that Malaysia has the highest proportion of science-based exports, followed in order by Singapore, Thailand, Hong Kong, Taiwan, Korea, India, Pakistan and China, and Indonesia. However, this ranking conceals significant qualitative differences in local content linkages and local technological input. Malaysia's leading position comes from semi-conductor exports, based on the local assembly plants of foreign firms, as we saw in Chapter 4. There is little proprietary about this activity, and this reflects in lower value-addition per worker in manufacturing (Table 5.7).

Going proprietary through process innovation

Some firms in developing countries have been brilliant process innovation-led followers. Particularly in process industries such as steel and petrochemicals and cement, a striking feature of the last twenty years has been the emergence of world-leading firms in the most unlikely places. We will briefly sketch two – Reliance and Ispat – and then draw common themes between them and Cemex. Each has developed proprietary technology through process innovation.

Reliance

Reliance has benchmarked itself against the best internationally for nearly twenty years, well before the Indian economy opened up. Reliance had a practice of building global-scale manufacturing facilities well before there was any economic imperative to do so. While many Indian companies were forced to restructure working practices to survive post-reform, Reliance was ready.

Table 5.6 Distribution of manufactured exports by technological categories (%)

	China[a]		Korea		Taiwan		Singapore[b]		Hong Kong[b]	
	1985	*1992*	*1980*	*1994*	*1980*	*1994*	*1980*	*1994*	*1980*	*1994*
Resource-based	4	6	7	4	9	7	7	3	2	4
Labour-intensive	67	58	50	28	54	33	17	9	66	54
Scale-intensive	18	11	26	27	9	14	21	11	1	4
Differentiated	5	17	14	36	24	31	50	46	17	21
Science-based	0	1	3	5	4	15	5	31	14	17

	Indonesia		Malaysia		Thailand		India		Pakistan	
	1980	*1992*	*1980*	*1992*	*1980*	*1992*	*1980*	*1992*	*1980*	*1992*
Resource-based	15	30	11	5	54	20	27	29	16	4
Labour-intensive	29	49	18	17	28	38	55	50	84	94
Scale-intensive	20	8	5	5	4	6	11	17	0	0
Differentiated	19	8	60	30	14	16	4	1	0	0
Science-based	0	1	4	43	0	20	3	3	0	2

Source: S. Lall, 'Technological change and industrialization in the Asian newly industrializing economies', in L. Kim and R.R. Nelson (eds) *Technology, Learning and Innovation*, Cambridge University Press, 2000, p. 35.
Notes: [a] No data for China are available for 1980, so starting year is 1985.
   [b] Figures for Singapore and Hong Kong are for total manufactured exports (including re-exports).

Table 5.7 Value-added per worker in manufacturing, 1990–94

	Malaysia	Singapore	Thailand	Hong Kong	Taiwan
Value-added per worker in manufacturing ($ per year)	12,700	40,700	19,950	19,500	–
	Korea	India	Pakistan	China	Indonesia
Value-added per worker in manufacturing ($ per year)	40,900	3,100	–	2,900	5,150

Source: www.worldbank.org/data/wdi2000

In 2000, Reliance was the largest Indian private company for both profit and sales. Over 1991–2000 profits multiplied nineteen times. Having started as a small textile concern in the late 1960s, Reliance in the early 2000s is a fully vertically integrated petrochemical firm. It ranges between the first and tenth positions in global volumes in its various businesses. In the mid-1990s, it was the world's largest integrated PET producer, the second largest producer of paraxylene and third in the production of purified terephthalic acid (PTA).

Reliance has long built global-scale manufacturing plants. In the 1980s, Reliance built a polyester plant with an annual capacity of 40,000 tonnes, equivalent to India's entire annual consumption at that time. Again in 1997, Reliance commissioned the world's largest single-stream ethylene cracker. These world-class plants have been built in record time. Reliance's first backward integration project in polyester yarn and fibre was completed in 17 months against a global standard of 26 months. For a PVC plant, Reliance took 24 months for project completion, three months below the global standard.

Reliance is also among the most vertically integrated companies globally. In polyester, value-addition from naphtha to final fabric is 7,000 per cent, providing significant raw material, freight and handling savings. Reliance practises what it calls sweat technology to consistently operate plants at over 100 per cent of capacity. Major savings have come from repeated de-bottlenecking of processes. For example, engineers at a plant manufacturing polyester yarn at 100 per cent capacity realized the main reactor had the capacity to take in more air. Investment in a new compressor increased capacity significantly at one-fifth the cost of a new plant. Sweat technology allows Reliance to push volumes and maintain margins; its profit margin of 19 per cent has been well above the 14 per cent of its leading global competitors Du Pont and ICI.

From its demonstrated mastery of shop-floor innovation, Reliance is now focusing on developing new technologies. The catalysis group in Reliance's research division is developing 'green technologies'. A joint technology development with National Chemical Laboratories (NCL) in Pune involved a novel non-polluting zeolite-based catalyst for manufacturing linear alkyl benzene being tested at Reliance's polyester yarn and fibre plant.

Reliance's global scale and ambition sets it apart from its Indian counterparts. International consultants and financial analysts routinely rank Reliance among the top ten Asian firms. There is, however, a qualification. Reliance's success has come from dominating the domestic market, which provides 95 per cent of its revenues. Sources maintain that this comes in part from close links with Indian politicians. The firm has benefited from a curiously favourable regulatory regime. The firm has also long benefited from the Indian structure of import duties. As India's petrochemicals sector liberalizes, however, Reliance will for the first time have to face foreign rivals on an increasingly level playing field.

Ispat

The LNM Ispat group in 1998 ranked among the top five in the global steel industry. Total sales of its three member units – Ispat International NV, based in the Netherlands, and the privately owned Ispat Indo and Ispat Karmet – were $6.5 billion in 2000. International sales grew at an average of 50 per cent per year in the second half of the 1990s. Ispat has plants in ten countries around the world including the US, Canada, Mexico, Germany, Kazakhstan and Indonesia. Over half of output is exported from ten plants to 150 countries world-wide. North America and Europe are the key markets accounting for 58 and 20 per cent of exports (Table 5.8).

Ispat's success comes from a number of factors, with acquisitions accounting for 60 per cent of its growth. Ispat has a tradition of taking over under-performing units around the world and turning them into some of the lowest cost producers in its field. This is in part achieved through greater capacity utilization.

Table 5.8   Ispat group in comparison with other global players

	Posco	Nippon Steel	British Steel + Hoogovens	Arbed	Usinor	LNM (Ispat)
Steel output[a]	25.6	25.1	22.5	20.1	18.9	17.1
Operating profit margin[b]	15.5	3.3	−2.8	0.7	2.0	6.6

Source: [a]*The Economist*, 8 January 1998; [b]Company Annual Reports.
Notes: [a] 1998, in million tonnes,
          [b] 1999 (%).

Cost control is possibly the most important success factor. Since 1998, Ispat International has reduced costs in all operating subsidiaries. Total sustainable annual cost savings realized since 1998 have exceeded $500 million, approximately 11 per cent of sales in 1999. Financial analysts rank Ispat among the lowest cost steel producers in the world today. Ispat's technological vision shows in the shift from traditional blast furnaces to more efficient mini-mills. R&D is important to the company at a time when many steel plants around the world are downsizing R&D budgets. The R&D centre at Ispat Inland in the US is being expanded and converted into a global resource centre for the group. This centre holds a number of patents in steel-making processes and steel products. The centre has also undertaken product development with several US auto-makers, including Ford. For Honda, a total of five new products help reduce the weight of its cars and improve fuel economy. A new steel was developed for Toyota, which will lead to more dent resistant outer body panels.

With global benchmarking for everything it does, Ispat can be considered a truly global steel company.

Lessons from Reliance, Ispat and Cemex

Each firm licenses international technology when it needs it, but then improves it further, leading to the building of proprietary assets and competencies. In Reliance and Cemex (see Chapter 2), the firm has emerged as a world-leader built around dominance in its own, protected, home market. All firms have moved rapidly up the value-chain by innovating in process innovation. Each firm represents what it takes to be good at process innovation – such as spreading best practice quickly around the group, rapid project execution and constant incremental innovation.

These firms permit us to illustrate more clearly what we mean by proprietary process innovation: the firms each 'own' assets and competencies that are distinctive relative to competitors (Table 5.9). It is not the particular assets or competencies that these firms own that matters but that they add up to a distinct and difficult to duplicate capability that is a basis for future competitiveness and therefore proprietary.

Going proprietary through product innovation

In many industries, at some point the ability to add value through process innovation reaches limits, and there is a need to move to product innovation. As Lundvall puts it:

Table 5.9   Proprietary assets and competencies in Reliance, Cemex and Ispat

Firm	Proprietary assets	Proprietary competencies
Reliance	Vertically integrated petrochemical complexes. World-scale manufacturing plants – largest single-stream ethylene cracker in the world.	Project execution capability – builds global-scale plants in record time.
	Degree of vertical integration among the highest in the world – translates into significant cost savings.	Over-utilization of capacity a regular feature of all plants – translates into ability to maintain globally comparable operating ratios even in slack periods.
Cemex	500 plants in 30 countries with over half of assets outside Mexico. Marketing operations in 60 nations.	Moved from 28th to 2nd position in the cement industry in the last decade. Ability to maintain the highest OPM in the industry. Provides a delivery guarantee to customers building itself a strong brand value. Aims to complete its global supply chain initiative by 2001.
	Highly profitable dominant market position in Mexico and Venezuela.	Demonstrated ability to develop new products and services – e.g. cement for extreme temperatures and the one-hour delivery window.
Ispat	Manufacturing facilities in 10 countries and marketing operations in 150 countries.	Ability to turn around poorly managed plants into efficient low-cost units – achieving some of the lowest costs per tonne for certain kinds of steel. One of the pioneers in the cost-efficient DRI and meltshop technology.
	Assets acquired at prices much below replacement cost.	
	Among the top 5 in the global steel industry.	Ability to spread best practices world-wide.

What seems to characterise both Japan and the Asian Tiger economies – as compared with other less successful developing economies – is that they have moved massively into new product areas where it was far from obvious that they had an original comparative advantage.[36]

Since 1991, as India's economy has opened up, firms have been forced to make processes more efficient to survive. New manufacturing methods have been introduced, and manufacturing efficiency has risen significantly. But change at the product end has usually come through abdication (selling out to foreign firms) or by licensing new product technology, which has become more difficult. Only in some exceptional cases, as we will see in Chapter 6, has change at the product end come in the form of investment in R&D and building proprietary product development capability aimed at the international market. Four Indian attempts at product innovation are Bajaj Auto, Titan and the Indian textile firms Bombay Dyeing and Raymonds.

Bajaj Auto

Bajaj Auto (BAL) is India's largest two-wheeler manufacturer and the third largest two-wheeler manufacturer in the world.* It licensed scooter technology from Piaggio in the 1960s, and then continued to make essentially the same model, with just a few cosmetic changes. Bajaj claims to be the world's lowest cost two-wheeler manufacturer, and has demonstrated its ability to innovate considerably in making its manufacturing process more efficient (see Chapter 4). Honda established a joint venture (Kinetic Honda) in India in 1983.† In the first few years after Honda entered, Bajaj Auto's market share went up. Since then, though, the Indian market has moved away from scooters to motorcycles, where BAL was second to Hero Honda and BAL saw its market share fall. BAL invested heavily in product development in the late 1990s, through both technology licensing and in-house development, as we will detail in Chapter 6. As the President of BAL put it, 'after eighteen years with one model, BAL released eighteen models in eighteen months' (see Table 5.10).

Table 5.10 New product introductions at Bajaj Auto, India

Launch date	Model name	Description
Jan 2001	Kawasaki Bajaj Eliminator	175 cc 4-stroke motorcycle
Jan 2001	Bajaj Chetak	145 cc scooter
Oct 2000	Kawasaki Bajaj Caliber	112 cc 4-stroke motorcycle
Oct 2000	Bajaj M80 Major 4Stroke	75 cc 4-stroke moped
May 2000	Bajaj Spice	60 cc 2-stroke scooty
April 2000	Bajaj Saffire	92 cc 4-stroke scooter
Jan 2000	Bajaj Spirit	60 cc 2-stroke scooty
Sept 1999	Bajaj M80 Major	74 cc 2-stroke moped
Jan 1999	Bajaj Bravo	145 cc 2–stroke motorcycle
Sept 1998	Bajaj Legend	145 cc 4-stroke motorcycle
Jun 1998	Kawasaki Bajaj Caliber	112 cc 4-stroke motorcycle
Feb 1998	Kawasaki Bajaj Boxer	100 cc 4-stroke motorcycle
Nov 1997	Bajaj Classic SL	145 cc 2-stroke scooter
1995	Bajaj Super Excel	145 cc 2-stroke scooter
1994	Bajaj Classic	145 cc 2-stroke scooter
1991	Kawasaki Bajaj 4S Champion	123 cc 2-stroke motorcycle
1990	Bajaj Sunny	50 cc 2- stroke scooty
1986	Bajaj M-80	moped
1986	Kawasaki Bajaj KB100	100 cc 2-stroke motorcycle
1981	Bajaj M-50	50 cc 2-stroke moped
1976	Bajaj Super	145 cc 2-stroke scooter
1972	Bajaj Chetak	145 cc 2-stroke scooter

* In late 2000, Bajaj was overtaken by Hero Honda as India's largest two-wheeler manufacturer.
† The joint venture with Kinetic ended in 1998. Kinetic continued to make scooters independently and Honda launched its own scooter in late 2001.

Titan

Titan is India's largest digital watch company. Titan entered the Indian watch market in 1987, and in five years had become the leading Indian watch firm, mainly through design, as we will describe in Chapter 7. The watch movement was imported for many years, though Titan now makes its own. Titan released an average of 100 new designs a year. Middle-class Indians went from wearing a smuggled Japanese watch to wearing a Titan, and the watch went from being something you had in order to tell the time, to a fashion accessory you had several of. In the late 1990s, Titan entered the European watch market, attempting to establish its own brand in secondary markets like Portugal, Austria, the Netherlands and Scandinavia. Titan's sales in Europe are estimated at about 100,000 watches a year in 2000, and argues that its new target of 300,000 is a number few international watchmakers, apart from Citizen and Seiko, can match.

Bombay Dyeing and Raymonds

In some markets there has been an attempt to build a local brand that would add value to an otherwise fiercely competitive business. Bombay Dyeing and Raymonds are two of the oldest names in India's oldest industry of textiles. Raymonds was founded in 1925, Bombay Dyeing in 1879. Both firms diversified away from textiles in the 1960s, 1970s and 1980s: Bombay Dyeing into synthetic fibre and chemicals, Raymonds into cement, synthetic fibre and steel. Both have refocused on textiles, with Raymonds selling its steel and cement units and essentially giving Reliance its synthetic fibre unit. Bombay Dyeing has also tried to sell its synthetic fibre unit, so far unsuccessfully. Both firms were early brand-builders in the Indian market, their names synonymous with bed-sheets and suiting. Both have recently also started focusing more on ready-made garments, Bombay Dyeing investing in a brand called Vivaldi for shirts and Raymonds buying (in late 2000) India's leading home-grown casual-wear brand Color Plus. Both have also invested in distribution, with Raymonds having 250 of its own stores plus 80 Color Plus stores. Both are attempting to move up the value-chain with these apparel brands; whether or not they succeed will depend on their success in learning to design and make new products.

New product proprietary innovation is hard

As Hobday says,

> only a small number of OEM suppliers have managed to generate new product innovations. Most are still dependent on their natural competitors for key components, capital goods, distribution channels, and high-quality brand images. . . . Many OEM suppliers continue to rely on a repeated cycle of catch-up, imitation, and incremental innovation. . . . Despite significant advances in manufacturing technology, all East Asian Miracle economies face unrelenting competition from lower-cost countries of the region. Lacking strong R&D capabilities and a thriving capital goods sector in electronics, the technological roots of the NIEs, by and large, remain shallow.[37]

Acer was one of the first firms to make the transition to OBM. Acer is one of Taiwan's leading OEM suppliers, by 1990 one of the largest manufacturers of PCs, monitors, fax machines and printers in the world. Acer was also one of the leading Taiwanese firms to attempt to build its own brand abroad, entering the US market in its own name. Stan Shih, the head of Acer, 'began Taiwan's Brand International Promotion Association in an effort to build up Taiwan's quality brand image abroad'.[38] This proved to be a costly strategy and Acer somewhat retreated back to OEM/ODM in 1993 after making losses. It then approached its OBM strategy more cautiously, avoiding the leading international markets and instead attempting to build brand leadership in secondary markets like Mexico, Russia and Finland.

The four Indian attempts at moving to product innovation also demonstrate how hard it is. All four firms have seen new product development as crucial to continued growth and profitability. Bajaj is struggling to maintain margins as it attempts to compete in a world where success comes from developing products people want to buy, not just making reliable old products well. Bombay Dyeing and Raymonds are attempting to move up the value-chain into garments, where distribution and image counts more than an old reputed name. Titan's move into handmade jewellery and Europe is the most ambitious attempt yet by any Indian firm to jump up the value-chain.

The example of the Indian software industry is also instructive since it illustrates both how much potential there is in the shift to proprietary products and how hard it is. As we saw in Chapter 2, the industry is a huge success story of growth, exports, new firms, and huge market valuations. But there has been almost no move to product innovation. We would argue in this case that the key missing element is the *crucial importance of wanting to*. To advance, firms must move to products even though it makes no short-run economic sense. India's leading software firms are flush with money and huge valuations, but product launches have so far come from new firms. The software firms have developed some proprietary process technology, in the category of *learning to improve production*. The leading established firms – TCS, Infosys and Wipro – have been trying, but are really still software factories. The key constraints they face are hiring enough skilled bodies fast enough.* Far from there being a pressing short-term need to move up the value-chain to products, the reality may be the opposite. In some interviews with Indian software firms in 1998, we came across cases of software firms like Infosys and Wipro starting off with development projects to develop a proprietary technology or even a product, only to abandon them later for lucrative contracts that required pulling out the best people. As a result the projects get shelved for indefinite periods or simply die.

Perhaps the most prominent illustration of this argument is the software firm Ramco Marshall, one of the few Indian firms to develop its own product, a branded enterprise resource planning (ERP) package. Ramco consistently made losses and, as Box 5.3 shows, has now retreated from products. The retreat from products was welcomed by financial analysts as Ramco saw its share price fall in the same period that those of Indian software service firms rose sharply.

---

* A Delhi economic think-tank was asked in 1999 by the Indian commerce ministry to prepare a report on India's negotiating position at the new WTO round. The draft report was prepared by Infosys, and strongly endorsed by many of India's leading software firms. Of the total report length of 66 pages, 34 pages were about easing visa restrictions so Indian firms could more easily export people. Completely missing was any concern with deepening the actual content of the work done by Indian firms or moving up the value-chain.

Box 5.3   Ramco and the retreat from products

In 1995, an article on the Indian software industry in *Business India* had the byline 'Very few (Indian) companies have dared to get into product development'.

Take the case of Ramco Systems. Ramco was one of the few Indian companies to do product development in the early 1990s, developing its own ERP software called Ramco Marshall. This involved 400 developers, making it one of the biggest software projects undertaken in India. Though tiny by the standards of Germany's SAP or SAS Corporation of USA, Ramco received a fair amount of recognition for its new product. Today it has more than 150 customers including 75 in India. However, the product's success has been moderate at best. By 1998 the product had earned 650 million rupees in revenues against 1 billion rupees in development and promotion. While other Indian software firms reported record profits based on services, the product led Ramco into losses. In fact, Ramco declared a profit from its Indian operations for the first time in March 2000. The challenge faced by the company was name recognition as it was 'still virtually unknown in North America' and had a 'great deal to learn about selling and marketing'.[39]

Ramco is currently moving from being a product-centred business to a services and solutions company similar to other Indian software firms. The idea is seen as a smart move by financial analysts. The company expects to get 60 per cent of revenues in 2003 from services, up from the current level of 5 per cent: 'Ramco seems to have got its act in the right direction by shifting from products to services and solutions.'[40]

However, the company is not abandoning products completely. It is now launching its indigenously developed enterprise application framework platform – a software product for software services companies which claims to reduce development times by 40–60 per cent. It is also improving its marketing infrastructure with a branch office in the UK, subsidiaries in the USA, Switzerland, Singapore and Malaysia, and strengthening partnerships with overseas companies.

So why not product innovation alone?

There are those that say that once proprietary capabilities have developed, there is no need to worry about manufacturing – just focus on proprietary product innovation. But this is not so easy for the technology-followers that are our subject. They do not usually have a distinctive technological competence that is protected by intellectual property rights or layers of complex tacit knowledge. There is therefore a need to continue to be good at the hard slog of process that we discussed in Chapter 4.

Earlier in this chapter we suggested that there is no *one* learning hierarchy. Indeed, the 'hierarchy' constitutes a whole *set* of things the firm must be good at relative to its competitors. Some years ago, David Teece identified the concept of complementary assets, where capturing the benefits of a particular innovation depended not only on the innovation but on other assets the firm had.[41] For example, if an industry is dominated by a few leading international brands, and a small independent firm comes up with an innovative feature, the leading international brands may capture the benefits. Take the example of a small cola-maker in Brazil coming up with an innovative bottle. Coca Cola and Pepsi may benefit much more than the Brazilian cola-maker as they have the necessary complementary assets of world-wide manufacturing, distribution and brand to take up and sell the idea.

This is where the OEM learning hierarchy has its greatest merit; it depends on manufacturing competitiveness. By being an OEM producer a firm also has a scale of manufacture that is global. When Acer entered the branded product PC market, it was doing so after it had established world-class manufacturing capability, then world-class design capability. It was fighting only on one front at a time – essential in such a competitive market as PCs. The same is true for Samsung in microwaves; coming up with a new microwave product feature makes sense for Samsung as it has the necessary complementary assets of world-scale production. In a case we will discuss in Chapter 7, a small company called Symphony in India introduced a clever new water-cooler with several attractive features – mobility, plastic mouldings, ease of use. However, one of India's leading white-goods firms, Videocon, took up the idea, developed its own mobile, moulded water-cooler and not only captured the benefits of the innovation but is generally considered to have introduced the innovation to the market! Symphony simply did not have the nation-wide distribution and brand that Videocon had as complementary assets. Raymonds' purchase of Color Plus makes sense precisely because of its complementary assets of a nation-wide presence through its own stores: at a stroke Color Plus multiplies Raymonds' outlets by four times.

Titan's attempt to enter the European watch market is interesting because it is attempting to jump straight up the learning hierarchy to make new products without having world-scale watch volumes. As its managing director, Xerxes Desai, said: 'We may even go for a strategic alliance, a kind of double-barrel brand with a foreign partner if our own efforts do not yield results. But we would obviously like to first try to go it alone.' If Titan had an OEM-scale of manufacturing volume this would make its push to establish its own brand internationally that much more viable. As Xerxes Desai said, 'Europe is costing us a fortune. Some of our shareholders may feel I am taking too long a view on Europe. But I firmly believe that unless Titan establishes a strong European presence, it cannot emerge as a world player.'[42]

This argument that manufacturing depth is needed to take advantage of product innovation may sound familiar to those who recall the emphasis on new manufacturing in Chapter 4. If firms did not get serious about manufacturing, the Japanese would keep trouncing them in one industry after another. But this has not happened. In some industries there has been a trend away from manufacturing, while the firms themselves seem to go from strength to strength. The growth of contract manufacturing in the 1990s was one of the less expected and more prominent features of change in the electronics global supply chain. Contract manufacturing accounted for 15 per cent of the $594 billion electronics industry in 1998, and this was expected to rise to 33 per cent of a $861 billion industry in 2003. Leading electronics firms like HP, IBM, Nortel and Alcatel have sold their factories to contract manufacturers like Solectron, which have emerged as major corporations, sometimes dedicating whole factories to just one customer.* This runs counter to our product *plus* process argument and is possible only because these firms, with technological leadership or OBM leadership internationally, have built a barrier to entry. Solectron and its peers have made manufacturing capability a commodity, to some extent! The question is, can Solectron become another Samsung? Will it introduce its own computer?[†]

---

*Solectron, the largest contract manufacturer, had revenues of $14 billion in 2000, with 65,000 employees in 45 manufacturing facilities world-wide. In early 2000, Solectron signed an agreement with Acer 'to form a strategic alliance to provide global design, manufacturing and service solutions for OEM-branded personal computers, servers and workstations' (Solectron web-site, 17 October 2000).

[†] This shift has not happened in autos, where there has been a move to specialized subassembly firms, but manufacturing remains core to the business.

Conclusion: what does it take?

To return to the process–product–proprietary grid (Figure 5.1), let us map the firms we have discussed in our mini-cases. We map both where the firm is today and where it was a few years ago (Figure 5.2). Some conclusions can be drawn from this grid.

All firms can add value, as we saw in Chapter 4, by absorbing slack or innovating on the shop-floor, even where this involves no proprietary or product innovation. This is hard-slog innovation, and is represented as movement within the left-lower quadrant. The maquiladoras represent a non-proprietary process position that has been stationary. So too does the Indian software industry, where the position represents higher value being added by each individual, but it is also relatively stationary.

The firm can also get clever and jump up the value-chain. This takes a move out of the left-lower quadrant into proprietary and product competence. A maquiladora would need to acquire the proprietary capabilities of an Ispat or Cemex, for example, or the product capabilities of ODM manufacturing. The move from OEM to ODM that Samsung or Acer made in the 1980s represents adding value by developing the competence to develop new products, with the product concept perhaps still coming from the buyer.

In this chapter, we looked at two cases of highly successful process proprietary innovation, Reliance and Ispat, which have also shown good value-added growth. They are, however, dwarfed by Cemex, our one firm that has arrived in the quadrant where it competes on an equal footing with the world's leaders.

Finally, a move into the most lucrative quadrant to operate in, that of proprietary products, is also the most difficult. Titan and Vitro are feeling their way along this path, and the way ahead is hardly easy. Moving into this quadrant takes competence at proprietary product innovation. Developing proprietary competence is all about R&D, to which we will turn in Chapter 6. Moving out of the box is hard, but the rewards of capturing the value-added that comes from branded products is also hugely attractive. With few exceptions, this is the only option to become a global player.

Product	OEM deepening – moving to 'higher tech' products e.g. Samsung and Acer in 1990 ODM		ODM (independent) or OIM OBM Cemex
	Chapter 5	Vitro Titan	Chapter 7
Process	OEM e.g. Samsung Microwaves 1989 Maquilas Maquilas in 2000		Ispat International, Reliance
	Chapter 4		Chapters 5 and 6
	Non-proprietary		*Proprietary*

Figure 5.2   Process–product–proprietary grid, mark 2.

6 Managing R&D in technology-followers

Introduction

In Chapter 5 we spoke of the need for proprietary technology and new product development to move up the value-chain. These are done with R&D. But what is R&D? Given the expense of R&D should follower-firms do it? What kind of R&D is relevant for these aspirant firms?

The normal mental construct for the role of R&D is the development of products new to the world, but R&D is a many-faceted activity. In an import-substitution environment, R&D can mean indigenization. In an environment of rapid catch-up, R&D can mean learning from other firms. In labs everywhere R&D means improving existing products. In some cases R&D can be not means but end, with R&D as the core business of the firm. Finally, R&D can mean research aimed at producing new knowledge. We will explore each of these and illustrate them with cases from NICs.

We go on to show how global R&D is concentrated: most is focused in a handful of countries and a handful of industries and firms. It is an enormously expensive enterprise. The R&D effort, of even the largest, most technologically advanced developing countries cannot match that of the major industrial nations or the largest corporations. Fortunately, they do not have to. An increased focus on R&D in NICs can pay rich dividends. Alone, though, this argument is hardly new: politicians and academics of every kind in NICs have been arguing the virtues of increased R&D for at least four decades. What matters is how this R&D is focused. Focus is far more critical to the success of industrial innovation than the level of R&D spending. We develop an argument as to how R&D can be focused in NICs on those activities that will force firms up the value-chain.

What is R&D?

Policy-makers, academics and business see R&D as a well-defined term. The prime minister of India exhorts the nation to 'treble the per cent of GNP spent on R&D to 2 per cent'. An academic studying responses to liberalization by firms in Latin America notes the 'absence of a strong R&D base'. A businessman in the US seeks to 'redirect R&D activities to research directly relevant to the firm's strategy'. All think they are talking about the *same* thing, indeed the same *well-defined* thing. This is not so. As we will see later in this chapter, it is the content of R&D that matters, and here understanding is very limited outside a few technology-leading firms. We will delve 'inside the black box' of technical change, to see what is actually happening when a firm is said to be doing R&D.

R&D in NICs has played many roles

The conventional role of R&D is the development of new products and processes. In 1998, Mowery and Rosenberg began their book on technological change in the US with Alfred North Whitehead's observation that:

> The greatest invention of the 19th century was the invention of the method of invention. It is a great mistake to think that the bare scientific idea is the required invention, so that it has only to be picked up and used. An intense period of imaginative design lies between. One element in the new method is just the discovery of how to set about bridging the gap between the scientific ideas, and the ultimate product. It is a process of disciplined attack upon one difficulty after another.[1]

From the late nineteenth century onwards, this 'disciplined attack' was institutionalized in in-house R&D departments in firms first in Germany (primarily in the chemical industry) and later also in the US (in both the chemical and electrical industries). By 1921, US firms employed just under 3,000 scientists and engineers in their industrial research laboratories. This grew to 46,000 in 1946, by which time leading industrial firms world-wide had established their own R&D laboratories. The period after the Second World War saw the greatest growth in industrial R&D, with US industrial R&D employment rising to almost 800,000 in 1996. R&D employment in firms in most developed countries also rose sharply in the post-war years.

In this section, we discuss five distinguishing roles for R&D in NICs. We do not imply that any of these roles for R&D are trivial: indigenization and learning from other firms is not necessarily an easy process. Neither is 'mere' copying. Particularly if the product involved is complex, and involves much tacit knowledge, indigenization and learning to become competitive are hard. As Nelson and Pack put it: 'there is nothing automatic about the learning business'.[2]

R&D as indigenization: India in the 1970s and 1980s

Almost all NICs went through an import-substitution phase, though as we saw in Chapter 3, the East Asian countries moved to export-promotion much earlier than Latin America, Africa or India. India took import-substitution further than most. Most R&D in India is done by the government in autonomous state-owned institutes, with just 26 per cent of national R&D spending (in 1991) done in the in-house laboratories of private and public sector firms.*

The content of Indian corporate R&D under India's inward-looking policies of self-reliance illustrates the range of activities that can be counted as R&D. In a pioneering effort by Ashok Desai in 1969 (with a follow-up study in 1980), research absorbed approximately 2–3 per cent of corporate R&D, development around 30–40

---

* In 1991, India spent $1.8 billion on R&D, 86 per cent financed by the state, and 74 per cent done in state laboratories. Of national R&D, 12 per cent was financed by the state but done in the in-house R&D laboratories of public sector firms – this should more properly be combined with private sector in-house R&D as we have done here. Since 1991, the share of corporate R&D has risen significantly. While the state still does well over half of national R&D as of 2000, the in-house share has increased to 35 per cent with almost all the growth taking place in the private sector.

per cent and operational investigations – problems of raw material supply, manu-facturing problems and customer's problems – the rest.[3] We would hazard that the proportion of R&D spent on 'operational investigations' dropped by 1991, largely as a result of a more formal separation of the R&D function both functionally and geographically, which insulated it from the demands of day-to-day fire-fighting. What can be termed development, then, constitutes the great bulk of R&D. Development, though, meant something quite different in India: indigenization. If it was imported, do it locally. The content of R&D in industry became the development of local materials and components, substitutions of items which were unavailable, and the development of local manufacturing processes. The objective was to get a product made almost entirely locally. Not only was indigenization almost the *only* objective of R&D but it was seen as the *only proper* objective of R&D. For example, *all* the awards introduced 'to recognize R&D effort' by the government and by various chambers of commerce, including those presented at the annual R&D summit, rewarded import substitution. Whether the product compared well with what was internationally available or was sold at a price that reflected international competitiveness was not a secondary concern: it was of no concern at all. The job of R&D was to indigenize the next product, not improve the existing one or manufacture it better (Box 6.1).

Box 6.1   R&D as indigenization – hydraulic excavators in India and Korea in the 1980s

The case of hydraulic excavators illustrates this objective of indigenization at any cost, to any time frame and with compromises in quality. A study by Edquist and Jacobsson compares the manufacture of hydraulic excavators in Korea and India in the 1980s.[4] In 1980, the twenty leading producers in the world produced 65,000 units between them, accounting for almost 90 per cent of global production. Both Korean and Indian firms started out as licensees.

Hyundai International obtained the first Korean licence for excavators in 1974 from Poclain of France, subsequently transferred to the state-owned Korean Heavy Industries Co. Ltd (KHIC) in 1980. Samsung Shipbuilding and Heavy Industries (SHI) acquired KHIC in 1983. The second firm to enter the industry was Daewoo Heavy Industries (DHI) which entered into a technical collaboration with Hitachi of Japan in 1977. By 1983, SHI alone was selling 633 units, fast approaching the size of the smallest among the twenty largest producers in the world (which produced 715 units in 1980).

India's leading engineering firm Larsen and Toubro (L&T) obtained the first licence also from Poclain in 1973 and production began two years later. By 1981, the total Indian market had grown to 240 units. In the early 1980s, five more producers entered the market, including a public sector company. Production volumes remained low, generally not exceeding 10–15 units each.

The growth paths of SHI and L&T make for an interesting comparison, given that both entered into a technical collaboration with Poclain of France (Table 6.1). Roughly the same number of years after start-up, SHI's production was nine times that of L&T's. While Samsung's price was 25 per cent higher than the international level, it was under half the L&T price. The main reason cited for the exceptionally high Indian price was the low production volume and significant loss of scale economies.

However, scale economies are not enough to explain the entire price difference. The more crucial factor was the excessive emphasis on indigenization. While output was one-ninth, local content was almost double. Its effect on cost is explicitly stated by the study: 'The process of indigenization . . . increases the cost of components. It also absorbs a large number of design engineers. The cost . . . increases exponentially after a certain point.'[5] The authors cite the cost of track chains which are 3–4 times of those produced in France and the price of an Indian engine which is 2.5 times the international level.

The number of design engineers reflects the indigenization drive. The number of L&T engineers is considerable not only in relation to Samsung but also compared with the Swedish firm Akerman (that ranked nineteenth in 1980). In 1984, Akerman produced 1,000 excavators per year of its own design, employing a similar number of engineers (38) as L&T. The authors report that L&T engineers spend a lot of time on non-productive work, such as complying with government regulations and finding substitutes for raw materials. The number of items which Indian designers have to design is 'ridiculously high'. Indigenization is carried on unabated in spite of facing acute problems such as 'problems with the supply of components of a high quality and performance'.[6]

Government policies have played an important role in the performance of industry in the two countries. While both Korea and India followed a policy of import controls and indigenization, India took this to extremes and there were other crucial differences. To support the infant industry, the Korean government provided preferential loans to excavator producers. The government financed most of the $76m invested in the construction equipment plant during 1974–78. The importance of adequate domestic demand for scale-economic production of excavators was recognized by the Korean government. A general policy in the early 1980s was to use the National Investment Fund (NIF) to provide credit to machinery users. The Indian government followed neither of the above policies. On the contrary, its support for the use of manual labour, in keeping with its policy of reducing unemployment, ensured that demand for excavators remained low.

These policy differences help explain some of the difference in development of the industry in the two countries. However, not all of it. There exist sharp attitudinal differences among the two companies.

While candidly accepting that 'R&D is a non-profit area', indicating the relative unimportance of R&D for profit-making at that time, Samsung nonetheless nursed ambitions towards developing its own design capability. 'The eventual target of our R&D and design efforts is to develop our ability to produce our own machine which can be suitable to this (Korean) market as well as overseas requirements.'[7] This view was complemented by a change in trade policy to expose domestic production to international competition and force them to '(1) develop own designs, (2) decrease their costs to international level, (3) improve the quality of the products, and (4) penetrate export markets'.[8]

In contrast, an L&T employee said: 'L&T goes for self-sufficiency instead of international competitiveness'[9] and 'do not foresee that we can ever compete internationally'.[10]

In hindsight, the authors remark that 'Given the small market and the very high price, it could . . . be questioned whether it was wise to start production of excavators at all in India'.[11]

Bringing the story up to date

The evolution of the two firms in the 1990s has been very much in line with these patterns. The Korean financial crisis of 1997 forced the chaebol to sell some of their better firms: Volvo of Sweden bought Samsung's construction equipment division in 1998. At that time, Samsung's construction equipment division exported 50 per cent of output to 60 countries. Samsung's technological capabilities in manufacturing hydraulic excavators seemed to be a key factor driving the acquisition: 'In particular, it was the range and reputation of Samsung's hydraulic excavators which made the acquisition so compelling. . .the strength of Samsung's product range complemented that of VCE [Volvo Construction Equipment].'[12]

A report of the US Department of Commerce in August 1999 brings out the contrast with India: 'Typically . . . (Indian) firms have foreign technical collaborations. They mainly produce lower-end construction equipment. To meet the demand for higher capacity and specialized construction equipment, these firms offer products from their foreign collaborators.'[13] As a result, demand for large capacity equipment and sophisticated technology is fulfilled mainly through imports, with South Korea itself having supplied India with over 1,000 hydraulic excavators and forklifts over 1995–99.

L&T still manufactures the Poclain models, but has recently entered into a 50:50 joint venture with Komatsu of Japan for new models. According to its latest annual report, the joint venture firm reported a loss of Rs120 million 'on account of lower price realization and high import material content' of the new model.

After two decades of forced indigenization, it is ironic that the Indian hydraulic excavator industry is today reliant on imports of both technology and finished product.

Table 6.1   Growth paths of SHI, Korea, and L&T, India, 1983

Firm	Output of excavators (units)	Price comparator[a]	Number of R&D engineers for excavators	Domestic content (%)
SHI, Korea	633	125	10–15	40–60
L&T, India	68	300	30–35	70–80

Note: [a] Approximate percentage of price in industrialized countries.

A general lack of access to imports forced much effort – useful and useless. This technical effort involved much learning. There is no question that Indian industry built substantial technical capability by learning to make almost everything locally. The key question is how much of this technical effort was worthwhile and useful in building internationally competitive products. Waste was rife. Indigenization resulted, for example, in locally manufactured printed circuit boards (PCB imports were banned until 1991 – *no* exceptions) with runs of 20 boards *per year* and a PC industry which in the early 1990s was shown to have added *negative* value locally.* But indigenization also resulted in forcing the local development of a range of intermediate components of some sophistication. India in 1991 had a large and fairly competitive casting, forging and PCB industry. While many suppliers produced what could charitably be called sub-standard products, there were also several that made products of a high enough quality to export to Germany. The same applied for many other industries. Indeed, even *profitable* firms in technology-intensive industries in India were characterized by contrasts – bad quality manufacturers co-existed with decent quality ones, and firms that imported everything in knocked-down form thrived alongside those who added significant value locally. In the process of indigenization, capabilities that were useful and useless developed simultaneously.

Overall, India's technological achievements by 1991 fulfilled Nehru's 'practical proposition' of making second-rate goods in the country instead of importing first-rate ones.

R&D as learning to catch up from other firms: Korea in the 1970s and 1980s

Howard Pack identifies East Asia's successful industrial development as coming from openness to foreign knowledge and ability and willingness to tap international technology markets.[14] Reading descriptions of technology acquisition in Korea (and Japan two decades earlier) in the 1970s and 1980s leads to another role for R&D as the unit that learned from foreign firms. Kim describes how Korean firms built capability in one industry after another:

> Although LG had accumulated radio design and production experience for several years, it was beyond the firm's capability to reverse engineer TVs . . . thus in 1965 LG found it necessary to enter into a licensing agreement with Hitachi. . . . The agreement included not only assembly processes but also product specifications, production know-how, parts/components, training, and technical experts, transferring a significant volume of explicit and tacit knowledge. . . . [LG] sent seven experienced engineers and technicians to Hitachi for . . . assimilating and mastering TV production technology . . . the engineers held group discussions every evening, reviewing and sharing the literature . . . their observations, and their training, facilitating rapid learning by the team; they played a pivotal role on their return home.
>
> The next step was to master production technology for color TVs, especially to compete in export markets. After being turned down by foreign firms for licensing technology, LG and two other major firms decided to enter into a joint research contract with the Korea Institute of Science and Technology (KIST). The R&D team worked round the clock for two years, searching and mastering foreign literature, reverse engineering foreign color TVs. LG finally developed a working model of its own color TV and mass production began a year later.[15]

* Local value-added was negative because the import of complete PCs was not allowed. As a result, firms imported components, boxes, screens, keyboards – all separately. The total cost in foreign exchange of importing such PC components exceeded the cost of buying it whole! See Sudha Mahalingam, 'The computer industry in India: strategies for latecomer entry', *Economic and Political Weekly*, 21 October 1989.

LG thus became the pioneer of Korea's TV industry. It produces more than 150 models with nine production bases overseas exporting most of what it produces. The company has also developed an extensive R&D network both in Korea and overseas. When Posco set up its first steel plant in 1970, it similarly actively invested in learning from other firms. Posco had sent 20 per cent of its work-force abroad by 1991. There are also stories from the 1970s of Friday evening flights from Tokyo to Seoul and the Sunday evening flight from Seoul back to Tokyo being packed with Japanese engineers moonlighting over the weekend at Korean companies.

The Korean engineers who formed technology-transfer teams became the core of the new R&D departments at their companies. Firms licensed technology and expanded investment in in-house R&D. Tables 6.2 and 6.3 show how licensing payments and in-house R&D spending rose dramatically in both Japan and Korea.

Table 6.2 Technology payments (in millions of current dollars)

Year	Japan	Korea[a]	Brazil	India	Israel	Mexico
1960	95	–	–	–	–	–
1965	170	0.2	–	–	–	–
1970	430	10	–	–	–	–
1975	710	20	–	–	–	–
1980	1,440	100	300	–	–	–
1985	2,075	303	150	25	50 (1987)	230 (1987)
1990	6,040	1,360	150 (1989)	70	70	380
1995	9,400	2,385	530	90	160	480
1998	9,000	2,370	1,075	200	210	450

Sources: Data for Japan and Korea till 1985 from H. Odagiri and A. Goto, 'The Japanese system of innovation', and L. Kim, 'National system of industrial innovation', in R.R. Nelson (ed.) *National Innovation Systems*, Oxford University Press, 1993, and IMF thereafter; data for Brazil till 1990 from C.J. Dahlman and C.R. Frischtak, 'National systems supporting technical advance in industry', in R.R. Nelson, op. cit., 1993, IMF thereafter; data for India, Israel and Mexico from IMF.
Note: [a] Data till 1985 is five-year averages starting from 1962.

Table 6.3 R&D expenditure by industry (millions of 1990 dollars)

Year	Japan	Korea	Brazil	India	Israel
1960	920	–	–	–	–
1965	1,870	0.3	–	–	–
1970	6,100	2	–	–	70 (1972)
1975	12,480	20	–	–	80
1980	23,280	50	240	70	210
1983	33,780	–	–	–	280
1985	52,025	1,310	310	140	500
1990	83,650	3,810	–	310	470
1995	–	9,370	2,350 (1998)	900	610

Sources: Data for Japan till 1980 from H. Odagiri and A. Goto, op. cit., 1993, Unesco (www.unesco.org) thereafter; data for Korea from L. Kim, *Initiation to Innovation*, Harvard Business School Press, 1997; data for India from Department of Science and Technology; data for Brazil from *World Competitiveness Yearbook* (2000); data for Israel from M. Trajtenberg, 'Innovation in Israel 1968–1997: a comparative analysis using patent data', *Reseach Policy*, 30, 3, 2001, pp. 363–89.

In Japan technology imports rose rapidly in the 1960s, increasing nearly five times. Then R&D rose rapidly in the 1970s to 1990s. In Korea, technology imports rose rapidly in the 1980s by roughly thirteen times and then R&D rose very rapidly in the 1990s. As R&D rose in both countries, though, technology imports also continued to rise. In other words, firms invested more and more heavily in technology, both through technology imports and R&D. Both were aimed at catching up with other firms through learning (Box 6.2).

Box 6.2   R&D as learning to catch up from other firms: Hyundai Motors in the 1970s

Hyundai began as an assembler of Ford cars in 1967. Following the Korean government's initiative in developing the national automobile industry (see Box 5.2 for more detail), Hyundai formed a task force to acquire basic production capability. In 1968 Hyundai entered an Overseas Assembler Agreement with Ford, to assemble Ford compact cars on a semi-knocked down basis. Besides absorbing packaged technology, Hyundai engineers trained at Ford sites and acquired significant tacit knowledge. There were conscious attempts to learn efficient manufacture: 'teams rehearsed operations by disassembling and reassembling two passenger cars, a bus, and a truck over and over to routinize procedures.'[16] The presence of Ford personnel at Hyundai also helped. To minimize production lead-time, engineers, technicians and construction workers lived together in makeshift quarters during plant construction. Kim credits this arrangement as generating intense personal interaction and accelerating knowledge conversion 'spirally' at all levels. As a result, Hyundai held the record (six months) among all Ford assembly plants for the period between groundbreaking and commercial production.

In 1973, the government's Automobile Industry Long-term Promotion Plan asked the three major car-makers, Hyundai, Daewoo and Kia, for detailed plans to develop a Korean car. Hyundai's strategy involved obtaining foreign technology from 26 firms in five different countries and integrating it itself to maintain independence from foreign suppliers. 'These companies provided opportunities for Hyundai engineers to tour not only their sites but also those of the leading automobile manufacturing plants that had used suppliers' technology.'[17] This helped in the formulation of a composite knowledge base that could be usefully related to physical operations, especially those involved in large-scale, modern automobile manufacturing systems.

The first Korean car (the Pony) appeared in 1975 with 90 per cent local content. Hyundai's share of the Korean market increased from 19 per cent in 1970 to 74 per cent in 1979 and it exported 62,000 cars during 1976–80.

During the second oil crisis Hyundai achieved its third major breakthrough. As car sales nose-dived the world over, Hyundai turned the crisis into an opportunity. The plan this time involved developing a low fuel consuming, front wheel drive (FF) car for launch in the North American market. In 1981, Hyundai licensed the engine, transaxle, chassis and emission control technology from Mitsubishi. It also sourced technology from other Japanese firms as well as from firms in the US, UK, Italy and West Germany. In all, 54 licences were signed in the four years to 1985.

Learning at this stage required three significant aspects: (1) adhering to US safety and environmental standards, (2) full computerization of design, manufacturing and parts/components handling, and (3) construction of a proving ground.

Besides obtaining explicit literature on CAD/CAM systems, the project team spent 14 months internalizing tacit knowledge which involved an in-depth study of Mitsubishi's system in operation and a comprehensive study of all available software packages. The knowledge gained by team members was 'socialized' by expanding the team to include two or three representatives from each related department.

In 1985, Hyundai completed the FF plant and exports to the US began in early 1986. Nearly 170,000 cars were sold in the US in that year alone and FF Excel became the best-selling import car in 1987, with sales in the US alone rising to more than 260,000.

As Hyundai moved up the learning curve, it invested more and more in R&D. Sales grew from US$6.2m in 1975 to $220.7m in 1986. R&D expenditure grew from $0.23m (3.5 per cent of sales) to $9.3m (4.2 per cent), with the number of researchers rising from 197 to 2,247 over the same period.

The role of R&D, at least until the mid-1980s, was primarily to learn. This included overseas training for scientists and engineers, from short-term training and observation to graduate degree programmes. The number of scientists and engineers trained abroad increased from 74 in 1982 to 351 in 1986. In 1984 Hyundai opened an Advanced Engineering and Research Institute to develop its own engines and transmissions and the Manufacturing Technology Center to design its production system. This was followed by the opening of R&D centres in Ann Arbor and Frankfurt in 1986 with the main purpose of monitoring technological change. Proximity to the US and European markets was meant to aid in designing and engineering new cars for these markets. In 1997, Hyundai opened an R&D centre in Japan.

Hyundai's success lay in pursuing a largely independent learning path, one which involved continuous heavy investment in acquiring foreign technology, actively learning from other firms world-wide through intense effort, and a rapid expansion of in-house R&D to complement acquired technology.

R&D as improving existing products

Development is the core of industrial R&D. At major international giants, the R part of R&D is a small part of a central research facility, which is itself part of total company R&D, more of which is focused on existing products. At GE, which spent $1.5 billion on R&D in 1997, the central corporate research lab accounts for 20 per cent of all GE's R&D spending and is the locus for research that is longer term and more blue-sky. Even this central lab has a rule that 15 per cent of spending must go on improving existing products.*

In NICs, a major role for R&D has long been seen as adapting foreign technology to local conditions. The scale of production may be lower or the skill levels different. In India, several companies have succeeded by introducing lower end products to expand the total market. India's largest consumer product firm is Hindustan Lever Limited (51 per cent owned by Unilever, the Anglo-Dutch multinational). HLL has long dominated the Indian soaps and detergents market, with brands that have been

---

* At the central lab spending is allocated: 15 per cent for improving existing products, 35 per cent for introducing successor products, 35 per cent for next generation products and 15 per cent for research without specific products in mind. *Financial Times,* 23 July 1996.

household names in India for over fifty years. In the 1980s, a small start-up company called Nirma grew rapidly by entering the market at the lower end and competing on price, tailoring its manufacturing, distribution, packaging and marketing to its low-cost strategy. HLL's market share for detergents fell as Nirma's rose, until HLL introduced its own lower-end brands and regained some market share.

HLL is probably the world's most successful rural marketing company. Shampoo was long considered a luxury product, and aimed primarily at the middle-class urban consumer. By meeting the poorer rural consumer's requirement for different price points, Hindustan Lever was able to grow the market to a point where by 2001 it commanded 80 per cent of the total shampoo market in rural areas and the rural share of total shampoo sales grew to 20 per cent from zero (see Box 6.3). Achieving this required a significant investment in R&D – not radical innovation, but many small changes in packaging materials and machines that made these lower price points economically viable.

Box 6.3   R&D as improving existing products: Hindustan Lever in India

Hindustan Lever Ltd (HLL), the Indian subsidiary of Unilever, is the country's second largest private company with a turnover exceeding US$2.2 billion in 1999. It has always been considered one of India's most professionally managed firms. The *Far Eastern Economic Review*, in 1998, ranked HLL India's most respected company for the fourth successive year on the basis of 'overall leadership' and a 'company others try to emulate'. *Forbes Global* ranked HLL as the number one consumer household company in the world in 2000. The company has long been a source of trained managers for Indian companies and now multinationals entering India, an indication of its own professional management. HLL has thrived under liberalization with turnover growing nine times and profits sixteen times between 1991 and 2000. From its long presence in India HLL is considered an Indian firm by the Indian consumer in spite of Unilever's majority shareholding. The company had the highest market capitalization on the Bombay Stock Exchange in 1999 and is known for creating brands especially suited to the Indian market, reinforcing its overwhelmingly Indian image.

Hindustan Lever has a history of innovation. In 1958, the company set up an R&D centre and by 2000 employed over 100 scientists and technologists. R&D at HLL has always focused on developing and adapting products especially suited to a low-income tropical country environment. One of HLL's first innovations was 'Dalda', a hydrogenated vegetable oil introduced in 1928, which has become a generic name in India for such oils.

A significant share of research at HLL is focused on improving existing products. One such example is shampoo sachets. Through a series of incremental innovations, HLL dominated the Indian shampoo market, even after the entry of foreign brands following economic liberalization in the 1990s. HLL's market share has risen from 40 per cent in 1987 to 66 per cent in 2000. In 2000 70 per cent of HLL's shampoo sales came from sachets.

To understand the logic behind sachets, consider certain characteristics of the Indian market. The total market for shampoo in India is around 30,000 tonnes. This is double the market in Thailand (15,000 tonnes) where Lever also operates. In per capita terms, however, Thailand consumes 250 ml per year to India's 30 ml. The potential for growth is huge, then, especially given that India is home to 28 per cent of world hair with 16 per cent of the world population (Indian women have longer hair!). The low levels of per capita consumption come from low penetration as well as low consumption. Just 20 per cent of the population in India uses shampoo as against 80 per cent in Thailand. Low consumption comes from low frequency of hair wash (once a week in India to thrice a week in Thailand) and relatively small levels of product usage. Cost underlies this consumer behaviour (so does water scarcity and prevalence of traditional alternatives). The company saw latent demand if cost could be tackled. The average Indian consumer saw an upfront payment on a whole bottle of shampoo as an unnecessary *investment*. More so because usage is infrequent. The answer lay in unitization of the product. HLL made shampoo more income-friendly by packaging it in 30-gram plastic sachets instead of one-litre bottles, which made it affordable to those with just a few rupees in their pocket. Within three years of the introduction of sachets, volume sales of shampoo more than doubled.

The idea of sachets was borrowed from Argentina and Brazil, where they were used as a sampling tool. The company needed to work along two lines – on the product and on its packaging. Packaging issues included cost of the material, its machinability, adaptability to local conditions like weather and transport, and amenability to printing and mass production. Above all it became important to control the overall cost of packaging very closely. As the unit product price dropped, the unit cost of packing came under pressure. Various materials were tried. HLL started with imported material, which it still uses. With continuous improvement the material cost of the sachet package was reduced by 40 per cent over 1995–2000. According to Dr Raghupathy, the head of the haircare division at HLL, this cost reduction has enabled HLL to keep reducing unit prices.

The other line development objective was to improve the product. The R&D department worked on a countrywide hair sample to take into account regional differences while working on product attributes.

Innovation spread backwards from sachets. Initially, HLL imported machines for manufacturing sachets. Pressure to contain costs led the company to source machines locally in 1993. HLL jointly worked with machine suppliers to decrease cost and improve efficiency. By 1997, the cost of the local machine had been reduced to a third of the imported one.

The sachet project involved twenty people in R&D. The haircare division currently spends 2 per cent of turnover on R&D. The team also drew from the global knowledge pool of Unilever. Inputs on basic research were sourced from Lever's global R&D centres, two of which are based in India. The team also interacted with Lever's R&D departments in various countries like Brazil and Thailand, which contributed to knowledge flows regarding adaptability to local conditions.

R&D *as* the *business*

R&D is *the* business in three different circumstances: transnational relocation of R&D facilities, contract research and research lab partnerships with local universities. Leading international firms increasingly locate development activity across the world. Countries such as India and Israel are emerging as major locations for doing R&D, based on the easy and (in India) cheap availability of skilled people. The objective is to produce R&D for the foreign parent, and is often quite removed from local operations, even of the same foreign parent. GE's R&D centre, discussed in Chapter 4, is an example. Another is the opening of the IBM R&D lab at the Indian Institute of Technology in Delhi in 2000, focused on developing new technology and reducing product development time. The GE and IBM labs are linked to parent research labs, not local sales and manufacturing facilities. Box 6.4 gives other examples.

Prasad Reddy identifies the move to locate R&D in some developing countries as a major and little noticed trend. He points out that 'since the mid-1980s, globalization of R&D has come to include efforts to gain access to R&D personnel as well as exploit the cost differentials ... [that is] facilitated by the availability of large cadres of research personnel at substantially lower wages and adequate infrastructure in these countries.'[18]

Table 6.4 tabulates transnational R&D activities. Note the concentration by field in electronics and software, and country – India. Around half India's total is software. Reddy attributes this to shortages of research personnel in OECD countries, in the fields of electronics and biotechnology and the increasing 'R&D intensiveness' of technologies raising concerns about R&D costs. His survey of India finds the availability of personnel to be the main attraction across all types of R&D activities and industries followed by low cost.[19]

As the level of knowledge embodied within particular technologies has increased dramatically, it has become exceedingly difficult for organizations to develop and maintain in-house expertise in more than a very few technologies. Firms focus more and more on a few core strengths, resulting in gaps which force them to tap expertise outside the organization. This includes R&D. Contract research is widely prevalent in pharmaceuticals. In 1999, world-wide expenditure on research and development by

Table 6.4   TNCs' strategic R&D activities in developing Asia – by host country and technology field (%)

	Hong Kong	Indonesia	Taiwan	South Korea	China	Malaysia	Singapore	India	Total
Biotechnology – food and plant genetics	–	–	–	–	7	6	3	4	3
Pharmaceuticals	–	–	–	–	–	–	4	9	7
Chemicals	–	–	–	–	–	6	4	4	4
Electronics	–	–	50	50	22	63	20	3	12
IC design and semiconductors	100	100	33	33	14	6	0	7	13
Software R&D	–	–	–	–	29	6	11	49	37
Telecom and networks	–	–	–	–	21	6	11	20	17
Computers	–	–	17	17	–	6	11	4	6
Engineering	–	–	–	–	7	–	6	–	1
Total (%)	100	100	100	100	100	100*	100	100	100
Number of R&D facilities /units/activities register	1	1	6	6	14	16	46	196	286

Source: P. Reddy, *Globalization of Corporate R&D: Implications for Innovation Systems in Host Countries*, London and New York: Routledge, 2001.
Note: *Rounding up error.

Table 6.5 Number of pharmaceutical contract research organizations (CROs)

Country	Number of pharmaceutical CROs
USA	468
UK	161
Canada	140
France	133
Germany	94
Belgium	37

Sources: www.acrpnet.org/whitepaper2/html/ii._contract_research_organizations.html; for Canada: http://strategis.ic.gc.ca/

pharmaceutical and biotechnology companies was estimated at $44 billion, of which (according to one estimate) $10 to $12 billion was outsourced. Approximately $5.5 billion of such spending was on preclinical/laboratory and clinical development.[20] Many firms have been set up as contract research organizations (CROs) to undertake this outsourcing of activity, as Table 6.5 shows.

Firms have also set up research labs in collaboration with universities. While most of these have been in the US and Europe, Glaxo has also established a lab in Singapore. The Centre for Natural Product Research (CNPR) at the National University of Singapore was established in 1993 as a collaboration between Glaxo Wellcome, the Economic Development Board of Singapore and the Institute of Molecular and Cell Biology. The centre operates high throughput screening for the discovery of biologically active molecules. High-throughput technology screens natural product extracts for new drug leads. It is the only centre in South-East Asia developing and operating this screening. According to Richard Sykes, the then CEO of Glaxo Wellcome, the centre which 'provides a forum for the interplay between Glaxo Wellcome's cutting-edge technology and experience and the Institute of Molecular and Cell Biology's strength in biomedical research will result in new and different approaches to the search for new drugs'.[21]

Box 6.4   R&D as the business: Astra and Biocon in Bangalore

We outline below two case studies by Prasad Reddy of international firms conducting R&D in India.

In 1985, Astra AB, the largest pharmaceutical company in Scandinavia, established its research centre in India. 'The primary driving force behind the establishment . . . [is] to gain access to scientific personnel, who meet the standards, requirements and needs of Astra' which is reinforced by 'the shortages of R&D personnel in the field of biotechnology in Sweden'. Reddy also mentions lower costs of conducting R&D in India as an important factor.

The main objective of Astra Research Centre India (ARCI) is to sponsor biomedical research on infectious diseases and develop novel diagnostics and therapeutics. The centre has been given the full responsibility for doing R&D on malaria, tuberculosis and other infectious diseases.

Nearly half of the fifty research personnel at ARCI hold doctoral degrees with most of the rest being postgraduates. Based on the type of R&D performed, Reddy categorizes ARCI as a global technology unit as work at ARCI relates to products marketed world-wide. The centre has filed 15 patents since its inception. Initially, the centre was given the task of developing products with a short-term time frame such as the preparation of several crucial reagents used in molecular biology research. This was to help build the R&D standard up to international level in terms of equipment and personnel. As Reddy mentions, 'Successful development of such products with a standard to meet global market requirements' has helped in this objective and 'the centre is now entrusted with the tasks of drug discovery.'[22] Besides joint projects with Astra's other R&D laboratories world-wide, the centre also caters to specialized needs such as supplying expertise in biotechnology, utilized in the initial stages of most drug discovery projects. This is expected to decrease now with ARCI getting into drug discovery itself and according to Reddy is a sign of the centre's competence to pursue independent R&D.

The second case is Biocon India Pvt Ltd formed in 1978 as an Indian joint venture with an Irish biotechnology company, Biocon Biochemical Ltd. In 1989, the Irish company was acquired by Quest International, a wholly-owned subsidiary of Unilever which took over its stake in Biocon India. The company develops and manufactures industrial enzymes, investing in R&D to generate new products, technologies and specialized applications. Success in research projects has meant a track record of commercializing at least two new products every year.

The establishment of Biocon India was driven by the availability of raw materials and low processing costs in India. Ready access to R&D personnel and expertise later led Quest to continue the joint R&D arrangement with Biocon. The company employs 115 people. Starting with an initial focus on solid substrate fermentation, the company had built a strong R&D base by the time its Irish counterpart was acquired by Quest. This included mastering of production technologies of certain enzymes and development of certain unique strains and process technologies through in-house R&D. Besides a formal agreement to manufacture certain enzymes exclusively for Quest, Biocon also develops new products in return for payment. Reddy mentions two reasons for this kind of arrangement – Biocon's strength in a field where Quest International lacks experience and the cost effectiveness of this method of furthering technologies in which Quest is interested. Reddy notes that while it is contract-based R&D, 'the total responsibility for product design and development is entrusted to Biocon India'.[23] For its exclusive projects Quest contributes about 50 per cent of the total R&D budget. In addition to its strong in-house R&D base Biocon collaborates with several Indian institutes and universities such as ARCI, National Chemical Laboratories and the Central Institute for Food Technologies. Focusing in-house efforts on application-oriented R&D, it sponsors research projects to take advantage of the expertise on pure science available in these institutes. Besides being cost effective this obviates the need to spend on research not directly related to product development.

R&D as research

In *technology-leaders*, research 'expands the base of knowledge on which existing industries depend and generates new knowledge that leads to new technologies and the birth of new industries'.[24] That view of research must, however, be coupled with our earlier discussion in Chapter 1 of how industrial innovation really happens. First, research tends to be less firm specific than product development, and proprietary innovation within the firm may well depend on knowledge through research at another firm or university, or indeed, as in the case of the swept-wing described below – research done in another country. Second, research's role in innovation is crucial to technical progress in two cases. Advance in certain fields, like biotechnology and semi-conductors, has close connection with scientific research. Third, there is a second broader role for research as one of 'technologies wellsprings' – to reinvigorate technical progress in a particular field.[25] Vincenti points to several examples of the fertile interaction of specific development efforts and research in engineering science. For example, the swept-wing for jet aircraft (which greatly improved aerofoil performance at high speed) was first applied by Boeing in the B-47 of the late 1940s. But where previous aerofoil designs were largely the result of empirical studies and experiments, the swept-wing drew on theoretical work done by German scientists during the Second World War.*

To illustrate this limited role for research even in technology-leaders, consider what Gordon Moore of Intel, one of the world's leading technology-based firms, has to say about research:

> Intel operates on the Noyce principle of minimum information: one guesses what the answer to a problem is and goes as far as one can in a heuristic way. . . . Thus, rather than mount research efforts aimed at truly under-standing problems and producing publishable technological solutions, Intel tries to get by with as little information as possible.
>
> While operating as it does may, at some point, cause Intel to miss a revolutionary idea that has the potential to wipe out established positions, having a large competent R&D organization has not been shown to be protection against change in a basic business paradigm.
>
> In its early years, the company looked to Bell Laboratories for basic materials and science related to semiconductor devices; it looked to RCA's Princeton labs for consumer-oriented product ideas; and it sought insight into basic materials problems and metallurgy from the laboratories at General Electric. Over time, Intel found that most of the R&D relevant to its needs was being done by companies such as Fairchild and Texas Instruments, which had evolved into the product leaders in semiconductors. Today, Intel looks to universities for much of the basic research of interest to it.
>
> The large, central research laboratories of the premier semiconductor firms probably have contributed more to the common good than to their corporations.[26]

In technology-followers, the role of research is even more limited. By definition, neither advancing frontiers in science-based industries nor innovating new technical paradigms is the province of technology-followers. As we will see later in this chapter, the roles of R&D in technology-followers that we propose simply do not require a

---

* Apparently one of Boeing's chief designers was in Germany after the Second World War studying German aviation research. The B-47 was well under development at that time, but when he came across the theoretical work done on swept-wings, Boeing swiftly but fundamentally re-designed the aircraft, drawing on both the German work and theoretical work in the US done by Robert T. Jones. W. Vincenti, personal discussion, 29 May 1997.

major research effort. There are some exceptions, where technology-followers should do research, but these are very limited.* Table 6.6 shows how the R&D spending of the twentieth largest international pharmaceutical firm ($515m) exceeds the combined spending of the twenty largest Indian firms ($69m) by a factor of seven. Average R&D expenditure of the top twenty Indian pharmaceutical companies was 2 per cent of turnover in 1999 vs. 14 per cent internationally. World-wide, pharmaceuticals is the most R&D intensive of all main industrial sectors, but, the disparity between R&D in leaders and followers is representative of industry generally. Box 6.5 discusses how the move from reverse-engineering to new drug discovery has led to major changes in the content of R&D within firms.

Table 6.6   Pharmaceutical R&D expenditures, 1999

Top 20 global firms	R&D expenditure ($m)	Top 20 Indian firms	R&D expenditure ($m)
AstraZeneca	2,923	Ranbaxy Laboratories Ltd	13
Pfizer	2,773	Wockhardt Ltd	10
Novartis	2,653	Cadila Healthcare Ltd	5
Johnson & Johnson	2,600	Lupin Laboratories Ltd	5
Roche	2,363	Sun Pharmaceutical Inds. Ltd	4
Merck	2,068	Torrent Pharmaceuticals Ltd	4
Glaxo Wellcome	2,045	Aurobindo Pharma Ltd	3
Bristol-Myers Squibb	1,843	USV Ltd	3
Eli Lilly	1,784	Pfizer Ltd	3
American Home Products	1,740	Dr Reddy's Laboratories Ltd	3
SmithKline Beecham	1,641	Panacea Biotec Ltd	3
Pharmacia & Upjohn	1,434	Nicholas Piramal India Ltd	2
Schering-Plough	1,191	Alembic Ltd	2
Boehringer Ingelheim	830	Novartis India Ltd	2
Amgen	823	Ipca Laboratories Ltd	2
Takeda Chemical	757	Orchid Chemicals &	
Schering	686	Pharmaceuticals Ltd	1
Sankyo	612	Glaxo India Ltd	1
Yamanouchi Pharm	531	Astra-Idl Ltd	1
E Merck	515	Cheminor Drugs Ltd	1
		RPG Life Sciences Ltd	1

Sources: *Financial Times Survey*, September 2000; calculated from CMIE Prowess Database.

* Briefly, the four exceptions are: (1) research in universities to improve science education of technical people, (2) organised research in specialty areas of importance where research would not otherwise be done world-wide, (3) research where local appropriability is a problem – say where a particular industrial sector is hugely fragmented in structure with hundreds of small firms, and (4) research as a ticket of admission to understanding and accessing work done elsewhere.

Box 6.5   R&D as research: Ranbaxy and the Indian pharmaceutical industry in 2000

The Indian pharmaceutical industry is seeing a clear change in the nature of R&D activity: a shift from reverse-engineering and process development to new drug discovery–product development. This shift is being driven by the 2005 deadline for recognition of product patents by India. Companies like Ranbaxy, Dr Reddy's Laboratories (DRL), Nicholas Piramal, Lupin, Wockhardt and others have recognized the importance of new products in maintaining their success and profitability and are increasingly focusing on the development of new chemical entities.

Ranbaxy, India's largest pharmaceutical company, with over 500 research personnel (150 PhDs and MDs and 240 postgraduates) illustrates this change well. New Drug Discovery Research at Ranbaxy began in 1995 and recently shifted to its R&D centre at Gurgaon in Haryana. The centre has an 80-scientist team and has been successful in developing three potential lead compounds, for which patents have been filed internationally, and is conducting clinical trials for two more compounds. Other potential molecules in the area of antifungal, urology and antibacterial are undergoing preclinical studies. The lead compounds are in the areas of cardiovascular and anti-cancer. This reflects a shift in the company's product line from antibiotics to these areas of greater international demand. R&D expenditure amounts to 4 per cent of sales, out of which a quarter is absorbed by new drug discovery research ($3.3m). This figure is tiny relative to the budgets of leading pharmaceutical companies world-wide, as we saw above.

Certainly research costs in India are a fraction of those in the West. The chairman of DRL has estimated his research costs to be 'one-eightieth of those of his MNC competitors'. Manufacturing costs are also lower, 'perhaps two-thirds of rich country levels'.[27] This helps firms like Ranbaxy as they strengthen their basic research activity but searching for a new molecule remains a highly time- and capital-intensive task. Present cost estimates for the entire activity of introducing a single new drug in the US range between $350 and 450 million, spread over a period of 10–12 years. The estimates include attrition costs and cost of failures, making new drug discovery research a highly complex and risky activity.

According to Dr Khanna, president R&D, Ranbaxy, investments and success rates vary from company to company, the success rate depending on the intellectual assets created by the company. Serendipity plays a major role in new drug discovery research. However, modern drug design tools such as combinatorial chemistry, high throughput screening* and general purpose platform technologies such as genomics, proteomics and bioinformatics promise to make discovery research more predictable in the future.

Recognizing the financial pressure involved in the activity, Ranbaxy has entered into several research tie-ups with publicly funded institutes and universities in India. It is working on the anti-cancer compound Campothesin with Indian government labs. The shift to basic research has not been easy. The company faces a number of difficulties, some in particular reference to India. Dr Khanna mentions the low availability of experienced

---

* Combinatorial chemistry enables rapid systematic assembly of a variety of molecular entities, or building blocks, in many different combinations to create tens of thousands of diverse compounds that can be screened to identify potential lead compounds. High throughput screening methods make it possible to screen vast populations of compounds via automated instrumentation: that is, complex workstations capable of performing several functions with the help of mechanical arms or simpler automated dilution devices. Orsenigo *et al.* 'Technological change and network dynamics: lessons from the pharmaceutical industry', *Research Policy*, 30, 3, 2001.

scientists in India, a ban on animal experimentation, lack of government incentives for R&D, lack of sufficient investment/funds and lack of a critical mass in pharmaceutical R&D in the country. With the substantial scope of subcontracting various stages of drug development, the absence of contract research organizations in India is a major impediment. Ranbaxy recently entered into a joint venture with Speciality Laboratories Inc., the largest single provider of specialized laboratory testing in the US, to undertake higher stage trials for its lead compounds. Ranbaxy has also joined CSIR and Cadilla, another Indian company, to set up a state-of-the-art toxicology bank in Lucknow.

Besides investing in-house in basic research, Ranbaxy is pursuing a wider strategy of spreading risk. Ranbaxy has been able to develop a marketing presence in over 40 countries world-wide with manufacturing facilities in six countries outside India. As Smith reasons, 'Since fixed costs – such as those for R&D and clinical trials – represent a considerable proportion of the total costs for developing drugs, pharmaceutical profit margins are largely contingent upon the number of customers reached'.[28] Ranbaxy has purchased assets from firms in both India and abroad to further this objective.

To support basic research, Ranbaxy is strengthening its core capability of developing and commercializing generic forms and novel drug delivery systems. It currently supplies 26 generic products in the US market and was second world-wide in producing the generic version of Cefaclor, a widely selling antibacterial, enabling it to compete with Eli Lilly in the US market.

Ranbaxy now plans to set up an R&D base in the US for early stage R&D. The centre would start with new drug discovery research and later take up new drug discovery systems and biotechnology research, the new growth area of the future. According to Dr Khanna, the 'USA is a leading player in pharmaceutical/medical research, both basic and applied sciences, so it becomes obvious and essential to monitor the latest developments in that country'. The centre is also expected to play a role in subcontracting specific stages of drug development.

Why do R&D in a technology-follower?

R&D as the expensive option

What is true for pharmaceuticals is true for industry generally: doing R&D is not the obvious choice for firms in NICs. R&D is hugely concentrated globally. The developed world accounts for around 95 per cent of total global R&D spending, and a still higher proportion of patents. Most R&D is done in a handful of countries: of a total of $526 billion spent on global R&D in 1998, the top five countries accounted for 87 per cent (Table 6.7). Within those countries, it is highly concentrated in a few industries: the top five industries – IT hardware, automobiles, pharmaceuticals, electronics and chemicals – account for 77 per cent of the total. And within industry, it is highly concentrated in a few companies: the top twenty companies account for 20 per cent of total global industrial R&D, the top 300 companies for 60 per cent (Table 6.8).

Patents can be used as one measure of R&D output. They are even more concentrated by country (Table 6.9) and company (Table 6.10).* The US and Japan dominate patenting by country. The tenth highest international patenting company in

---

* Patents have the advantage of being well documented and internationally comparable across industries, but the disadvantage of missing almost all incremental innovation in all industries, and most innovation in industries such as mechanical engineering and food.

Table 6.7   Total and industrial R&D expenditures, 1998 (in $ million)

Country	Total	Industry	Country	Total	Industry
USA	227,900	171,300	China	6,700	3,000
Japan	122,300	88,100	Brazil	5,900	2,400
Germany	49,800	34,000	Taiwan	5,300	3,300
France	31,100	19,200	India	2,300	450
UK	24,000	15,700	Singapore	1,500	900
Italy	13,000	7,000	Mexico	890	180
Canada	9,400	6,000	HK	350	30
Sweden	8,800	6,600	Thailand	200	10
Netherlands	8,300	4,200	Malaysia	195	270
Korea	8,100	5,900	Indonesia	190	90
Total for 46 countries				526,000	368,200
Share of top 5 (%)				87	89
Share of top 10 (%)				96	98
Share of NICs (%)				6	5

Source: *Financial Times*, September 2000.

Table 6.8   R&D expenditures of top 20 international companies, 1998 (in $ million)

Company	Total	Company	Total
GM	7,900	Lucent	3,680
Ford	6,300	Ericsson	3,280
Hitachi	4,990	Toshiba	3,160
Daimler Chrysler	4,980	Sony	3,100
IBM	4,710	VW	3,010
Matsushita	4,700	Motorola	2,890
Siemens	4,660	NTT	2,820
Toyota	4,340	Microsoft	2,800
Fujitsu	3,780	Honda	2,790
NEC	3,730	Intel	2,510
R&D expenditure of top 20 companies			80,104
R&D expenditure of top 300 companies			237,350
Global industrial R&D expenditure			396,030
Share of top 20 in total R&D expenditure of top 300 international companies (%)			34
Share of top 20 companies in global industrial R&D expenditure (%)			20
Share of top 300 companies in global industrial R&D expenditure (%)			60

Source: *Financial Times*, September 2000.

Table 6.9   Number of US patents, selected countries

	1963–84	1986	1990	1994	1998	Total 1963–98
Total	1,416,600	70,860	90,366	101,680	147,520	2,770,440
USA	970,240	38,130	47,390	56,070	80,290	1,701,090
Japan	105,510	13,210	19,530	22,380	30,840	390,340
Germany	108,850	6,860	7,610	6,730	9,100	211,760
UK	57,480	2,410	2,790	2,230	3,460	94,440
Taiwan	570	210	730	1,440	3,100	16,290
South Korea	170	50	230	940	3,260	11,290
Israel	1,700	190	300	350	750	6,640
Mexico	1,190	40	30	40	60	1,760
Hong Kong	300	30	50	60	160	1,170
Brazil	400	30	40	60	70	1,080
China	110	10	50	50	70	720
India	260	20	20	30	90	700
Singapore	50	3	10	50	120	600

Source: www.nsf.gov, Science & Engineering Indicators (2000).

Table 6.10   US patents in top international and top Indian corporations

Top 10 international corporations (1998)		Top 10 Indian corporations (1995–99)	
International Business Machines Corp.	2,660	CSIR	95
Canon Kabushiki Kaisha	1,930	Individuals	54
NEC Corporation	1,630	Texas Instruments	16
Motorola Inc.	1,410	Ranbaxy Labs	13
Sony Corporation	1,320	Dr Reddy's Research Foundation	10
Samsung Electronics Co. Ltd	1,300	Hoechst Aktiengesellschaft	10
Fujitsu Ltd	1,190	Lupin Labs	9
Toshiba Corporation	1,170	GE	6
Eastman Kodak Company	1,120	Panacea Biotech	6
Hitachi Ltd	1,090	National Institute of Immunology	5

Source: www.nsf.gov, Science & Engineering Indicators (2000) and *Businessworld*, 25 December 2000.

the US, Hitachi, received over 1,000 patents in the single year 1998. The top Indian patenter, CSIR, received 95.

Most studies of R&D in developing countries point to the low proportion of R&D as a percentage of GDP or turnover (see Table 6.11), usually with the objective of arguing that R&D spending must be increased to build local technological capability.

We find these comparisons virtually meaningless. In terms of scale, the highest spending NIC in 1987, Korea, spent $4.5 billion on corporate R&D, which is about what one firm, General Motors, spent in the same year. Glaxo Wellcome alone spent well over $2 billion on R&D each year, more than the *total* pharmaceutical sector in the NIC column (every firm and government lab in all six countries) in Table 6.11 added together!* In 1998, India's total R&D spending in over 1,000 industrial labs came to $450m. Stanford University in the same year had an R&D 'budget' of $410m.† The point is that technology-followers cannot hope to compare to technology-leaders in R&D spending. Fortunately, they do not have to, because the role of R&D in a follower environment is quite different. The reason stems from our earlier analysis of innovation in followers: the essential difference is that the future is known; it is the uncertainty involved in technology-leading innovation which adds much to the cost of doing R&D. As Rosenberg puts it, 'Quite simply, the vast majority of attempts at innovation fail'.[29] Although numbers to back up this assertion are hard to come by, a consulting firm reported in a now dated study that well over half of all R&D projects were simply cancelled.‡ A share of those which are completed are not considered to have come up with anything useful enough to patent. Even more, 90 per cent of what finally does get patented is never commercially used. Putting this together, one can indeed conclude that the R&D process is expensive, with the bulk of spending leading to no useful commercial application. Anecdotal evidence from technology-leaders such as HP and Glaxo is consistent with this analysis over time.

Table 6.11   R&D as a percentage of GDP, 1987 and 1997

Country	1987	1997	Country	1987	1997
US	2.9	2.7	Korea	1.8	2.7
Japan	2.8	2.9	India	0.9	0.7
Sweden	2.7	3.9	Taiwan	0.9	2.0
FRG	2.6	2.3	Brazil	0.6	0.8
UK	2.3	1.8	Singapore	0.9	1.8
Canada	1.5	1.6	Mexico	0.3	0.3

Sources: All data from www.unesco.org except Germany (O. Keck, 'The national system for innovation in Germany', in R.R. Nelson (ed.) *National Innovation Systems,* Oxford University Press, 1993); Taiwan (S. Lall, *Building Industrial Competitivenss in Developing Countries*, Paris: OECD, 1990); and Brazil (C.J.B. Dahlman and C.R. Frischtak,'National systems supporting technical advance in industry: the Brazilian experience', in R.R. Nelson, op. cit.).

* The merger between Glaxo Wellcome and SmithKline Beecham has been driven largely by the expected R&D benefits of a larger resource base. R&D expenditure is expected to rise to $3.7 billion making it the largest spender in the pharmaceutical industry world-wide. *Financial Times Survey*, September 2000.

† Also, the number for universities is hugely understated since the availability of cheap but highly skilled labour (graduate students) does not show up in the numbers. Stanford number from www.nsf.org, India from *World Competitiveness Report*, 2000.

‡ A report from a management consulting firm from 1982 indicates that for every 100 projects that enter development, 63 are cancelled, 25 become commercial successes and 12 are commercial failures. See D. Leonard-Barton and J. L. Doyle, 'Commercializing technology: imaginative understanding of user needs', in Rosenbloom and Spencer, op. cit.

Nelson argues that industrial technical progress happens in a simultaneously wasteful and powerful way.* It is precisely the wasteful attribute of technical change that makes R&D expensive in a technology-leader. In a technology-follower, much of the waste has already taken place before the follower begins work and the uncertainty involved is thus a different order of magnitude.

Given this analysis the key issue for R&D in followers is not 'how much R&D?' but 'what R&D?' R&D in followers needs to be focused in five specific ways to move followers up the value-chain. First, formal R&D effort can usefully complement process innovation. Second, R&D teams can play a crucial role as the firm's 'learners' of knowledge produced elsewhere. Third, doing R&D can have intangible spin-off benefits for the rest of the organization. Fourth, an increasingly important role for R&D is to tap external sources of knowledge and to co-ordinate this knowledge with in-house effort. Fifth, and increasingly importantly, the move up the value-chain to more attractive markets depends on a firm's ability to develop proprietary product designs, which is the subject of Chapter 7.

The role and organization of R&D in technology-followers

As a complement to shop-floor innovation

Most problems which arise on the shop-floor are best solved there. But some problems which arise in manufacturing need an organized and focused team effort, drawing on the special skills of an R&D department. An obvious role for R&D in a technology-follower is to be the solver, though of last resort, of problems that arise on the shop-floor.

Rosenberg shows that the establishment of the first chemical research lab in the US in the late nineteenth century was for troubleshooting in the production of Bessemer steel. The formation in 1902 of the American Society for Testing Materials was induced by equally practical concerns of problems associated with the production of tile pipe, stone, slate and iron steel, to meet the day-to-day needs of the construction industry.[30]

In their study of a rayon plant in Argentina, Katz *et al.* mention the 'trouble-shooting' nature of the R&D efforts of the firm: 'the firm is trying to respond to problems or urgent requirements of the production process by stepping up its commitment to knowledge-generating activities', as the demand for in-house R&D grew over time:

   1937: The 'start-up' period.
   1944: Expansion of installed capacity with the incorporation of 12 additional
          machines in the spinning section.

---

* Nelson describes capitalism as an 'engine of progress', that is simultaneously wasteful and powerful. It is *powerful* because it is capable of generating many alternative approaches to technical change and then has institutions in place (firms and markets) to select the best alternative. But this approach is also *wasteful*, in that there is frequent duplication of effort (several firms working on the same thing), much work done that turns out to be fruitless, and certain socially useful areas where no work is done because the benefits are not apparent enough or appropriable enough to justify effort by any one firm. R.R. Nelson, 'Capitalism as an engine of progress', *Research Policy,* 19, 1990, pp. 193–214.

1946: Introduction of high-speed spinning through the incorporation of 'tube spinning' technology.

1951/2 and 1957/8: Changes in process technology due to raw materials substitution and process optimization efforts.

1962: Substitution of capital for labour through the installation of new washing and purification equipment.[31]

In a study of a Mexican steel firm, Perez and Peniche (1987) report that 'the innovative efforts carried out . . . [are] mostly of the "trouble-shooting" kind' and that 'previously existing and newly emerging production problems absorb almost the whole of the firms' innovative capacity'.[32] Kim, too, provides several examples of the role of R&D in de-bottlenecking process plants and adapting imported technology to local raw materials to improve local manufacturing.[33]

This argument is consistent with Nelson's analysis of why industrial R&D takes place primarily in specialized laboratories, and why these laboratories tend to be in-house. First, in many fields, bringing about significant technical change requires a concentration of people trained in science and engineering that is most easily found in a distinct institution – the R&D laboratory: 'The differentiation of the people involved in R&D from those involved in production, and the requirement for dedicated equipment and organization led naturally to the specialized laboratory committed to inventing and distance from on-line production.' Second, although R&D needs to be distinct and separate, it also needs to be *closely and permanently* connected to the firm:

> To be effective, industrial R&D generally needs good communication channels to the firm whose problems are being addressed, and who will in the end use the product of R&D. . . . Thus, while there are exceptions, where effective and sustained industrial R&D is important for competitive success, a firm is going to be forced to establish a long-term relationship with a research and development laboratory which, in turn, is committed to it. . . All this strongly pulls towards having an in-house laboratory.[34]

In technology-followers a specialized R&D laboratory will provide that concentration of people both skilled and qualified enough, sufficiently removed from day-to-day routine, to solve bigger and longer-term shop-floor problems. This group of people cannot be at the R&D laboratory of the technology-leader or a national laboratory or a university – they have to be within the follower-firm. Only then will the laboratory be primarily responsive to the problems of the firm and develop the long-term formal and informal communication channels needed for a close relationship.*

As the formal learning unit of the firm

So R&D needs to be organized as a distinct in-house unit. In technology-leaders, organized R&D is usually seen as the formal *innovating* unit of the firm. In a

---

* Although this is an issue peripheral to this chapter, our analysis explains why the autonomous government or non-government R&D lab, so beloved in NICs from India to Mexico, has contributed so little to technical change in local industry.

technology-follower, R&D should instead function as the firm's formal *learning* unit. In particular, R&D must build absorptive capacity to be able to access work done in other firms. This absorptive capacity is primarily a function of prior related knowledge, which 'confers an ability to recognize the value of new information, assimilate it, and apply it to commercial ends.'[35]

R&D thus performs the role of a gate-keeper that plugs into external storehouses of technological knowledge. It is quite likely that the knowledge a firm must access from the outside is highly specialized, requiring advanced training even to understand it. An R&D group usually contains people who are ideally suited to carry out this gate-keeping role (particularly valuable in a technology-follower where the availability of people experienced in the field will be lower). To understand R&D being done elsewhere may also require not only adequate training, but also doing R&D. Doing R&D amounts, then, to a 'ticket of admission' to research done elsewhere.[36] This 'learning' role is of great importance in technology-leading firms.* In technology-following firms, it becomes R&D's reason for existence. For several Korean firms, the R&D department played the key role in transferring imported technology such that capability was built in-house for subsequent project execution.[37]

Ronald Dore argues that building *learning capacity* is the crucial technical capability for firms in followers. This learning capacity includes 'the information-gathering network that can survey what is available in the world, detect new developments, judge what is worthwhile buying and learning in detail.'[38] Dore even invents an acronym for this capacity, IWTRC, for Independent World Technology Reconnaissance Capacity. Leading Japanese firms' ability to scan the world horizon for useful developments has long been praised. The four leading Korean chaebol have set up and bought firms in California to function as 'outposts' that would, together with doing R&D, 'serve as an "antenna" for information on research activities in advanced countries'.[39] Kim[40] documents several dozen such examples: in electronics, LG has laboratories in Tokyo, Sunnyvale, Chicago, Germany and Ireland; Samsung has them in San Jose, Maryland, Boston, Tokyo, Osaka, Sendai, London, Frankfurt and Moscow; Daewoo has two in France and one in Russia; Hyundai has laboratories in San Jose, Frankfurt, Singapore and Taipei. In automobiles, Hyundai has technical centres to monitor technological change in Michigan and in Frankfurt. In semiconductors, Samsung, LG and Hyundai have bought firms in Silicon Valley as a way of monitoring advances. Organizing for this learning role requires that individual R&D engineers see themselves as technology-keepers, a broader role than gate-keeper (see Box 6.6), with responsibility for tracking useful knowledge inside and outside the firm. In a technology-follower, this useful knowledge will be overwhelmingly technological, not scientific. Recruiting freshly minted scientists and engineers directly from university will generally keep a firm adequately up-to-date with scientific knowledge.

---

* Indeed this argument is based on W. Cohen and D. Levinthal, op. cit. and R.R. Nelson, op. cit., 1992. Both papers talk of technology-leading environments. The learning and creating roles of R&D are closely related – an earlier paper by Cohen and Levinthal is even titled 'Innovation and learning: the two faces of R&D', *Economic Journal*, 99, 1989, 569–96.

Box 6.6   The importance of technology-keepers in technology-followers

As we saw above, R&D in a technology-follower functions as the firm's learning unit, playing the role of a gate-keeper by building absorptive capacity and becoming a *technology-keeper.*

What does it take to 'keep' technology?

Effective technology keeping has at least three distinct roles:

1 Boundary spanning and gate-keeping: to track advances in the area wherever they may happen. This will involve a combination of keeping track of what other firms in the field are doing, reviewing the relevant technical journals, and being 'plugged into' those people networks that matter. For example, in the area of computer networking, the technology-keeper would need to read the many magazines on networking, be plugged into what other firms in the country and abroad are doing with networks, and be a part of a network of people at other firms (local software engineering firms, say) who tend to keep abreast of developments in the field.

2 Codification: this external knowledge needs to be 'captured' in some permanent form – collections of articles, reviews of new products of other firms, and so on, all put together to represent the state of 'kept' technology. Codified knowledge provides a base for further advance. Only if knowledge is codified can it become permanent, communicable and improvable. If an individual comes afresh to designing a new generation of an existing product, drawing on previously captured learning could shorten the learning curve dramatically and enable the organization to learn from its past to avoid mistakes and fruitless paths.*

3 Communication and utilization: knowledge is useless to an organization unless it is used. And the knowledge kept by the keeper may be useful in very different work areas. A crucial technology-keeper role is to make knowledge – from external or internal sources – available wherever in the firm it is needed. Codification permits knowledge to be communicated more easily. But knowledge may also need to be translated into a form that is understandable to whoever needs to use it. The average manufacturing engineer may understand nothing of the terminology of metallurgy, but may benefit greatly by knowing of some advance in welding techniques. The technology-keeper's role would be not just to codify, but to translate and then communicate the knowledge to those specific individuals in the firm who would benefit from the knowledge. An essential technology-keeper role is to know which person in the firm would benefit from the knowledge he or she keeps, and to see that that knowledge gets to that person. This means both passively making knowledge available – say in the form of indexed manuals in the company library or a shared database on a computer network – and actively searching out those who would benefit from the knowledge to get it to them, and then being available as a resource when questions arise.

---

* *The Economist* makes precisely this point in an article on corporate amnesia. By cutting out layers of management hierarchy, firms remove individuals, particularly middle managers, who hold vital tacit knowledge gained from the experience of how the firm has done things in the past. See *The Economist*, 'Fire and Forget?', 20 April 1996.

As a source of intangible spin-off benefits for the firm

Apart from playing a direct role in technical change, R&D can provide significant intangible benefits to the firm. First, as Ronald Dore says, 'Self-reliance is always a virtue, especially when it comes to technology', referring to our earlier discussion about a firm's need to combine openness to outside knowledge with the cultural confidence to improve what is learnt from the outside (Chapter 1). R&D, with its collection of 'higher qualified' people, can set the tone for discourse on technology. Second, R&D can play a useful role as a change agent for a firm. As technology-followers start looking to international markets, aspects such as product finish and packaging require a quantum leap. R&D can play a 'demonstrator' role of setting new standards that match the best internationally. Indeed, one of the most effective ways of building absorptive capacity is by bench-marking against competitive products. Bench-marking, of course, should extend across all key firm activities, but R&D is a natural place to begin the process, because it directly feeds into product development – an activity the firm is doing for the future in any case. Third, doing R&D can help in attracting some good technical people who are needed by the firm but who would not otherwise join.*

These intangible benefits are just that: vague and difficult to measure. But the role of nucleus for new attitudes and new procedures, and attracting more technical people, is potentially important.

As co-ordinator and integrator of a global knowledge system

In a recent review of innovation in firms, Keith Pavitt argues that co-ordinating research done outside the firm is emerging as another face of corporate R&D. This 'third face of R&D' is a result of the 'continuously increasing number of technological fields that firms must monitor and master'. He continues:

> Firms at the centre of complex or fast-changing supply systems – be they physical supply systems as in the automobile industry, or knowledge supply systems as in pharmaceuticals – must also have the means to co-ordinate change in these systems, especially when they are designing and implementing major changes. Empirical studies show that such firms maintain in-house a systems integration capability: first, in order to monitor and stimulate improvements by suppliers within the modular constraints of established systems; and second, in order to integrate major changes periodically into new and improved systems. With increasingly systemic complexity, it is likely that a growing share of corporate technological activities are being devoted to these activities. In addition to innovation and imitation, corporate R&D now therefore has a third face: co-ordinating change and improvement in increasingly complex external product and knowledge networks'.[41]

---

* There are parallels: in Brazil, some universities do R&D as a way of attracting good teachers; whether or not anything valuable comes out of the research is secondary. And some technology leaders like HP, IBM and AT&T have to commit to doing some basic research to attract the best technical minds.

A key role for R&D, then, is to co-ordinate these external sources of knowledge and connect them up with in-house effort. We have seen several of these sources earlier in this chapter. For example, learning from other firms, contract research, subcontracting to a research subsidiary in a developing country and setting up listening posts to monitor other firms.* To these can be added pooling patents with competing firms and accessing knowledge from universities where industry-sponsored projects provide an increasing share of university research budgets.

As a firm nears the technology frontier in specific fields, this role is becoming more important for many technology-followers. For example, the Indian pharmaceutical firm Ranbaxy (see Box 6.5):

- formed (and later dissolved) a joint venture with Eli Lilly to conduct joint development of pharmaceuticals in India;
- established an R&D base in the US for early stage R&D;
- entered into collaborative research arrangements with the Indian Institute of Chemical Technology for new drug discovery research and with the University of Bath in the UK for new drug discovery systems;
- licensed a drug to Bayer for royalties on world-wide sales by Bayer. In turn, it has bought from Bayer its generic drugs subsidiary in Germany to give it access to the European market;
- entered into a joint venture with Speciality Laboratories of the US to undertake higher stage trials for lead compounds;
- collaborates with Cadilla, another leading Indian pharmaceutical firm, and CSIR to set up a state-of-the-art toxicology bank in Lucknow.

Ranbaxy's head of R&D, Dr Khanna, emphasizes that its aspirations to be a 'research-based international pharmaceutical company' require that it rethink the role of R&D. Ranbaxy needs to simultaneously draw on a range of external knowledge sources, while managing and channelling rapid growth in in-house R&D.

Conclusions: organizing for effective R&D in followers

The follower-firm must organize for effective R&D. This involves:

- Reconceptualizing what R&D is for: in countries with long histories of import-substitution, the role of R&D meant indigenization. Moving from R&D as developing locally the same things that were previously done abroad to R&D as developing products to sell globally takes much change. It takes the skills we spoke of in Chapter 5 and will talk of again in Chapters 8 and 9.
- Co-ordination within the firm: playing R&D's role as solver of last resort for shop-floor problems requires that there be systematic linkages built from the shop-floor to R&D, such that the right problems (and only the right problems so R&D is not kept from doing anything else) are referred to it. Playing a technology-

---

* The Circle Bar in Santa Clara has been the source of many anecdotes of this exchange and its importance to technology development in the semi-conductor industry of the 1970s.

keeping role requires that the firm establish systems to document and share knowledge.

- Co-ordination beyond the firm: the role of gate-keeping and co-ordinating external knowledge with local effort requires that R&D set up systems to track what is being done elsewhere, and that the firm consciously match in-house effort with external sources of technology. None of this is easy.
- Concurrent engineering: in Chapter 5 we argued that even as firms move towards the frontier, as long as they are operating within a technology-follower paradigm being efficient at manufacturing is essential to success. A key source of this efficiency is an effective product development to manufacturing interface. Japanese firms, and Korean firms too, have long been role models for concurrent engineering, for involving other functions in the product development process early on so that time-to-market is low and initial manufacturing efficiency high. This meshes perfectly with the shop-floor innovation we discussed in Chapter 4.
- Creativity and innovation: as firms move to conceptualizing their own new products, the mix of effectively implementing what is known and innovating incrementally and constantly has to be leavened with a dose of bigger jumps in product features. This takes creativity and what management gurus like to call discontinuous innovation. The precise attributes of no-waste and widepread and cross-functional capabilities that make Japanese and Korean firms such good incremental innovators, hold them back from the more creative jumps. We will return to this key issue of how to balance the skills of incremental innovation with the skills of making creative jumps in Chapters 8 and 9.
- Independent product development capacity: finally, and perhaps most importantly, is the development of technology that is proprietary to the firm, including new products. These new products will not be based on new technology, but will be new product conceptualizations: they will, in short, need to be new designs. The firm thus needs to build design capability, the subject of Chapter 7.

7 Design leadership for technology-followers*

Introduction

The most important role for R&D in technology-followers is the development of a technology base that is proprietary to the firm, including the development of new products. New products will not be based on new technology but will need to be new product conceptualizations: they will, in short, need to be new designs. As we saw in Chapter 6, a key role of R&D is to deliver an independent product development capability to the firm. New products fall on a scale that ranges from homogenized low-cost, usually mass produced items, to high value-added items. Incremental innovation, process innovation, design for manufacturability and optimizing the supply chain are all critical at the homogenized end.[1] The high value-added end offers some of the most attractive opportunities, but to be at the high value-added end demands the ability to define design specifications. The development of products that meet the *particular* needs of a local market also requires design capability. Thus it is necessary to recognize the importance of design, and the distinction between design and technology.

We start by explaining why design is important to firms, both for technology-leaders and followers. We argue in this chapter that the role for R&D in followers is to push out the design frontier while following the technology frontier. Using work done by Jim Adams on the soft aspects of quality, we advance an argument as to how this can be done. The role of R&D in NICs, then, is less one of research and development, more of development and design. Focusing on the dual role of the R&D function in followers, of efficient frontier-following and effective design leadership, provides the potential for firms in NICs to move substantially up the value-chain of global manufacturing. Finally in this chapter, we report on a comprehensive design-leadership exercise undertaken in 1999–2000 between four leading engineering firms in India. We use this exercise to illustrate both the potential and the challenges involved in building design capacity in firms that are not used to conceptualizing products themselves.

What is design and how is it distinct from technology?

By design we mean the deliberate conceptualization of a product to achieve certain desirable characteristics. These characteristics apply at different levels and include

* This chapter is jointly authored with Jim Adams. It has also benefited greatly from the inputs of Ed Pearce, the experienced product designer mentioned in the section on the IDMM story.

aesthetic factors that apply to the emotions and performance factors that affect function. A new design – a new form and function – is concerned with 'matching techniques and markets'.[2] In the case of consumer products, design tends to be market driven with technology providing the capability to meet new market needs. Design plays a different role over time. Walsh indicates that,

> A shift in emphasis may be observed in the life cycle of an industry or technology, from an early period of designing for experimentation and technological innovation, through a period designing for technical improvement, lower cost and ease of manufacture becomes more important, and finally to a mature phase where a multiplicity of design variations, fashions, styles and re-designs within product ranges aimed at different market segments predominates.[3]

When possible, technology-followers should operate at the later stages.

We argued in the introduction to this chapter that technology-followers should be concerned with new design. This argument rests on the premise that the design and technology frontiers are somewhat separable. It is quite feasible to push out the design frontier while remaining a technology-follower. Design and technology are quite distinct in this respect.

Why do good design?

We argue that design should be undertaken for both objective and subjective reasons. First, and most objectively, a good product design enables firms to move up the value-chain and improve margins. We deal with several examples. Second, design has a high reputational effect that works at the level of the individual designers, the firm and indeed the country. The design and production of an outstanding product positively affects other products designed by the individual designer, the company and sometimes country. This leads to a virtuous circle which steadily increases expectations and performance: a designer or design team in an environment where doing good design is the norm wants at least to meet the standards of that environment, and if possible exceed them. This in turn leads to better-designed products, which improves the environment, and so on. Finally, not just designers but all employees are motivated by working for a firm that is perceived as being good at design. They are proud of being part of an organization known for producing outstanding products. This spirit leads to a strong urge to catch-up in followers. We will deal with each of these issues.

To move up the value-chain

By pushing out the design frontier, a technology-follower can capture the higher value-added market segment. Three examples from India of *new* designs with *old* technology illustrate the importance of design innovation in moving up the value-chain. Among the most successful products in the Indian market in the last few years have been Titan watches, Videocon air-coolers and TVS Scootys. Titan entered the watch market in the mid-1980s, a market dominated by a public-sector firm which made reliable, though unfashionable, watches, and Japanese-brand smuggled digital watches. In five years,

Titan became the leading Indian watch firm, mainly through design – Titan released an average of 100 new designs a year. Middle-class Indians went from wearing a smuggled Japanese watch to a Titan, and the watch became a fashion accessory with subsequent advantages to Titan because an individual might own several. Air-coolers were long available in India, as sheet-metal affairs knocked together in small, local workshops.* Videocon introduced air-coolers that were made out of moulded plastic components with a variable speed fan, an integrated water-circulation system and wheels to make the unit mobile.† The combination of mobility, less mess and modern appearance greatly expanded the market for air-coolers. The TVS Scooty product is essentially a moped in scooter clothing. The two-wheeler market in India has a clear hierarchy of desirability from moped to scooter to motorcycle. The Scooty provides a scooter look-alike at an in-between price.

All three examples are attempts to use new design within an existing technology frontier to move up the value-chain. The air-cooler and the Scooty illustrate product development to meet the *particular* needs of a local market. All three products sold at higher prices than products with similar technology; design provided the premium – design was used to add value and get a better quality product.

Thus, a significantly new design can be seen as an intermediate point on the innovation continuum, as a jump in the capability of a product drawing on an existing technological paradigm, but going beyond incremental improvement.

Reputation – at three levels

As we said earlier, a key reason for designing world-class products has to do with the positive effects that reputation for good design can bring to country, firm and individual designer.

Country

To illustrate this argument, let us do an exercise. If a product were to be produced in one of the following countries – China, Denmark, Germany, India, Italy, Japan, Korea, Sweden, Switzerland, Taiwan, United States – for which country of origin would you be willing to pay more for the product?

Now answer the questions: from which of the countries listed above would you pay more for a car? How about a computer? A chair? How about a pharmaceutical product like a vaccine? A machine tool? A pair of shoes?

Conducting this exercise produces several conclusions. First, some countries have a reputation that is cross-product. Countries like Germany and Switzerland have a reputation in general for high-quality products. Similarly, countries like China and

---

* An air-cooler is a cheaper alternative to the air-conditioner, selling for about one-fifth the cost. It does not have a compressor, being essentially a fan that blows through circulating water. The cost difference was greatly aided by the Indian government, which – deeming air conditioners a luxury good – taxed the compressor that went into an air conditioner at around 200 per cent.

† As described in Chapter 5, Videocon did not actually introduce this product, but Symphony a small company did. Videocon was able to eclipse Symphony because of its brand and distribution network.

Korea have a reputation for cheaper products. Second, even more countries have a reputation for particular product ranges, such as German cars, Danish furniture, American computers, Italian clothes. If you get more specific the effect of the reputation becomes even more marked – luxury cars (Germany – Japanese automakers have had to work hard to move into the luxury segment), raincoats (the UK – no prizes for guessing why!), or precision lathes (Switzerland – think watches!).

For value-added, a country benefits greatly by having a high reputation for product quality. Product quality depends heavily on good design. After the Second World War, a great amount of effort in Japan was put into improving the reputation of Japanese consumer products through achieving superior design and manufacturing. That was one of the main goals of Akio Morita for Sony Corporation.[4] It paid off handsomely.

Firm

The reputation of a firm not only allows it to price for good profit but also affects other products. Sony's efforts paid off not only for Japan, but also for Sony. Since Forbes Marshall makes the world's finest vortex meter, people will assume their steam traps are good too. Hewlett Packard built a reputation for outstanding products in the instrumentation business. When the company moved into computer products, this reputation moved with the product line. Nokia has maintained an outstanding reputation for design even though its first seventy-five years were in the forestry products business. So much for the normal management consultant's advice to 'stick to the knitting'! Indeed, Nokia has prospered through design, unlike its rival Ericsson. Their share of the market was similar just three years before, in 1997. In an interview in the *Financial Times*, Nokia CEO said that Nokia phones were preferred because of 'the design and lifestyle portrayed by the phone. People find them functional and easy to use'. Nokia phones simply look neater and sleeker than Ericsson's. 'And it is the look of the phones and their functionality – rather than any pronounced technical superiority which has given Nokia its edge. "Ericsson is a technology-driven firm full of engineers. It has never looked at phones from the consumer end" . . . [Ericsson] has appointed a new head of design among a range of measures designed to improve the appeal of its phones.'[5] Companies such as IBM can withstand product failures much better than companies without a long history of outstanding products.

Companies who consistently design outstanding products have high employee motivation, especially among technical personnel. It is rewarding to be part of an enterprise that is one of the best at designing outstanding products, especially if you are directly involved in that process, but even if you are only in a support role.

Individual designer or design team

The ability to design outstanding products rests eventually on the individual designers and design teams that actually do the work. Here the 'virtuous circle' applies. Schools are better able to teach single skills than the broad integrative skills needed to be an outstanding designer. Much of the latter must be learned on the job by working with experienced and outstanding people. Outstanding designers are therefore needed as mentors and leaders. The more of them there are, the faster the educational process can proceed. Design is usually a team effort. Designers inspire each other, help create new ideas, trade knowledge, and criticize each other's work. Much of the excitement of the design process in industry stems from working with bright and motivated people in a team.

The need for outstanding designers in increasing product quality can be seen in the success of consulting design firms, such as IDEO or Italdesign or IDEA. Such firms retain sizeable numbers of outstanding designers and are experienced in working with large numbers of firms on large numbers of product types. Their employees are used to working with each other and are uniformly proud of the ability of the firm to do an outstanding job of product design. They have vast backlogs of approaches to problems, which can often be put to use in other areas. Even though their fees are high, their clients consider them most worthwhile in adding to the pool of designers and design teams in their companies. As a side benefit, these 'outsiders' often teach and inspire the company design staffs to do better work. As is the case with countries and with firms, better designs create better designs.

Living up to your reputation is, of course, critical. It often requires a long time before a country, firm or individual designer/team acquire a reputation for designing outstanding products. It is possible to lose one's reputation more quickly, in which case it will take even longer to regain it. It is easier to maintain a reputation for good quality than to lose and regain it.

Motivating technical people

Motivating technically skilled people is critical. For those employed in firms that design and manufacture products, motivation is strongly influenced by the quality of the output. As an example, Harley Davidson has highly motivated employees. Many of them are themselves bikers and most of them value the 'cruiser' type of motorcycle. They are fiercely proud of the dominance of their product and the highly successful business that has been based on it. This is a far cry from the days when Harley Davidson was almost bankrupted by the Japanese. Its comeback was driven through a total focus on design. Harley's share of the heavy motorcycle market in the US dropped from 100 per cent in 1972 to 14 per cent in 1982, before bouncing back to over 50 per cent in 2000. Apple Computer is another example. Although its market share is relatively small and the company has had its ups and downs as a business, most of their employees are convinced, quite simply, that Apple computers are designed better than competing PCs. This keeps them excited about their work and able to withstand business fluctuations.

Why is the motivation higher at Harley Davidson than at Enfield in India? Both make motorcycles that are quite traditional in design. Harley Davidson has modernized engine and suspension, increased reliability, and has removed inconveniences such as oil leaks. However, there is an obvious and direct link between modern Harley Davidsons and those of forty years ago. The Enfields manufactured in India are almost identical to those manufactured in England in the 1950s. Why were they not upgraded in reliability and performance and why are Enfield employees not as motivated as those at Harley Davidson? This is a classic chicken-and-egg problem. Motivated technical people produce improved products, but the motivation often comes from being confident of the high quality of the products. Something has to happen at Enfield so that the product becomes world class. Once this occurs, the motivation of technical staff will take care of itself. Oddly enough, in the case of Enfield, this should not be too difficult to achieve. There is a strong desire for 'retro' motorcycles – i.e. motorcycles that are reminiscent of the past (Box 7.1). Triumph, which almost disappeared through neglect of its product, is now strong again through radically modernized and improved designs. It has recently released a nostalgia-provoking update of its classic Bonneville machine. What could be more classic than the Indian Enfield? Its market potential should be great if its performance and reliability were up to modern standards. A widely heralded and sought-after Enfield would do great things for the motivation of not only the Enfield technical staff, but all their employees.

Box 7.1   Enfield

In 1955, the Indian government needed a solid and reliable motorcycle for its police and army. The Bullet was chosen as the most suitable bike for the job and the government ordered 800 of the 350 cc model, an order beyond the company's ability to fulfil. The parent company in the UK sold its design to Enfield India, a subsidiary firm in Madras that started manufacturing them. Between 1955, when production began in Madras, and 1994, when Enfield was bought by the Delhi-based Eicher group, little changed in design and manufacturing process. In 1970, the parent company in the UK ceased production. Production continues exclusively in India of the original 350 Bullet, using many of the original machine tools and dies from the original British parent factory. Most parts are still hand finished. Indian-built Enfields are now exported to some 26 countries, including the UK.

Over the years, many more modern motorcycles were introduced in India, and by 2000 licensees of Honda, Kawasaki, Suzuki and Yamaha dominated a market of 1.4 million units. Enfields continued as before – with policeman and farmers continuing to buy machines that can be repaired anywhere (and often needing to be). In the 1990s, a small niche market began to grow of motorcycle fans attracted by a design that was not just retro but old.

Since 1994, after the takeover by the Eicher group, the company has undergone considerable reorganization. Volumes have increased from 16,800 units in 1994 to 25,400 units in 2000. Capacity utilization increased from 47 per cent to 65 per cent over the same period. In the five years to 2000, Enfield has introduced six new and restyled models that improve performance and reliability while retaining their classic look, feel and sound. For example, there has been a shift to hydraulic brakes that give better deceleration and longer lining life. International designers have been hired to revamp old models. Swiss and British designers and an Austrian engine design firm have been hired for new, larger capacity motorbikes.

The company has set up two new plants doubling total capacity to 50,000 units. Inspired by the success of Harley Davidson in the US, Royal Enfield has also introduced motorcycle gear like jackets, boots, helmets and other riding accessories such as custom seats and luggage.

What is good design? Moving up the value-chain with 'soft' quality

But if technology-followers need to push out the design frontier, won't they be subject to the same uncertainties, high cost and 'waste' of technology-leading R&D? Strangely enough, the opposite may be true. Unlike technological research the success of design is defined directly by its effect on the user. There are many techniques to assure that this effect is positive. Market research is just one example. By finding out what customers really want, it is possible to design products that are likely to be quite successful in the market-place. It is possible to go even deeper in understanding the customer. Need-finding is a systematic exercise to articulate user needs which are unmet and usually non-obvious.

Deciding what is needed is by no means self-evident. It is distinct from market research – which finds out what customers *want*, not identify what they *need*. In carrying out this need-finding exercise, a focus on moving up the value-chain is vital – from the business standpoint this is the whole point of doing design.

Using multiple techniques – ranging from market surveys, to anthropological studies, to partnering key customers, to building scenarios of the future   can lead to a more 'imaginative understanding of user needs' that characterizes a firm such as HP.[6] Hindustan Lever, the Indian subsidiary of Unilever, has long been one of the three largest investors in R&D in the Indian private sector. The main objective of its R&D operation is to develop products suited to the needs of Indian consumers. For example, some years ago, HLL developed a range of bar detergents suitable for use in cold water hand washing, to suit Indian consumer practices.[7] More recently, as we saw in Chapter 6, HLL has supplied products like shampoo in small sachets, as Indian buying power seemed to prefer many smaller purchases (see Box 6.3).

In addition to defining user needs, there are many aspects of 'good' design that are essential to outstanding products. Jim Adams has identified several of these that add value for customers. They include:

1   *Performance and cost*   A feeling of getting more for less. Although performance and cost might seem obvious and easy to measure, they are not. Perception of performance in a car does not come simply from the speedometer; the height of the occupants, the noise, the responsiveness of the steering, the suspension, and many other factors contribute. The cost includes not only fuel, but amortized purchase cost, insurance, maintenance, and opportunity cost because of other products that were affected by the purchase of the automobile. Value can often be most easily determined by focusing on perceived performance and cost factors as well as actual ones. Many people seem quite pleased with the performance/cost ratio of 'luxury' products such as Bang and Olufsen stereo equipment, even though straightforward testing of music reproduction might make one reach a different conclusion.

2   *Human fit*   This includes not only physical fit, but consonance with the senses and the brain. Obviously, there are many factors that compete with this in the design process. A large amount of effort goes into the design of airplane seats, but the desire of the airline to maximize the number of passengers on board may conflict with this effort. Even though people may initially put up with poor fit, over time their attitude toward the product will turn sour. For example, since the advent of digital electronics, the number of non-standardized control options has increased. In the US the majority of owners of VCRs do not know how to fully programme them. It is not that people are too dumb to learn to programme a VCR. The problem comes because they are also being asked to programme a number of different clocks, kitchen utensils and other devices. This probably produces a cognitive overload and one that is bound to result in increasing resentment of all digital devices. Devices that fit customers well are bound to be

more successful in the market-place. The computer mouse seems to be more in tune with the user than approaches such as the track-pad. In India the Videocon air-cooler adds value by being mobile.

3   *Consonance with global constraints*   The need to remain sensitive to scarce resources and the pleasure people gain from a beautiful environment. As the population grows this will become an increasingly important design constraint. Even though an NIC may not have severe environmental constraints on product design, value can usually be added by exporting to countries with well-developed economies. Environmentally friendly companies in many countries are able to charge a premium for their products, and some whole businesses, such as the Body Shop, are focused on environmental concerns. ISO 14000 provides a new international standard for environmental certification; many companies work toward certification in order to be seen as being in synchrony with global concerns as well as committed to the environment. Taj Hotels of India have begun a 'green' programme using recycled water, with little placards in each room explaining what they do. Such moves are consistent with future product directions.

4   *Craftsmanship*   People appreciate products that are well manufactured, assembled and finished. The difference in performance between two competing products may be less than the difference in how they 'feel'. Materials like leather upholstery and wood continue to appear in modern luxury cars, even though they are somewhat inconsistent with modern industry, because they give people a feel of craftsmanship.

5   *Emotion*   How does the product appeal to the emotions? Will the user love it or hate it? Will it cause joy and excitement, or anger and boredom. Products that are rather similar (say pick-up trucks) are advertised and probably sold on the basis of emotion. Television advertisements show the truck heavily loaded and careering through rough terrain far removed from a road. Often such ads have little to do with the probable use of the truck, but seem to appeal to the buyer. Consider the thrills from roller-blading or from the world of fashion. Passionate arguments arise between users of Apple and PC computers concerning their various advantages. The difference between the two types of computer is in all probability less than the passion in the arguments. When the Indian firm Telco launched its small car in January 1998, it took out full-page advertisements in the national press saying 'Isn't it time for some Indian engineering?', a clear appeal to the emotions since its main competitor was a 50–50 joint venture between the Indian government and Suzuki of Japan.* Telco's publicity campaign, the first to our knowledge by any Indian firm that consciously pushed Indian technology, proved hugely successful. When bookings for its new car, called, naturally, the Indica, began in January 1999, Telco hoped to sell more than the 30,000 units of its first-year production. Booking required paying 100 per cent of the price of a car, and Telco was overwhelmed by 130,000 people depositing the full value of the car. This resulted in their collecting an amount that exceeded the total 17,000 million rupee cost of the whole project (they subsequently had to return over half this, as they were not be able to meet the total demand for over a year).

---

* In 1998 there was a highly publicized squabble between Suzuki and the Indian government, with much rhetoric aired about Japanese technology. It is noteworthy that Telco's car was released by the Minister for Industry, the source of much of the rhetoric in the fight with Suzuki.

6   *Elegance and sophistication*   Is the product a clean and efficient solution to the problem? Is the form consistent with the function? Does it appeal to users with large amounts of experience with products of its type? Is it visually elegant? The package a product comes in conveys much about the product: Titan watches were the first in India to come in display boxes with clear plastic covers. Their higher-priced range went into a glossy sleeve – the package conveyed elegance.

7   *Symbolism*   Can the product symbolize something beyond itself? Think of cosmetic packages that symbolize that the user is as beautiful as the actress using the cosmetic in the advertisement. Consider the space shuttle, which symbolizes heroic technological accomplishment to the US. To the user, the Scooty we spoke of earlier symbolizes a higher station in life than the equal capacity moped. One of the authors of this book has used Titan watches as his favourite choice of gift for friends abroad to symbolize the design capability of modern Indian industry. We gain part of our identity from the products we use. A well-designed product helps us build the identity we desire.

Improving such aspects of quality in NIC firms helps them to move up the value-added scale. But that means a firm must be able to define its own design specifications, and not be satisfied with status-quo designs from outside. Instead, firms can use their absorptive capacity to learn from the technology-leader, and then create improved designs using need-finding and paying attention to various aspects of product quality.

Building design capability is hard

Building design capability in the Korean chaebol

The leading Korean chaebol consciously set out to acquire design capability as a part of the drive to develop their own higher value-added products. Kim shows how Hyundai consciously acquired style design capability in the 1970s as a part of its own car development:

> It selected a team of five design engineers to study literature related to auto styling, then sent them to Italy to participate closely in the design process with Italdesign engineers. . . . For a year and a half, the highly motivated team shared an apartment near Italdesign, kept a record of what they were learning during the day, and conducted group reviews every evening. . . . These engineers later became the core of the design department at Hyundai, and one became the vice-president in charge of R&D.[8]

Hyundai has more recently established the Hyundai Styling Studio in Los Angeles 'to sense the needs of American consumers'.[9] Similarly, LG Electronics has a design R&D laboratory in Korea and the LG Design and Technology Center in Ireland. Samsung has been among the most active chaebol in acquiring design capability, establishing the Innovative Design Lab and the Samsung Art and Design Institute (in association with the Parsons School of Design in New York). Samsung also has an active collaboration with IDEO of Palo Alto (the world's largest product design firm) to train its own designers. It also hired a designer from the British design firm Tangerine as its head of European design.[10]

The IDMM story

Two of the authors of this chapter, Naushad Forbes and Jim Adams, decided to apply these ideas on the importance of design to technology-followers to a small sample of firms in India. Integrated Design for Manufacturability and Marketing (IDMM) is a course taught at Stanford University as a co-operative venture of the School of Engineering and the Graduate School of Business. Fifteen teams of graduate students, each consisting of two engineers and two MBA students, work on developing a new product from initial product concept through to final working prototype. Recent product assignments have included a bicycle light, ski-carrier, can-crusher for home use, personal beverage container, camping light, wake-up device, mini camera tripod and water-filter for backpacking use.

The programme in India was jointly sponsored by four Indian firms, covering seven very different product areas. Godrej and Boyce had three projects (a home study centre, a door closer and an electric fork-lift), Forbes Marshall two projects (a boiler efficiency monitor and a vortex flow meter), Godrej Sara Lee a mosquito mat for the rural market and Telco an internal component of the Indica car. The projects were fairly divergent – ranging from consumer products, to consumer durables, to industrial products – and varied in complexity – from a small mosquito mat that would sell for 2 cents to a fork-lift that would sell for $20,000. We argue that if design techniques could work for so wide-ranging a set of products, they should apply fairly universally.

The IDMM design process – the essential elements

The essential elements of a good product design process are as follows:

*   Need-finding. The objective was not to go out and develop something the development engineers thought the right product or to ask customers what they wanted, but to discover their underlying unmet and perhaps non-obvious needs. See Box 7.2 on need-finding or market research.
*   A 'wheelbarrow full of ideas'. To generate many alternative concepts and gather as much information as possible all around the project – to suffer from a surfeit of information, if anything.
*   Prototyping – multiple and over time. The objective is to embody alternative concepts in physical prototypes as a way of coming up with a better overall product, forcing up issues earlier rather than later; and to prototype throughout the development process as a base for learning.
*   Cross-functional teams. To work in an integrated way, covering product development, manufacturing and marketing. Cross-functional teams are at the heart of concurrent or simultaneous engineering, the approach whereby firms speed up the product development process by carrying out the production engineering and initial marketing tasks of the project concurrently with design and other traditional phases of product development. In modern product development, this has replaced the traditional 'over the wall' approach in which designs are passed to manufacturing and marketing is not present until late in the cycle.
*   Detailed market testing. To use current quantitative market research techniques to test the outcome of the need-finding exercise against the consumer population in an analytically rigorous way.

- To be innovative in a design sense. To push out the design frontier, offering functionality and aesthetics that set a new standard for the organization, for the country and, if possible, even internationally.

IDMM in India – the mechanics

The basic content of IDMM was provided in the form of five three-day workshops attended by all the project participants spread between September 1999 and July 2000. These workshops were conducted by four Stanford faculty members, from design, science technology and society, marketing and mechanical engineering. An experienced product designer on sabbatical from the leading design consultancy IDEO spent six months in India working regularly with each project group as it went about each stage in the design process. Table 7.1 shows how three of the faculty collectively assessed the performance of each group.

Rather than cover individual differences between groups, we draw some general conclusions that run across the groups, dealing in turn with what was easy, what was hard, what worked and what did not. We will then turn to what we learned from the IDMM project for improving design capability in a technology-follower generally.

What was easy

Cross-functional teams worked easily. Most groups arrived at the first workshop with members drawn from product development and manufacturing (all seven groups) and (for four of the seven groups) marketing. Other functions were involved in the product development process in four of the groups, and there were subsequently fewer problems encountered in the transition to manufacturing and sales. However, these groups were chosen to ensure cross-functionality. It was not clear whether this would have happened had the groups been formed in the traditional way rather than for this exercise.

What was hard

Getting the groups to physically *prototype* was extremely difficult. There was a reluctance to physically embody a concept, and a great reluctance to physically embody

Table 7.1 IDMM in India: performance of groups

	A	B	C	D	E	F	G
Need-finding	5	4	2	4	3	1	5
Wheelbarrow full of ideas	5	4	1	2	3	3	2
Prototyping – multiple	5	4	1	1	3	1	3
Prototyping – over time	5	4	1	1	3	1	2
Cross-functional teams	4	4	2	5	4	4	3
Public review to top management	5	5	4	3	2	2	5
Detailed market analysis like Conjoint	1	1	1	4	2	1	2
Trying something new/risk taking	4	2	2	1	2	1	4
Impact of programme overall	++	+	+	=	=	=	+

Notes: 1=low; 5=high.
   + positive; ++ strongly positive; = minor impact.

more than one concept or to do it again as the project carried on. People seemed reluctant to commit themselves to a specific design, rather preferring to delay to a hoped-for time when the final answer would become apparent. This in spite of the fact that each time a group did prototype they learned a great deal and changed the design as a result. Rapid prototyping not only of stages in the evolving design, but of alternate directions, is vital to high quality output.

Trying new things was also hard. The groups were reluctant to try out new materials or shapes or sensors when these were suggested. Some of this could be associated with Indian industry culture – there is no premium on doing new things, and four decades of inward-looking policies meant (as the section 'What is R&D' in Chapter 6 argued) that firms saw product development as indigenization. Skills to develop new product concepts were therefore relatively undeveloped. As an example, one of the teams was physically given a new and much cheaper sensor to try out: it had not been tried out even after six months had elapsed. A lack of familiarity with the technology concerned meant additional obstacles to trying out new things like the new sensor concept. One might associate this reluctance with a lack of knowledge, but the problem is deeper.

Indeed, prior knowledge and experience sometimes forms mental blocks against trying out new things. There is often an underlying sense of the existing approach being best, and a lack of openness to try outside ideas that could initially appear silly. The three groups that were most resistant to trying out new ideas and external suggestions came from three different organizations. Their members had the most prior experience directly related to product development and the groups were the best resourced of the seven in terms of sheer product development hours available for the project. However, there was much reluctance, for example, to try out unconventional product shapes or colours, or to go after a different market. One group saw the critical success factor as unit selling price, and therefore cost. While unit selling price is undoubtedly key in a market like India where a lower price point can greatly expand the market, there was a conscious refusal even to consider a higher-specification product for other needs.

What worked

Need-finding was done well by most groups. In the case of two projects (the home study centre and the boiler efficiency monitor) the product concept changed completely as a result of the need-finding exercise. The Godrej furniture group set out, as Box 7.2 shows, to develop a home study centre for children. The rough concept they had in mind was a kind of modular desk that would grow with the child. Their need-finding showed that the primary unmet need was space: to study (children studied with their books on the bed and their knees on the ground); and to play, given small Indian homes. This insight directly changed the product to a bunk-bed with a desk and ample storage underneath.

Similarly, the Forbes Marshall boiler-efficiency product also changed radically through need-finding. The group started with a concept of a product that would monitor boiler efficiency, based on the oxygen percentage of the exhaust gas. Customer observation showed that the conventional way of measuring boiler efficiency was via the fuel to steam ratio, which was calculated in a notoriously imprecise manner. This insight led to conceptualizing a whole product family of boiler-efficiency products, with the first product being a precise monitor of boiler steam to fuel ratio, with boiler efficiency monitored through a PC link.

Box 7.2 Need-finding for a home study centre

The Godrej and Boyce Office Equipment team, when tasked with need-finding for a pro-posed children's study centre, took advantage of a convenient and co-operative resource and headed into their Hillside housing colony. There several co-workers had volunteered their homes and made their children available for interviews.

The first visit was with a 17-year-old young woman who had just finished a set of exams. She shared the room with a sibling, in this case an older sister who was studying at the university. This lead to questions about how the two shared the space. Was light an issue? Noise? Which of them had put up the movie posters? Who was neater? Since the desks were located in the bedroom a conversation developed around how differing schedules were managed. Were there problems with music-listening preferences? Where would they go when issues like these arose?

Later the discussion turned to the desk colour (grey). The young woman emphatically stated that she hated it: 'It looks like surplus furniture from Daddy's office.' The Office Equipment team took note; colour was important.

The second visit of the evening was with another pair of siblings who were sharing a small room. In this case a boy and a girl with a seven-year age difference. Not surprisingly they described a greater conflict in sharing the space. They also shared a desk, which their father had commissioned a local cabinetmaker to make. A conversation developed around the decisions he had made in specifying the design. The children contributed their thoughts about what was successful about the desk, as well as what they didn't like. How did they share? How did they manage two people's storage needs? What had they changed as they had grown older? The team was graciously allowed to photograph the desk for posting in the team's project room.

Afraid that two visits to the families of Godrej employees was not a representative sample, three team members capitalized on holiday trips and sales calls to visit additional families in other parts of the country. They reported back to the group with more snap-shots and new anecdotes. Many of the issues that had been seen in the Hillside colony were the same elsewhere.

The team felt they had uncovered two important insights: space was tight, and children of different ages had different needs. With this in mind, they proceeded to develop three quick designs to be prototyped prior to an upcoming IDMM workshop. Each design was meant to address storage and study needs, but each was aimed at a different age-group: 'tots', 'teens' and 'titans'.

The 'teen' model was a desk/cabinet combination that the team had been thinking about for some time. The 'titan' model was a more elaborate version of this. For the 'tots', however, the team opted for something different and in their eyes a bit more risky: a combination bunk bed-desk-cabinet. At this point, the group consensus was that the bunk-study combination, while an interesting idea, was not going to be the design of choice.

A local cabinetmaker quickly built three rough prototypes, and installed them in a quiet corner of the group's office. The result was immediate and unexpected; anyone who happened by, from local office personnel to senior managers, was struck with the bunk-desk combination. A quick review with some local children (including one whom had been interviewed) confirmed the excitement. The excitement seemed to be independent of age-group.

Much to their surprise, the team members themselves where excited about the concept. They had come up with something new, and it was not what they had expected.

What did not work

Systematic market research did not work. Except for the mosquito mat group, which had a practice of using formal marketing techniques, the groups did not use any of the market research techniques covered. Clearly the level of knowledge of the groups themselves, and their organizations as a whole, was weak in terms of formal marketing knowledge. We would argue that this reflects a general weakness in marketing as a field in most newly industrializing countries, indeed in most countries relative to the US (see Box 7.3).

Box 7.3   Conceptualizing the right new product: need-finding *or* market research

Market research asks customers what they want. It does so using qualitative and quantitative techniques of data gathering, using sophisticated statistical tools to analyse the data and form a precise picture of customer preferences. Standard market research techniques would begin with the use of a questionnaire asking customers what they want. The techniques used today would include qualitative techniques such as the use of a focus group that would be asked to comment on a product's features while the group's interaction was observed from behind a one-way mirror. Quantitative techniques are also important, such as conjoint analysis, where customer preferences were elicited through a carefully crafted statistically reliable process, and then used to build a computer model that permits asking 'what if' questions. For example, would a customer be willing to pay more for a product painted green and with a particular feature set?

The field of design has generally been somewhat contemptuous of market research. The general approach is that if you ask customers what they want, they will tell you they want what your competitors give them. As such, one would always be playing product design catch-up instead of product leadership. Instead, as we saw earlier, need-finding is a technique aimed at discovering customer needs rather than wants. If these needs are non-obvious and unmet by anything similar today, they will not emerge however careful and thorough a depiction of wants that is the objective of market research.

> Unless it emphasizes needs, qualitative social research can only create a picture of the customer's experience; it will not uncover ways to improve that experience. Even the most detailed description of customer's behaviour and environments won't help product developers if it doesn't expose opportunities for action. Because many needs are apparent only after they've been solved, research focused on needs suggests opportunities that competitors may not recognize. [Indeed] companies can find that their customers express a desire for an improvement only after a competitor has created it. This forces marketing into the reactive role of asking for things that the competition already has. Developers, in turn, find themselves working toward a deadline that has already passed. When linear improvements fail to provide a decisive advantage, new opportunities must be discovered in advance.[11]

The IDMM approach combines both techniques – drawing on market research expertise from Marketing in the Business School and need-finding from the design programme in the School of Engineering. What emerges is that asking the question 'need-finding *or* market research' is the wrong question. Instead, one needs both techniques are needed, and the right question is what mix of the two would be appropriate to the product being developed. For example, no amount of market research around a sample population would have uncovered the need for space that led to the Godrej bunk-desk concept.

But in the same way, no amount of need-finding would uncover what particular combination of product features (including such variables as size, colour, texture, modular add-ons) would be most desirable, nor how much a particular market segment would be willing to pay for the final product concept. The combination of the two allows for a superior product development process. Need-finding provides the overall product concept and desirable feature set, and market research provides market-representative information on what combination of features would sell to how many at what price.

Learning from IDMM – why building design capability is hard

Improving design capability is not easy. It involves building the capability to do many different things. First, good design implies the ability independently to conceptualize one's own product in a manner that meets needs that no one else's product meets today. This requires the skills involved in need-finding and the market research skills involved in testing various product features for market acceptance and creativity. Second, the firm needs in-house designers who have high aesthetic standards and are willing to try out new things. Trying out new things is a skill that can be learnt, indeed has to be learnt. Finally, the product concept has to be manufactured to good quality and able to be sold quickly. Firms in Korea and Taiwan, used to working to demanding schedules in a highly competitive manner with demanding OEM customers, have a great advantage. Learning from our IDMM experience, we can suggest the following:

1   The importance of dedicated product development resources. This sounds obvious, but for four of our seven groups, all group members also had other major responsibilities. The result was that projects suffered from lack of focus on a day-to-day basis, and progress was instead driven by the deadlines formed by the external reviews and workshops rather than an internal project plan. The two groups that combined dedicated product development resources – people who woke up each morning worrying only about this project – *combined* with a challenging project plan, made the most rapid progress.*
2   The ability to tap into external sources of aesthetics and design. The product development process occasionally needs specialized inputs, in the form of trained product and industrial designers, who may well need to be brought in from design consultancies or design departments at universities. The firm needs to build in-house the ability to *recognize* good aesthetics and not necessarily the ability to do good aesthetics. This needs to be complemented with the willingness to tap into external resources.
3   Physical prototypes are key: they permit trying out product features, which greatly reduces later problems, and also communicate the product concept to other people in the organization. These prototypes initially need to be built in order to evaluate alternative concepts, and to be carried out throughout the product development process as ideas emerge. Firms building design capability need to practise proto-typing – cheap and simple model shops and forcing each development engineer to

---

* One group had a dedicated product development resource, but no detailed project schedule. They achieved even less than the groups with no dedicated resource.

prototype until it comes easily are features we intend to build into any future IDMM experiments!

4   A product champion in top management: a strong product champion in top management has been indentified as a key feature of successful innovation. Having top management directly involved in the product development process made a great difference to some projects. Involvement means investment of time and ideas to drive the project forward, not merely supporting a worthy process through an occasional presentation. Regular reviews that are high-profile and public played a key role in pacing the IDMM projects, and communicating concepts to others in the organization – vital for drawing in external support.

Conclusions: from R&D to D&D

As firms try to add more value to their activity, product innovation becomes increasingly key, and the role of R&D includes building independent design capacity for the firm. Product development in NICs is less a matter of research and development than of development and design.

This discussion implies a trajectory applicable to all industries. Certainly design can add more value in industries with more differentiated products – consumer electronics more than steel, for example. As we saw in Chapters 5 and 6, though, the move to product innovation must be driven by the firm's ambition. So too with design. The drive to build design capacity has to come, often, from a simple desire to build beautiful products – creating an environment where building products that appeal to the emotions comes naturally. The crucial distinction is between the design and technology frontiers – it is possible for firms to push out the design frontier without pushing out the technology frontier. It is to how to build a culture for innovation in NICs that we turn in Chapter 8.

8 Building a culture for innovation

Introduction

This chapter addresses culture at two levels. How does culture in firms reflect the national culture, and go beyond it? And second, what cultural attributes are required to build the technical capabilities demanded in Chapters 4, 5, 6 and 7?

Although we have tried to make our bias apparent as we have gone through the book, there is an underlying assumption that all nations, firms and individuals will choose to move up the value-chain as fast as possible.* This assumption is not valid, and we deal explicitly with how the *choice* of moving up the value-chain can be fostered – at least at the level of the firm. This will to develop must be widely shared in the firm if it is to grow value-added rapidly.

We begin with the characteristics of *national cultures* that impact on firm innovation – starting, dangerously, with cultural stereotypes. We argue that culture is not determined, neither does it alone determine whether a society is good or bad at innovation. Rather, cultures that value change and experiment can be encouraged and constructed. We present situations of relatively successful and relatively weak innovative environments (Box 8.1).

We then go on to look at how some firms build innovative cultures in very unpromising national environments. Companies can choose to become world-class in difficult circumstances. A firm's culture can be constructed that does not reflect its national stereotype. We give examples from India and Zimbabwe to illustrate our argument.

Finally, and most importantly, we identify what it takes to build a culture that moves a firm up the value-chain. What culture makes a firm good at the widespread, continuous, shop-floor improvement we discussed in Chapter 4? Where does the desire to move to proprietary and product innovation come from? What culture builds the kind of R&D capabilities, including design, that we discussed in Chapters 6 and 7? How does one get better at creativity and exploring new ideas so one can develop world-beating products? As we will see in this chapter, the cultural attributes needed for these different objectives may well conflict, and the firm needs to find the right balance.

---

* This assumption exactly parallels that made by economists of profit maximization. The assumption that the driving motive for all economic actors is to maximize profit, can cause major errors in policy conclusions, and lead to neglect of the true motive behind the actions of individuals and firms.

Box 8.1   Culture's comeback?

Many books on innovation refer little to culture – emphasis is on the economic, financial, organizational, production system, enterprise, entrepreneurship and creativity. A few books mention culture in passing, preferring to move quickly to more tangible factors for improving innovation. A very few have made culture the focus of their interest, for example in questions of why certain nations, like the UK, seemed to decline industrially, and why some countries have been so spectacularly successful, like Germany, Japan and the East Asian industrializers

Of those books that make culture the focus, many present culture as determinant. One, by Lawrence Harrison, looks at Brazil, Taiwan, Korea and Japan and contrasts them with Hispanic Latin America. His book concluded: 'In the case of Latin America, we see a cultural pattern, derivative of traditional Hispanic culture, that is anti-democratic, anti-social, anti-progress, anti-entrepreneurial, and at least among the elite, anti-work.' And the same author says 'What has been demonstrated in this century . . . is that democratic capitalism does a better job of promoting human progress and well-being than other systems'.* This is the kind of approach that has given the study of culture in industrial and national development such a bad name!

But culture is making something of a comeback. Culture matters in considerations of success and failure in innovation. It is important not because it determines which economy and nation will be successful and which will not. Rather it is an essential part of the total picture of building indigenous technological capability in particular and development in general. It affects which policies will work, since practices need to accord with cultures. Culture is important in the sense that some styles and practices are more amenable to successful innovation than others. The German model of innovation inspired many in the 1960s and 1970s. The Japanese model followed by the East Asian miracle became ubiquitous in the 1980s and early 1990s. Silicon Valley in the USA and the Third Italy are examples of successful innovation at the regional level. And at the level of the firm, studies of innovation have always emphasized culture. In short, culture matters for innovation.

National culture and cultural stereotypes

The collaboration that led to this book began in 1990 when the authors taught a course with Jim Adams called *Comparative Technology Policy*. The idea was to try out different explanations for innovation success. We came from three different countries – India, the UK and the USA. It became clear to us at the beginning, and also to students, that each of us had a serious critique of our own nation's innovation culture. In fact, we were more critical of 'our' nation's innovation style than our colleagues and other students (this still shows in this chapter – the British and Indian stereotypes are by far the harshest!). That set the scene for an open and serious debate. All alternative comedians and their audiences know that it is more insightful, and funny, to critique one's own culture than someone else's. We had worked in ten other countries, and our

---

* L.E. Harrison, *Who Prospers? How Cultural Values Shape Economic and Political Success*, New York: Basic Books, 1992, p. 10. 'Democratic' would be a peculiar adjective for each of Brazil, Taiwan, Korea and Japan for much of the last century, and 'capitalism' would also define their system imprecisely for some of the period.

class included students from eleven countries. Since then, in related courses, we (and invited professors) have discussed seriously a total of twenty countries, but perhaps more important, we have experienced and studied a huge variety of sectors, firms and institutions – from NASA to the Indian bureaucracy to the UK university to Hewlett Packard to Forbes Marshall to Samsung. The amazing result of all this has been the ability of everyone to critique 'their own' culture whilst looking for what it is that makes successful innovation within it and outside, debating the different meanings of 'success'. Our idea in discussing stereotypes in this chapter is to 'open up' discussion in a similar way to how our classes became 'open' and serious international learning experiences.

Japan as fashion

Even though the shine has gone off the Japanese model since the late 1990s, Japan has been headlined as the success story of the twentieth century. Japan is the key to debates on new organizational forms. For example, Japanese manufacturing techniques are now established all over the world.[1] Many observers were so impressed and astounded by Japan's rapid growth that they believed it must be culturally determined – that there was something in the Japanese psyche that allows huge leaps in comparison to other nations. What were the cultural characteristics perceived as accounting for the Japanese miracle?

'Japanese trust one another; they naturally work hard; they are loyal to the group rather than being individualists; and they are harmonious and co-operative' says Campbell,[2] making clear that he is setting up a stereotype to question. Dore cites Confucian perspectives of 'bonds of friendship and fellow-feeling . . . and a sense of loyalty and belonging – to one's community, one's firm, one's nation – and the sense of responsibility which goes with it'.[3] Dore goes on to give 11 distinctive characteristics of 'the Japanese', including: they work hard, are well educated, work co-operatively in large corporations, are managerial and production-oriented, not shareholders, use complex subcontracting systems, have clear income policies and harmonious labour relations, are thrifty savers, and are good at co-operating. We should emphasize that later Dore goes beyond this bare stereotype. These cultural norms are said to have determined the success of Japanese industrialization.

There is another more negative cultural characteristic that goes with the cultural characterization of a regimented, disciplined, hard-working, co-operative nation – the lack of creativity, the brilliance at imitating incremental innovation, the weakness at truly radical innovation of completely new products and processes, and the low number of risk-taking entrepreneurs. Another cultural stereotype is that the Japanese are workaholics who live in tiny houses ('rabbit hutches' one UK government minister once said) and have a rather low quality of life.

The example of Japan shows the fashion-oriented nature of national stereotypes. In the 1950s Japan was the country known for cheap imitations.* By the 1980s it was the country of world-beating products and turned into a model of success for others to emulate. By 2000, the stereotype was tarnished by economic recession and the fashion was 'I told you so, Japan cannot win in the long-term'.

---

* Indeed, this was a much older perception: a *Punch* cartoon of the 1890s shows a Japanese tailor copying an Englishman's clothes perfectly – right down to the patch in his trousers!

It is the Japanese and East Asian cultural model that took Japan from cheap imitations to quality production – that is the model others wish to emulate. But can such cultural attributes be transferred? 'If the Japanese cultural perspective is taken to its limits, it would mean that the production methods and organisational systems are moulded by cultural norms to produce a unique management system that cannot be replicated outside Japan.'[4] Highly successful Japanese plants in the UK and US prove they can.

Box 8.2   Hitachi

Dore's classic volume *British Factory, Japanese Factory*,[5] is a book-length comparison of the Japanese firm Hitachi and the British firm English Electric. Here is Dore on Hitachi of 1970:

'Employment with Hitachi is in principle for life'[6]

'The first principle of our firm is "sincerity". This above all is the basis of our company's reputation. . . . The second principle is the spirit of forward looking positivism. . . . It is precisely this spirit which should prompt each of us to develop the limitless potential which lies within us, to sharpen our wits and redouble our energies. It is this spirit which should make even a moment's slackness a matter of grave self-reproach, as we seek to attain a level of technical skill and managerial efficiency which not just in Japan, but also in the world at large, will be recognized as in the highest class. The third comes harmony. . . . That we have been able first to accomplish our mission to produce all-Japanese electrical machines, that we have been able to go further, develop our skills further to the point at which they outstrip world levels, diversify widely under integrated leadership and create one of the biggest firms in our country, is to be attributed precisely to the fact that each individual opinon is listened to. . . . But the decision once taken, all cooperate in a common endeavour to move triumphantly forward to the common goal'[7]

'Hitachi directors have nearly all graduated to their position after a lifetime of work in the firm'

'Hitachi's management organization is fitted into a pyramidical arrangement of teams, sections and departments . . . responsibilities are assigned to groups and can be shunted around among individuals within them'[8]

'Hitachi's organization relies on maximising cooperation between managers'

'Foremen in Hitachi are leaders of their team, expected to take a direct part in the team's work, rather than supervisors set over a work team'

'Their role is less specific, more diffusely extending to concern with the general well-being of members of their team. There is a good deal of sociability between the foreman and his subordinates outside of the work situation'[9]

'Hitachi workers are more likely to express a sense of pride in their work. One among several reasons for this is that Hitachi workers more easily accept the firm's legitimacy'[10]

England

Japanese cultural characteristics are often contrasted with those of England and the USA. English cultural characteristics are said to be individualistic, gentlemanly among the elite, happy to stagnate, without mass education, with weak technical training, not flexible, good at financial deal-making in the City of London, but not interested in manufacturing, brilliant at producing a few Nobel Prize winning scientists, terrible at exploiting their discoveries. The English culture is associated with disdain for production and constant harping back to rural bliss.[11] An absence of any industrialists, perhaps since Josiah Wedgwood of the eighteeth century, in a list of popular heroes, illustrates the attitude to industry The stereotype is of elitist disdain for engineering, for 'dirty' production, and happiness with humanities and classics, and resistance to change in any form. Scientists are called 'boffins', not usually a derogatory term so much as one of affectionate distance. Barnett, in his assessment of Britain's situation after the Second World War said:

> If Britain after the war was to earn the immense resources required to maintain her cherished place as a great power and at the same time pay for New Jerusalem at home, she had to achieve nothing short of an economic miracle. Such a miracle could only be wrought through the transformation, material and human, of her essentially obsolete industrial society into one capable of triumphing in the world markets of the future. Had all the most important groups and institutions in that society been willing enthusiastically to throw themselves behind the process of transformation, it would still have been difficult enough to achieve, given the scale of the inherited problems. But instead of such willingness there existed the massive inertial resistance to change which was so manifest in the history of Britain as an industrial society.[12]

Until the 1980s that would have been a reasonable analysis of the cultural inertia to change in Britain, but such a characterization cannot explain the massive transformation during the 1980s and 1990s.

Box 8.3   Barclays Bank: 'What's the word: small?'

The large bank Barclays fits the English stereotype in several ways. First, it is not a manufacturing company, but a major financial services company. Second, it is one of the oldest names in English banking, and represents the 'old-boy' network that stereotyped the City. Indeed, as a book on Barclays amusingly illustrates, this network of family management led to Barclays becoming a 'timid beast'.[13] *The Economist's* review of this book on Barclays notes:

> He [the author, Martin Vander Weyer] has had privileged access. His father, Deryk, worked for Barclays for 47 years, becoming deputy chairman. When he was surprised to discover how much people were earning – his own pay had by 1991 risen to £100,000 a year – he suggested that perhaps earnings should be more closely related to performance: 'People looked at me as though I was mad'.

> The son thinks Barclays would be in better shape now if Deryk had become chairman, but the Weyers were not Bevans or Barclays or Tukes or Trittons. They were not one of the families that had run Barclays since the amalgamation of 1896. Family members were placed on a special list, and got the pick of the jobs. They were set deeply in their ways, and intolerant of audacious young men who questioned them. As late as the 1960s, two grandees in the Lombard Street office, a Barclay and a Bevan, decreed that fish be eaten with two forks, in the manner of East Anglian Quakers. When both were on holiday, an opinionated sprig declared that it was time to join the modern world and eat fish with one fork and a knife. When the grandees returned, they informed the sprig that he would soon receive a new posting; the choice was Australia or Barbados.
>
> From its origins, Barclays was, to an unusual degree, designed for the comfort of its own executives, rather than the maximum strategic thrust in its marketplace.'[14]

USA

The US cultural stereotype is of the lone thrusting individual whose entrepreneurial 'can do' spirit builds an enterprise from scratch to global leader. American history is narrated through such individuals, from Carnegie and Rockefeller, to Ford, to Bill Gates. Indeed, American children study history through heroes, which include industrialists and scientists (and which other country has industrialists as heroes for its children?). When one of the authors went to the US as a college student in the 1970s, one of the more popular dormitory decorations was a full-length poster of Einstein, sharing wall space with The Who. Success at high-technology is key to American self-perception – witness the public trauma which went on for months after the Challenger disaster. More subtly, Rosenberg asks 'why are Americans poor imitators?', drawing a comparison with Japan.[15] He attributes this primarily to low learning skills, which come out of success. A perception of being well-ahead led to an attitude of Not-Invented-Here (NIH), of not needing to learn from the rest of the world.

India

The Indian stereotype is of a culture of *chalta hai* or let it be – where time commitments have little meaning, and products are not delivered on time. Four decades of indigenization fostered India's own version of NIH, where little was sought from the outside world. NIH in India, though, had a fatal exception: FIB, because Foreign Is Better. We are reminded of the cartoon by R K Laxman (Figure 1.2), the great Indian cartoonist, who has a doctor looking into a patient's eye saying: 'You have some foreign matter in your eye. Would you like to keep it, since it is foreign?'

The lack of a competitive environment led to other problems:

- A lack of interest in 'finish' – the choice was between one poorly finished Indian product and another.
- A lack of value of people and time – people are cheap so can be added at will. Employment can become the whole objective of the production unit. Indeed, there are several states in India today where 97 per cent of the budget is salary.

Many ministers see this entirely seriously as the whole point of government, both at the national and state level.

India also took the British bureaucracy and improved it: as a colleague once pointed out, it is not corruption that makes the Indian bureaucracy unique, but corruption combined with competence. Not only will your application for whatever require a bribe, but a bureaucrat will also find the mistake you made on page 73 of copy 8 and reject it.

Korea

Korea is a good contrast to India. The objective was usually to build the biggest plant in the world, as quickly as possible, using the best, indeed, highest technology. *The Economist* survey of Korea was titled 'Quickly, Quickly' – to depict a country in a hurry to catch-up. An inferiority complex with Japan led to a conscious copying of the Japanese model, but there is no doubt in Korean minds who is culturally superior. As most of our Korean students have pointedly remarked, Japan got its language and culture from China via Korea:

> By 1994 Korea ranked second in the world in shipbuilding and consumer electronics, third in semi-conductor memory chips, fifth in textiles, chemical fibres, petrochemicals and electronics, and sixth in automobiles and iron and steel.[16]

> No nation has tried harder and come so far so quickly from agrarian poverty to industrial prosperity as Korea.[17]

> Koreans work incredibly long hours, from morning to night, 'like robots', some Japanese say. Their comments echo American complaints about the Japanese. What made Koreans work so hard? There appear to be at least six situational factors: (1) the national trait of tenacity, (2) *han* psyche, (3) conditioning during school days, (4) physical environment, (5) 'beat Japan' spirit, and (6) experience of deprivation.[18]

> While Koreans admire and attempt to emulate Japanese economic success, the old generation has a vivid memory of a brutal and exploitative Japanese occupation. A sense of 'beat Japan' – to settle old scores in all fields – is a major source energizing Koreans. This spirit has been ingrained in the new generation through indoctrination in schools.
> This hardworking trait is well reflected in the Korean language. The first Korean word foreigners learn, *pali pali*, meaning 'hurry up, hurry up,' is the word most frequently spoken by Koreans. They use it to mean not only 'speed up' but also 'don't be lazy'.[19]

> National identity among Koreans is so strong that despite their strong animosity toward North Korea, South Koreans side with North Koreans in sport matches against Japan. Such strong nationalism may be a factor in the pursuit of independent strategy.[20]

However, the perception is also of an uncreative people. Kim, in a later piece, argues that creativity must be enhanced for Korea to compete in the future.[21]

A few years ago, one of us asked the head of a joint venture partner what difference he saw between his Korean and Indian operation. His Indian operation, he said, was always very conscious of making do, of being poor and therefore managing with an old machine or less powerful computer. His Korean operation always had to have the very latest machines and computers, whether or not they could use them.

Germany

One cultural characteristic of Germany, and of German industry, is of an extremely efficient and disciplined system. 'What strikes a foreigner travelling in Germany is the importance attached to the idea of punctuality, whether or not the standard is realised. Punctuality, not the weather, is the standard topic of conversation for strangers in railway compartments.'[22] The German work-force is well trained and has high craft skills. The key characteristic of the German work-force is its strength in depth. More than one half of shop-floor workers has vocational level qualifications.

Conclusions

What can we learn from these stereotypes? They are powerful because they are so ingrained. It is easier to reinforce cultural characteristics of 'German efficiency', 'Indian bureaucracy', 'American entrepreneurship', 'Japanese quality', than to notice any differences over time, as with the change in Japan from 'cheap imitations' in the 1950s and 1960s to 'quality products' in the 1980s. But remember that these are indeed stereotypes – they represent extreme positions. The range of experiences within any one country will always be greater than the difference between countries. Later, we discuss how firms can go beyond their national stereotype. We will first use the stereotypes to construct some building blocks of an effective culture for innovation.

Moving beyond the stereotypes

Culture is a pattern of shared values, beliefs and agreed norms which shape behaviour – 'the way we do things around here'.[23] A culture represents the culmination of a range of historical experiences that shaped this pattern. It may not seem as if war or partition has anything to do with the ability of the firm to innovate, but the experience can leave behind fears and ambitions that may be useful or damaging. In Korea, the trauma of Japanese colonization, civil war and partition brought a sense of backwardness that was shared by government, business and citizen alike, and fed directly into a will to catch up.* As a firm or nation catches up, the balance between learning (the Japanese stereotype) and creativity (the US stereotype) must change. Dore summarized this well twenty years ago in his distinction between Indigenous Technology Learning Capacity (which he said India needed more of) and Indigenous Technology Creating Capacity (which he said Japan needed more of).[24]

---

* North Korea and South Korea's very different development paths starting from the same cultural point in 1956 illustrate the fundamental point that culture while important is not determinant.

A shared sense of backwardness

A key cultural characteristic for follower-nations is a shared sense of backwardness. In the 1960s, one of the seminal concepts in economics was Gerschenkron's idea that collective awareness of 'backwardness' was key for a follower-nation to industrialize.[25]

Gerschenkron suggested that there were 'advantages of backwardness'. First, the follower could learn from the mistakes of the pioneers; it could start with institutional arrangements of which the pioneers only discovered the virtue long after they had institutionalized less suitable arrangements.

Second, there was the sense of backwardness, shared by the intellectuals and political leaders of the late-developing country, which provided a charter for state action to mobilize resources and to take initiatives and risks.

A will to develop

It was not only a shared sense of backwardness, but also a shared will to catch up – 'the will to develop' – that was a key trigger in Germany, the USA and Japan in the nineteenth century. Dore identifies this shared will to catch up as key to development in Korea (vs. the North and Japan), Taiwan (mainland China and Japan), Singapore (Malaysia, after Singapore was expelled from the Malayan Federation) and Hong Kong (mainland China).

Dore talks of the embedding of the 'sense of backwardness' in the development of a sense of nationhood. He argues that, in the case of Japan, South Korea and Taiwan, this has been key in the growth of a shared national interest which integrated in the public and private sectors 'a shared perception of national problems'. Also, at the level of implementation, 'the sense of shared, overarching national interest is also important for the effectiveness of policy'.[26]

Transformation of a shared sense of backwardness into a shared national will to catch up has been true in diverse political systems, from the China of Mao Zedong to Singapore under Lee Kuan Yew, who was once asked if economic reform in much of the world would permit other countries to enjoy the same kind of growth as East Asia. He replied: 'Getting the fundamentals right would help, but these societies will not succeed in the same way as East Asia did because certain driving forces will be absent. If you have a culture that doesn't pay much value in learning and scholarship and hard work and thrift and deferment of present enjoyment for future gain, the going will be much slower.'[27] And in Meiji Japan, the population 'did not expect the state to provide a minimum level of welfare for every citizen in the way that is normally expected even in the least developed countries today. So it was possible for the Japanese government to hold back consumption and concentrate on long-term investment, making the Japanese people forgo jam today in order that their grandchildren could have more jam in the distant future, in a way that is rarely possible for the developing countries of today.'

In firms, this will to develop can come as effectively from a shared sense of backwardness. At Forbes Marshall, the company has measured and compared its value-added per employee against its foreign joint venture partners for several years. It aims to close the gap in five years, becoming a developed company in a developing country (Box 8.4).

Box 8.4   Forbes Marshall's Vision Statement

Our Vision

Is to be a developed company in a developing country, pursuing market leadership in our chosen fields of Steam Engineering, Process Control and Utilities Management.

Dedicated to growth and an increasingly international presence, committed to being a role model organization for our customers, suppliers, society and members.

These goals are pursued by each person having a stake in the system, where he or she can see a direct link between individual implementation, what the organization achieves, and what the individual gets from the organization's achievement.

A will to learn from others

Another key characteristic is the will to learn from others, associated with cultural confidence. The objective is to avoid the NIH–FIB combination we discussed earlier: having the openness to learn from others and not close off from the outside world together with enough confidence and self-reliance to question what one has learnt. 'Learn from the best, and improve the rest.'

A classic example of a country that gave up looking outside for ideas was China in the fifteenth century. The Chinese produced many of the key innovations that were of fundamental importance to modernity: the compass, gunpowder and paper. Landes reports that the Chinese undertook, between 1405 and 1431, at least seven major expeditions to explore the waters of Indonesia and the Indian Ocean. Landes suggests that these flotillas did not go to learn but to show off Chinese grandeur to the barbarians.

> The flotilla far surpassed in grandeur the small Portuguese fleets that came later. The ships were probably the largest vessels the world had seen: high multideck junks ... testimony to the advanced techniques of Chinese shipbuilding, navigation and naval organization. The biggest were about 400 feet long, 160 wide (compare the 85 feet of Columbus's *Santa Maria*). ... The first of these fleets, that of the eunuch admiral Zheng He (Cheng Ho) in 1405, consisted of 317 vessels and carried 28,000 men. ... Yet this Chinese opening to the sea and the larger world came to naught, indeed was deliberately reduced to naught. ... The abandonment of the program of great voyages was part of a larger program of closure, of retreat from the hazards and temptations of the sea. This deliberate introversion, a major turning point in Chinese history, could not have come at a worse time, for it not only disarmed them in the face of rising European power but set them, complacent and stubborn, against the lessons and novelties that European travellers would soon be bringing. ... Why? ... To begin with the Chinese lacked range, focus and above all, curiosity. They went to show themselves not to see and learn. ... They had what they had and did not have to take or make. Unlike the Europeans they were not motivated by greed and passion.[28]

Cultures can change

What makes this quote from Landes so enjoyable is how unrepresentative it is of China at the beginning of the twenty-first century. No country better illustrates a will to learn from the best everywhere. Consider two anecdotes:

*   A few years ago, a cartoon had Ronald Reagan toasting Deng Hsao Ping. Reagan's toast is 'To Peace, Justice, John Wayne and the American Way'. Deng's is 'To Your Technology'.
*   China announced that if the 2008 Olympics were held in Beijing, the state would ensure that every one of Beijing's twelve million citizens would be able to speak English by then.

Change in culture is partly a change in external perception and partly reality – change that is consciously crafted or happens from historical circumstance. The East Asian model illustrates how perceptions of culture can change. Japan in particular has gone from being famous for cheap products in the 1950s and 1960s, to whipping many leading western industries in the 1970s, 1980s and early 1990s, to being the subject of concern as a drag on global growth by the late 1990s. A popular book of 1990 was James Fallows' *Containing Japan*, which argued for concerted government–industry action in the US to compete with the Japanese industrial machine. Ten years later we have Michael Porter asking 'Can Japan compete?' – about just the same industries and firms.[29] Reality in Japan has undoubtedly changed much less than the external perception.

The Japanese experience is representative of East Asia generally, which went from model to caution in external analysis between 1997 and 1999. Consider a few popular book titles:

1995–97	1999–2001
The East Asian Miracle	Rethinking the East Asian Miracle
Asia's Miracle Economies	The End of the Asian Model
Asia's Next Giant	East Asian Corporations: Heroes or Villains
Imitation to Innovation	Model, Myth or Miracle?
	Tigers Tamed: the End of the Asian Miracle
	East Asia in Crisis: From Being a Miracle to Needing One

At the level of firm culture, much of what was seen as a natural reflection of Japanese culture – lifetime employment, consensual decision-making, worker participation – was itself artificially and purposefully constructed after the Second World War. Labour relations in the pre-war Japanese firm were very different. The example we cited in Chapter 4 illustrates this too: when western academics studied quality circles in Japan in the early 1980s they were struck by their voluntary nature and the spontaneous participation of shop-floor employees in problem-solving. But as we saw, when quality circles first began around 1960, groups were often formed on the orders of superiors, and employees had targets and quotas for suggestions. By the 1980s, these were well-enough engrained to be voluntary participation – and that is the culture that observers saw and tried to emulate. There are two lessons in this: first, to be clear on motive – what result one is trying to achieve. And second, the appropriate culture, the way things get done, is different over time – voluntary is great when an ethic of volunteering participation has set in.

Conclusion

To summarize: not only can cultures change (e.g. China – fifteenth century and twenty-first century) but they can be changed (e.g. Japan – labour relations in 1930 and 1970; quality circles in 1960 and 1980). It was the will to work at it, within organizations and outside them, that produced the will to develop in Japan both during the Meiji period and after the Second World War. The will to develop can be fostered; openness to the world and confidence to change what is learnt is needed – self-reliance and the confidence to 'learn from the best'. These changes in culture are much easier to bring about in firms. But how do firms organize against the grain of their national cultural patterns?

Follower-firms: organizing against the grain

It is a reasonable hypothesis that national cultural stereotypes might be represented in their firms. The national style is likely to be connected to 'national' firms. For example, if the national industrial innovation style is to do internally what has been invented elsewhere, as in India from the 1950s to the early 1990s, then it is no surprise that most significant Indian manufacturers had R&D units that worked on indigenizing products. If the government pushes 'biggest quickest' policies, then it is easier to see how the big Korean chaebols ended up building the world's biggest heavy industry plants and shipyards. Posco's growth can be pictured as a small – but rapidly growing – part of a nation's push to have the biggest the quickest. Some of our earlier examples presented firms that behaved as though they were a micro-image of the macro-national stereotype.

However, there is no clear, hard and fast relationship between national culture and firm culture and behaviour, though often it is possible to guess which country is the main base of a particular firm. At the level of the firm, the search for unique competencies is usually a search for difference – to focus on the characteristics that bring competitive advantage. There are firms which operate at odds with national cultural style – like Reliance in India for example, or Ofco in Zimbabwe. It is possible even in the most difficult national circumstances to find some firms which are breaking the mould – which are innovative and creative in their own ways.

What can we learn from them? Can they become the node for a major transformation? This book is premised on world-class companies in developing countries. In the very same policy environment there can be dramatically contrasting firms.

Reliance Industries (Box 8.5) is a good example of a major company whose culture differs markedly from the Indian cultural stereotype. 'Korea in India' is a simple way of describing the biggest, quickest, culture with which it constructs its plant. Reliance's company culture, based on rapid response, massive economies of scale, 100 per cent plus capacity utilization, top-down vision and creative use of engineering skills, make it a strong fast follower-firm. Ofco (Box 8.6) illustrates how one company in Zimbabwe began a hard-slog transformation towards new manufacturing.

Box 8.5 Reliance Industries: Korea in India

Reliance Industries is probably India's most visionary company, which has always benchmarked itself against the best internationally. This is thoroughly reflected in the company's culture. Reliance has a record of being the quickest off the mark in many areas. For instance, it was the first Indian company to get a Moody's and Standard & Poor rating, the first Asian issuer of a 100-year Yankee bond. Stressing the importance of timing, Anil Ambani (the son of the founder) says, 'Market opportunities don't wait for anybody. It's a moving train and you have to run really fast if you want to catch it.' The decision on the 100-year bond was taken in less than two days: 'The opportunity to do the deal was open for only a few hours and so we had to move really fast', according to Mathew Panicker, MD Reliance Europe.[30]

The company was also the first in the world to build a cryogenic terminal at –138° C in deep seas for transferring ethylene to their downstream PVC and PET plants. Anil Ambani recalls: 'Everybody told us ethylene transfer is unsafe and definitely not possible in a country like India. But once we proved that we can do it, and do it safely, others in the world are copying it.'[31]

Speed is a prominent feature of Reliance's operations. Reliance's track record in project implementation consistently beat world standards: 17 months for PFY while the global time was at 26 months; 16 for PSF as compared to 26; 24 for PVC which was three months ahead of world schedule. As Hital Meswani, executive director-Hazira put it, 'In order to build a world-class plant you need to build in the shortest possible time, then stabilize, and that too at the least cost'.[32]

Its world-class scale production means that it ranges between the first and tenth positions in its various businesses. Constructing global-scale plants reflects in its culture. Mukesh Ambani reports a conversation with his father: 'If we tell him about a project of size x, his standard question will be "Why not 5x?".'[33] When Reliance decided to set up a university in Jamnagar, it sought 10,000 acres because Stanford has 9,000! Reliance plants are made to 'sweat': all operate at a capacity utilization of 120 per cent. This is one of the reasons why Reliance was able to offset the pressure on margins in 1996–97 despite a slowdown in the petrochemicals market. It reported an operating profit of 19.1 per cent against Dupont and ICI's 14 per cent.

Reliance also emphasizes its thoroughly professional culture in its working environment. According to Mukesh Ambani: 'we de-personalize things and talk about professional integrity and coherence. Reliance today doesn't depend on just ten or twenty people. Even if you take ten people out from any combination, the day to day running of the company won't get affected. That's the extent to which we are institutionalised.' He further says, 'We work in concentric circles, rather than in straight ranks but there is always a centre of accountability'. According to Lalit Jalan, senior vice-president heading the polypropylene business in 1997, 'It is rationality that runs through the company at all times'. Moreover, this 'vision and drive . . . come from the top management and percolates down to the ranks'. Their belief is reflected in the following statement: 'There is a lot of difference between saying "I think so" and "I know so". We pay attention to that difference.'[34]

Reliance seems to be well positioned for the future. Mukesh Ambani asserts 'We can deal with the risks in the petrochemicals like the process design risk, feedstock risk, operational risk or the market risk as well as any one else in the world.' Commenting on future developments, Anil Ambani says, 'If the administered pricing mechanism for petroleum is lifted . . . then the way we have configured the Jamnagar refinery, Reliance will be globally competitive,' and adds, 'Reliance will get listed on Wall Street because we want to benchmark ourselves with the top 100 companies of the world.' As he further puts it 'Impossible is not a word that exists in our dictionary'.[35]

Box 8.6 Ofco

At a very different level from Reliance is Ofco in Zimbabwe, which manufactures more than 300 products, including office furniture and shelving units. It was one of several firms that went through change instituted by a big consultancy, Price Waterhouse, using Japanese manufacturing techniques called the Kawasaki Production System (KPS). An example is the innovative layout change. The KPS consultants had recommended a cellular layout to allow for flexible production. But senior management 'stumbled upon an alternative and innovative way of achieving flexibility'.[36] The heavy presses and guillotines were located together in a U-shaped cell and the lighter machines all placed on mobile trolleys and wheeled near the presses depending on the product being manufactured. This meant the factory was in constant flux with light machinery being moved and hooked up whenever appropriate.

How did this kind of change happen when other firms in Zimbabwe found it much more difficult? The behaviour of management and work-force was key. 'The Factory Manager, who was responsible for much of the reorganisation experienced initial hostility from the shop floor . . . this was reduced when he worked on the production line himself to show that the proposed changes were feasible.' He tried 'to elicit the desired changes from the work-force rather than prescribing what these would be at the outset'.[37]

Can we have 'developed firms in a developing country', as Forbes Marshall's Vision Statement says (Box 8.4)? Firms can develop the will to change through fostering their innovative capabilities – but this entails major cultural change. Firms can be innovative and can learn to innovate in difficult environments. It involves the fostering of creativity and celebration of innovative success, whilst continuing with the day-to-day slog of continuous improvement.

Building a firm culture for innovation

Of exploitation and exploration

As we saw in Chapter 4, continuous improvement is key to building technological capabilities in all followers. But this key attribute, the ability to continuously improve, can conflict with being creative. March takes on these issues with his distinction between exploration and exploitation (Table 8.1).[38] Continuous improvement is all about exploitation, creativity about exploration.

Table 8.1 Terms associated with processes of exploitation and exploration

Exploitation	*Exploration*
Refinement	Search
Choice	Variation
Production	Risk taking
Efficiency	Experimentation
Selection	Play
Implementation	Flexibility
Execution	Discovery
	Innovation

Source: Adapted from J.G. March, 'Exploration and exploitation in organizational learning', *Organization Science*, 2, 1, 1989, pp. 71–87.

Getting better at exploitation

Chapter 4 gives many clues about what is needed culturally to be good at continuous improvement. It takes a culture that believes in educating the whole work-force, that believes in improved quality systems, that establishes systems to improve products and processes in a widespread and continuous manner, that is able to implement improvements so that they are 'owned' and done by everyone in a firm.

If we had to choose one word to sum up what firms must do to get better at exploitation it would be implementation. Many years ago the economist Harvey Leibenstein proposed a theory of X-efficiency.[39] X was the gap in productivity between firms in developed and developing countries, which used the same technology. The key reason for the productivity gap, it turned out, was not technology, or equipment, or employee skills. It was implementation, firms in developing countries simply used less of what they knew.

The conflict between continuous improvement and creativity, between exploitation and exploration, is different in different cultures at different points in time. Japan and South Korea have both been excellent at exploitation. But there is a point where to move further ahead in innovation requires getting better at exploration. This simple idea is also powerful. It is well understood that continuous improvement is not enough, but we must distinguish between the role of continuous improvement and creativity at different moments of development.

Getting better at exploration

What does it take to get better at exploration? We look briefly at three elements: building creativity, rewarding innovation and fostering difference among the work-force.

Fostering creativity

Building a culture for innovation involves both the construction of an environment that encourages creativity, and also the creation of environments that balance the necessary creativity with the day-to-day implementation of improvements, often the implementation of things that everyone knows to be 'the right way of doing things'.

Can creativity be stimulated? Tidd *et al.* make the point that 'management cannot directly change culture – but it can intervene at the level of artefacts – by changing structures or processes – and by providing models and reinforcing preferred styles of behaviour. . . . Changing this culture is not likely to happen quickly or as a result of single initiatives'.[40]

Although it is not easy and there are no simple models, there are experiences and approaches. For example, Rickards[41] made a list of the most popular factors associated with creative organizations:

*   Open communications systems, that encourage ideas
*   Reward systems that encourage creativity, and do not discourage getting it wrong
*   Freedom of choice, wherever possible, for individuals in their work organization
*   Diversity of views present through selection procedures – appoint diverse types of staff
*   Diversity of views encouraged through encouraging leadership
*   Constructive attitudes at senior levels as 'role models'.

Again at the micro-level, including personal behaviour as well as organizational, Adams used the company Synectics' approach to creative problem-solving, giving examples of actions that lead to it, and actions that inhibit it (see Table 8.2). Lest such an approach seems a bit open, it is important to note the Synectics developed it to allow groups to interact in a way that produces a result. It 'has concluded that the problem is not so much producing a concept but rather allowing a group to interact in a way that the final solution will be implemented'.[42]

Creativity cannot, however, be fostered in a vacuum, and the firm needs more than a supportive culture. Some firms have formal rules allocating and even protecting time for creativity, building innovation alliances with customers who would demand more, and setting formal rules for the proportion of new products in the company's product range.

The best known example of an organization that has institutionalized creativity time is the US company 3M. It has developed a culture that encourages individuals to follow up interesting ideas and allows them 15 per cent time without any rules. If the idea looks promising, there are venture funds to enable more thorough exploration. 3M will back such ideas and give the innovator the responsibility to run the business (Box 8.7). By this means of internal venturing (intrapreneurialism) 3M has set up a whole range of businesses, and its headquarters is a 'mecca' for companies in search of ideas and inspirations, though 'it's hard to emulate a culture that has been percolating since the turn of the century'.[43]

Table 8.2   Actions that lead to, and inhibit, creative problem-solving

Actions that lead to creative problem-solving	*Actions that inhibit creative problem-solving*
Take on faith, temporarily suspend disbelief, assume it can be done, share the burden of proof	Put the burden of proof on her or him, ask questions, cross-examine, give no feedback, be non-committal, put on a stony-face
Set up win-wins, make it no-lose	React negatively, discount/put down, be cynical/sceptical, insist on early precision, correct
Support confusion/uncertainty, value the learning in mistakes, use ambiguity	Point out only flaws
Stay loose until rigour counts	Assume no value, make no connections, be impatient, nitpick, interrupt, be bored
Optimistic, see the value in, focus on what is going for the idea, assume valuable implications	Be pessimistic, preach/moralize, be judgemental, be critical, disapprove
Deal as an equal, eliminate status/rank, give up all rights to discipline/punish	Pull rank, get angry, scare
Accept, connect with, join, be open to, wholly available	Be dominant, command, order, direct, threaten/warn, demand
Credit, acknowledge, attentiveness, listen, be interested, show approval, give early support	Blame, name call, set up win/lose, be competitive, make fun of
Protect vulnerable beginnings	Inattention, act distant, do not listen, do not join, use silence against

Source: J. Adams, *Conceptul Blockbusting*, New York: Perseus, 1990.

Box 8.7   Innovation at 3M, and elsewhere

3M: • keeps divisions small
• tolerates failure
• motivates champions
• stays close to the customer
• does not kill projects.

Hewlett-Packard urges researchers to spend 10 per cent of their time on their own pet projects.

General Electric jointly develops products with customers.

Johnson and Johnson gives freedom to fail.

The Japanese electrical company Matsushita had another problem – its staff were working too many hours and this affected creativity:

> Matsushita discovered that inefficiencies at work were blocking the creativity of its employees and taking away their personal time. . . . To solve this problem Matsushita set a goal in 1991 to reduce annual working hours to 1,800 hours. Osamu Tanaka, general manager of the programme, made clear that the idea was to enhance employee creativity rather than simply lower working hours or costs. 'We do not need [this programme] if we want to reduce working hours. We can just tell employees that the company will not pay for any overtime work. . . . We have wanted to improve the productivity of our staff organization through this project. . . . How can anyone be creative if he works until twelve midnight everyday? . . . You cannot make original products just by looking at plans at the office every night.'[44]

What followed was a major change process since new work practices and systems had to be developed in every division to allow hours to drop (from around 2,036) to 1,800. Self-organizing teams were set up in every division and no specific details were given on how it should be done.

Another approach that organizations can establish is to allow and implement space for creativity, to build boundaries around innovative activity by taking staff away from their normal jobs. Such ring-fencing requires support from the top of the organization. Even then, there can be difficulties. The large Indian software firm Infosys tried to build innovative product development teams to develop new software products. But each time, the urgency of demands to expand routine software business destroyed the time given to the teams. Finally, Infosys decided to spin-off some 'green-field' product development teams into independent subsidiaries so that they were not hijacked by day-to-day pressures.

Incentives for success, trying and failing

All organizations reward success, but innovative organizations treat failure and not trying differently. A less innovative organization rewards success and punishes failure, tolerating inactivity. A more innovative organization also rewards success, but tolerates failure and punishes not trying. The antithesis of an innovative organization is the Indian bureaucracy. If you do not take a decision, there is no penalty, but if you take the wrong decision you can be in trouble. That is a powerful incentive to take no decision. Our colleague Jim Adams once did a two-day programme on creativity for one of the leading West Coast banks in the US, which was greatly concerned that its staff were not innovative enough. At the closing dinner, Jim asked the vice-president who had organized the programme how serious they were about creativity – 'Oh, very serious!' Jim then asked the vice-president how much money he could spend without prior approval – he got a figure. Jim asked what would happen if he spent that same amount on a project that turned out to be a total failure – 'I'd be fired,' said the VP. Innovation requires actual change, not just lip-service.

Fostering difference

A cultural stereotype of Japan and other East Asian countries is of the regimented work-force, working together in a uniform way, from uniforms for all grades of staff, to Tai Chi for all staff in the morning. Clearly such approaches have played a part in tremendous productivity increases. There may, though, come a time when a more creative environment may be necessary with more tolerance of difference. Tolerance of purple hair may produce dividends in some organizations in India and Japan, but is not likely to be an issue in Silicon Valley.

Sometimes, more rarely, a whole geographical space for creativity and innovation is encouraged, or just grows. One rather unusual such attempt by a network of firms is to build a Silicon Valley culture in Bangalore! (Box 8.8).

Box 8.8   Silicon Valley in Bangalore

In Silicon Valley perks decide a company's fate. With high staff turnover rates that are continuously on the rise, Silicon Valley companies have switched to using soft perks to attract talent. Most are transforming their corporate offices into resorts with add-ons such as tennis courts and gyms. Novell, for example, has a $130-million campus in San Jose with volleyball, basketball and tennis courts, a gym, an espresso bar and even a restaurant. Sun Microsystems' Menlo Park campus has several restaurants including Java Java (an upmarket eat-out) and a fitness centre called fit@sun.

Software companies shower as much attention on food and fitness as on programming. Free Coke, soda, fruit juice and popcorn are now out and gourmet meals are in. Sun's Java Java serves delicacies such as porcini mushroom and cheese ravioli. Lucent Technology has hired an executive chef for its Coyote Creek Café, while AutoDesk has lured the chef of *Star Wars*' George Lucas to whip up gourmet meals for its employees. Some companies such as Oracle, however, farm out the catering to specialists such as Bon Appetit management company. Oracle is renowned for its Japanese noodle bars complete with baby grand pianos. Fitness facilities are also big on the agenda of several companies. In addition to the latest gizmos, companies offer classes on yoga and tae-kwon-do. Sun's fit@sun offers lessons in kickbox aerobics. Sun also assists its employees who want to adopt children by doling out stipends. Companies also give other perks which include dry-cleaning services, massage therapists and ergonomics experts.

The culture is fast becoming a part of Bangalore, India's Silicon Valley. An increasing number of organizations are creating or emphasizing a corporate culture to give people something to hold on to in fluid times. This is a meaningful strategy considering attrition rates of the order of 21 per cent and replacement cost per employee estimated to be between 60,000 and 100,000 rupees.

Take the example of Bangalore-based Infosys. Employees are taken to the office about 45 minutes away from the city by bus; and the day starts with breakfast, in consideration for the many single employees. Dormitories are provided for those who want to sleep over. There is a gymnasium for breaks during the day. A creche for children anticipates future needs of a staff whose average age is just 25 years. The company also offers a service called Personal Touch that takes care of personal chores for employees while they are at work. This ranges from delivering parcels to booking train tickets to setting up preschool facilities for the employees' children.

At NIIT the perks include compulsory 'offs' for individual employees on their birthdays; dating allowances; automatic celebration allowances added to paychecks in a birthday month; an allowance to 'do something nice' for elders in the family; paternity leave; an automatic provident fund account for children; annual calendars featuring crayon scribbles by employees' children instead of expensive paintings.

At VeriFone India, the software development centre for transaction automation devices, a 24-hour work facility and support system contains gyms, a swimming pool, sauna and an all-day creche. The entire work-force follows a TGIF (thank God it's Friday!) tradition where they get together in the canteen for beer and snacks. Says M.G. Balakrishna Rao, development manager, 'On an average, a software engineer spends close to 55 hours a week at his workstation'. And with the level of concentration that the job demands, the challenge for software companies is to cut the monotony in the job. For VeriFone, this included creating a different ambience in each of the four floors as well as ensuring that the panoramic view outside reflected into every corner of the workspace.

Companies like Sonata Software aim to foster specific cultures. Engineers working on off-site development projects for German companies are provided with language classes at work. Families are encouraged to participate in after-work activities that range from casual get-togethers to the orchestrated extravagance of Sonata Day, an annual day that has all employees participating in dances and drama.

Institutionalizing the after-hours concept in the industry is the elite gathering of the software heavyweights, the beer drinkers association of IT (BAIT). The annual gathering that provides an informal setting for industry interaction aptly matches the open culture that most software companies are building into their everyday work environment.

Even the government seems to have swung into action. According to Karnataka State Electronics Development Corporation's (KEONICS) chairman and managing director S.M. Pattanaik, 'We are under extraordinary pressure from companies in . . . [software and electronics] sectors to provide various kinds of support for them . . .'. Recognizing the high staff turnover rates in the software exports industry, according to Pattanaik '. . . providing a small township . . . [with] amenities like posh housing, gardens, swimming pool, health centres' would provide for a better environment for work (*Business India* 1997). Thus were born the plans for a 1,000-acre Electronic City. About 200 to 300 acres were proposed to accommodate the township, which is to have anywhere between 3,000 to 5,000 apartments.

Conclusions

March argues against a single-minded focus on either exploitation or exploration – a balance between the two is essential. For nations or firms, the balance exploitation–exploration depends on the actual situation at any time and place. At the level of nations, it is possible to argue that Japan and South Korea require more exploratory capabilities, while in Silicon Valley more emphasis on exploitation may improve innovation success. India might need to get better at both.

Most firms must also constantly think about the balance between the need for a more creative environment and the need to make sure that innovation is exploited to produce more value-added. 'The effectiveness of any specific organization will depend on whether the balance is in line with its potential ... The practical question is not "How does the organization get a creative climate?", but "how do we get the right balance between openness and control?"'[45]

In this book we have become used to discussing the 'soft' dimensions (of design and quality for example). Culture is inherently 'soft' and 'intangible', which can devalue it in the eyes of those who prefer the 'hard' and more easily measurable. It is precisely these 'soft' elements that must be embedded into firm routines if firms are to become innovative.

The comeback of culture has led to the insight that mindsets are different for the different innovation skills we have discussed in the different chapters of this book. The firm has to determine what it must be good at to make the next jump up the value-chain. Does it take the hard slog of widespread, continuous, incremental innovation on the shop-floor? Here the task is to implement in a hard-nosed way all that the firm knows must be done. But if the task is to build technology that is proprietary, then the firm must get more comfortable with uncertainty and the soft concepts of aesthetics and emotional appeal. Or, hardest of all, must the firm do both at the same time?

In Chapter 9, we examine how the firm must get the balance right between hard slog and cleverness in organizing for innovation.

9 Organizing for innovation

From followers to leaders

Introduction

We began this book by asking how firms in NICs can come from behind, learn from the best and then close the gap and move ahead as world-beating champions. How can firms go beyond being 'merely the drones who make products according to the strict and narrow confines of the role assigned to them by the multinational technology inventing firms'? How can they pass 'the rest to become the best'?

The immediate answer to this question is straightforward – that they should be competent 'drones'! Firms must organize to be effective at incremental shop-floor innovation – as we saw in Chapter 4. No firm aspiring to move up the value-ladder can afford to neglect these manufacturing capabilities. But our answer goes further: in later chapters we showed firms that had got clever and built proprietary and product capabilities.

In this final chapter, we first recap key conclusions from each chapter to suggest how successful firms can address questions of future strategy by asking how drones can get clever. How can firms organize both to be good at shop-floor continuous innovation and to move beyond the rest? We use the process–product–proprietary grid from Chapter 5 to map out choices for developing proprietary technology and new products.

Throughout the book we have used various strategic concepts, though we have not named them as such. Second, we formalize these key concepts of technology strategy and use them to map choices that must be made to grow value-added. Firm choice will be constrained by where they are now – their current assets and capabilities. But firms set on moving from follower to leader must also make choices about where they wish to go, and what investments must be made now in assets and capabilities to get there. This adds up to a technology strategy for innovation. In Chapter 2, we described five cases of successful firms at different points on the value-added spectrum. Using this strategic perspective, what questions must these firms answer to advance further? We will use the cases presented in Chapter 2 to illustrate concepts, simplifying the actual challenges facing firms.

Finally, we consider the role for national policy in pushing firms up the value-chain in the early years of the twenty-first century.

How can 'drones' get clever – organizing for innovation

Organizing to add value as a 'drone'

In an unprotected world the entry point is wage competitiveness. In Chapter 4 we focused on improving manufacturing through shop-floor innovation (Box 9.1). We argued that the new manufacturing is essential but as means to improvement, not end – the end is innovation to add value. This hard-slog gradual improvement is key because competition is with firms not just from Japan, the US and Europe, but also from Brazil and China. So if firms compete on wages, there is always labour some-where willing to work for still lower wages.

Box 9.1   Chapter 4: Innovation on the shop-floor

- There is no one best set of new manufacturing practices. Each new manufacturing technique is useful in itself, and adopting several techniques together has synergistic benefits. What is best for a particular firm will depend on context – the industry it is in, the environment in which it operates and its ability to implement widespread changes in shop-floor organization.
- New manufacturing must be seen as means and not end. The end objective is innov-ation and firms should not get stuck in the techniques. TQM and people involvement are important to the extent that they lead to shop-floor innovation.
- A key element, often forgotten, is absorbing slack. Simply working harder and elimin-ating waste has great potential in growing value-added.
- The firm should see itself as part of a potentially dynamic network of raw material suppliers, capital equipment makers and demanding customers. The key word is 'potentially': the firm should consciously foster its suppliers getting stronger and its buyers getting more demanding.
- Software should be seen as a capital good – it is key to industrial process improvement and transaction efficiencies with suppliers and buyers.

Consider the process–product–proprietary grid we set up in Chapter 5 (Figure 9.1): technology followers start competing internationally in the non-proprietary/process box of our grid. Some might even be outside the grid (they do not compete with international firms). They need to improve just to enter the grid, as TBL did in the early 1990s.

Once in the grid, firms begin the hard slog of improving process capabilities. The maquiladoras are examples of competing internationally on wages and not moving to develop proprietary or product capabilities. But firms should be seeking to add value as efficiently as they possibly can. Within the process/non-proprietary quadrant, firms can begin by absorbing slack and following the lessons summarized in Box 9.1.

Other firms we have met in the book have made significant movement within the process/non-proprietary box. Korean and Taiwanese firms in the late 1980s moved rapidly to producing more sophisticated products within the same OEM arrangements (Figure 9.2). Indian software firms have moved towards higher value services but not proprietary products. TBL has developed process capabilities much more than product capabilities.

Organizing by getting clever: from process to product and proprietary

Moving up the value-chain from hard slog means capturing innovation rents by moving to proprietary or product technology, or both (Box 9.2). These moves involve getting clever by gaining the assets and competences to jump quadrants. Building these new capabilities is hard and firms need strong will to abandon capabilities which

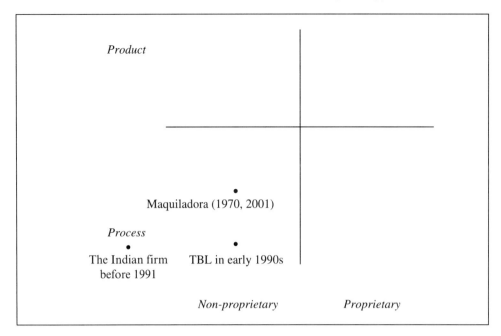

Figure 9.1   Process–product–proprietary grid, mark 3.

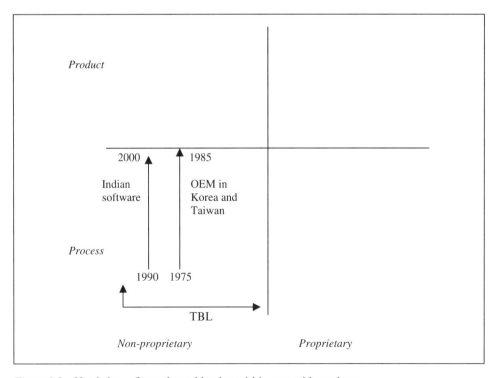

Figure 9.2   Hard slog – firms that add value within one grid quadrant.

have worked well in the past. In short, this move requires strong entrepreneurship: the ability to articulate a vision of the future and the will to make it happen.

Moving quadrants can happen in one of five ways (Figure 9.3). After adding value within OEM, between the early and late 1980s East Asian Miracle Firms moved from OEM to ODM (Figure 9.3a). Such a move in microwaves and computers was much harder than in garments, and produces much higher value-added. What did it take to make this move? Principally, the will to attract the buyer to the idea of the local firm doing design. To make it happen required local designs and engineering skills acceptable to buyers. These new designs were essentially detailed designs done within the EAM firm to a concept provided by the OEM customer. For example, a customer could ask for a larger or more powerful oven to be designed by Samsung. Hero Cycles is a good example of a firm that has moved significantly towards specialized, more design conscious, higher value-added bicycle products. But it has just started its journey towards more proprietary products.

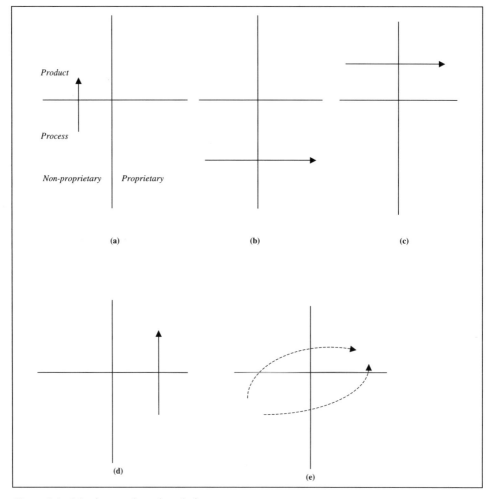

Figure 9.3   Moving up the value-chain.

Reliance and Ispat (Figure 9.3b) developed the capabilities to move to proprietary processes. They first invested in plant capacity that was ahead of market demand, running these plants at efficiency levels that set international bench-marks. They then developed their own proprietary process technologies that further added value.

A third transition was Korean and Taiwanese firms as they moved from ODM to OBM (Figure 9.3c), after adding value within OEM (Figure 9.2) and moving to ODM (Figure 9.3a). As Hobday points out, the transition from ODM to OBM often went through an intermediate Own Idea Manufacture (OIM) stage, where the EAM firm conceptualized a new product from scratch and convinced the foreign buyer to promote it. The firm had also been successful selling the product in its own name in its domestic market. With globally efficient manufacturing plants and a demonstrated independent new product development capability, the firm then moved to OBM, and introduced its own brand internationally.

Box 9.2 Chapter 5: From process to product and proprietary

- At some point, moving up the value-chain requires a shift to the firm capturing innovation rents from proprietary and product capabilities.
- East Asian firms moved up the learning hierarchy from OEM to ODM to OBM.
- Competing internationally is a key but insufficient means of forcing firms up the value-chain (the maquiladoras).
- Entrepreneurship (the crucial importance of wanting to) is key.
- Going proprietary is hard. It involves building new assets and competences. World-scale and cheaply established manufacturing plants that operate at bench-mark efficiency levels are such assets (Reliance, Cemex, Ispat). Outstanding project execution capability or the ability to quickly spread best practice around globally dispersed manufacturing plants are such competencies.
- Hard-slog process innovation continues to be important and cannot be abandoned in technology-followers as firms develop proprietary capabilities. This process capability can be the key complementary asset that would allow the firm to capture the innovation rents from a move to product or proprietary.

Cemex demonstrates the 9.3d transition, as it moves from a globally leading manufacturing operation to the development of new products, such as extreme temperature cement. Finally, 9.3e represents the most difficult move up the value-chain as the firm *attempts* (hence the dotted line) to move directly to its own international brand, as Titan has tried. Vitro, too, has moved quite rapidly towards developing new and proprietary products. As we described in Chapter 2, major innovation is a rising proportion of its total innovation activity.

R&D capabilities

Chapter 6 argues that there is a special role for R&D in followers (Box 9.3). Although followers cannot match leaders in spending, they can focus R&D on enhancing shop-floor innovation, to learn from other firms and to build independent product development capability.

Box 9.3   Chapter 6: Managing R&D in technology-followers

- Technology-followers cannot hope to match technology-leaders in spending, do not have to and should not try to. R&D must be focused on those activities that bring the firm to the technology frontier, not advance the frontier itself.
- The focus for R&D in firms is to:
  - (a) complement shop-floor innovation by being closely tied to but distinct from manufacturing (Reliance);
  - (b) be the formal learning unit of the firm, trading and accessing external knowledge, sharing it internally and codifying the firm's own knowledge (Reliance);
  - (c) set the tone for unfamiliar territory such as aesthetics, finish and packaging (Forbes Marshall);
  - (d) attract more qualified people who can be the firm's change agents (Ranbaxy);
  - (e) co-ordinate external sources of knowledge and connect them with in-house effort (Ranbaxy, Bajaj Auto);
  - (f) build product development capacity so the firm has design freedom to independently conceptualize products (Forbes Marshall, Bajaj Auto).

A number of firms have built new proprietary technology without expensive R&D units. Reliance is a good example of a company that has moved to develop proprietary technologies via process innovation (see Figure 9.4). Reliance has R&D units which operate closely with implementing units. Reliance has also sponsored research at national laboratories – on catalysts, for example. Its in-house R&D units have the

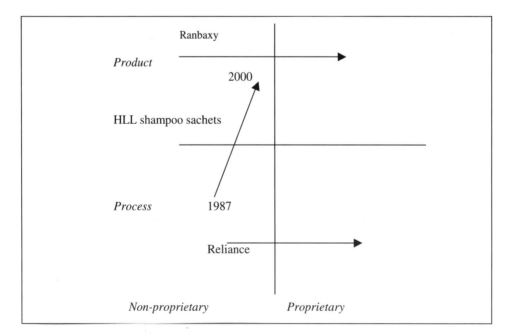

Figure 9.4   Building R&D capabilities.

responsibility of co-ordinating work done at these laboratories with in-house effort. In 2000 Reliance emerged as India's second-largest corporate spender on R&D. But growth in R&D spending came in the 1990s, *after* Reliance had established its pre-eminence in project execution and manufacturing efficiency.

Hindustan Lever has used R&D to deliver small improvements in product tech-nology (shampoo sachets) and process technology (cheaper packaging machines for sachets). These small improvements have led to major gains in market share and penetration of the Indian rural market.

Ranbaxy, the drug firm we met in Chapter 6, has also used R&D to move up the value-chain. Ranbaxy has until recently been in the non-proprietary/product box, as the bulk of its products are generic and reverse-engineered drugs. It built an effective R&D capability focused on reverse-engineering. Its more recent investment in research under its New Drug Discovery programme to find new molecules is precisely an attempt to move to proprietary and product (and internationally patented) technology. Its efficient FDA-approved manufacturing plants for generics are a useful comple-mentary asset for this new drug development programme.

Design capabilities

Design provides the potential to innovate in products without pushing out the technology frontier (Box 9.4). Firms have invested in design capabilities in different ways to move up the value-chain. Titan began as a product innovation based firm, has strong design capabilities, and is now developing proprietary products – it is selling internationally through its own brand (Figure 9.5). Bajaj is now developing a steady stream of new products after decades of variants on a single model. In motorcycles, it has gone from licensing new designs from Kawasaki to undertaking joint design and

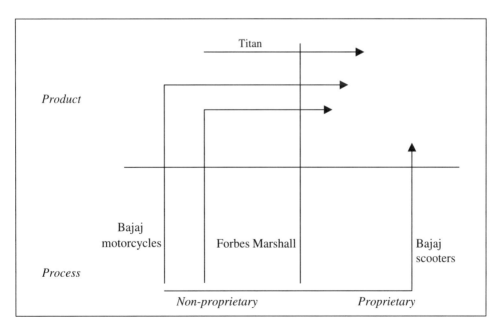

Figure 9.5   Building design capabilities.

development of new products. Bajaj recently announced that it was setting up an assembly plant in Brazil to enter the market with a Kawasaki-branded (but Bajaj–Kawasaki designed and owned) motorcycle. In scooters, Bajaj has bought technology for new engines and shapes from various sources to integrate into a range of proprietary new designs. Exports are still very limited, but new designs will be crucial to enter international markets in a serious way.

Forbes Marshall previously made a range of steam engineering and control instrumentation products with technology provided in joint ventures. R&D till 1991 was indigenization. For the past five years, it has been independently conceptualizing products new to the world and attempting to sell them internationally. It now has a small but direct presence in six countries, including the US.

Box 9.4   Chapter 7: Design leadership for technology-followers

- Design is key.
- The design frontier can be pushed forward independently of technology.
- Pushing forward the design frontier is key to adding value in technology-followers, and must be a focus for R&D.
- Design requires a mindset that is comfortable with aesthetics and emotions, and a culture confident enough to push out product parameters.
- Value can be added to products by targeting emotional appeal – such as craftsmanship, elegance, symbolism and human fit – product attributes that go beyond technical specifications.
- A combination of systematic need-finding and market research is most effective in uncovering what customers will buy (and pay a lot for!).
- The IDMM experience suggests that building independent design capability requires:

    (a) developing prototyping skills and using them – getting it wrong first time round is vital to designing good products;
    (b) dedicated product development resource to keep projects moving;
    (c) a product champion in top management.

Culture

Finally, what are the cultural requirements for innovation (Box 9.5)? We have already emphasized the need for entrepreneurship to make things happen. National policy and culture influence whether the bulk of firms can make the kind of changes we propose. Firms can transcend their national cultures, though most do not. Cultures can be constructed at both national and firm level, but it is certainly easier for a single firm to break the mould and organize against the grain.

As we saw in Chapter 8, issues of culture go much further than this. What are the cultural characteristics required to be good at learning from others?

Organizing for *exploitation* requires, as Dore pointed out, that one begin with a culture of humility – to learn from the best world-wide. Learning from the best means first developing the capability to identify what is best (Dore's Independent World Technology Reconnaissance Capability) and then to work consciously at acquiring it. When Hyundai's engineers practised assembling and dis-assembling Ford cars until they had mastered the process, they were investing in hard-slog learning. When a Bajaj

---

Box 9.5   Chapter 8: Building a culture for innovation

- Cultural attributes are key to building innovation competencies in firms. Firm cultures reflect their national cultures but can transcend them.
- The starting-point is a strong will to develop, to move up the value-chain, which can be fostered through a shared sense of backwardness. Firms can publicly compare themselves with their peers around the world to foster this sense.
- Firms need to be open to learn from the best wherever they may be, but have enough confidence to improve the rest.
- The cultural attributes essential to being good at the hard slog were key to EAM – exploitation of existing knowledge. These attributes are distinct from those needed for exploration – creative searches for new solutions.
- Getting better at exploration involves getting better at creativity, rewarding innovation and tolerating failure, and breeding difference and dissent in firms.
- What matters is balance – followers becoming leaders may need to get better at exploitation or exploration, or – hardest of all – both simultaneously.

Auto quality circle makes a process more reliable such that they get it right first time, they are eliminating waste in the manufacturing process. When HP Singapore's engineers re-engineered a calculator to reduce assembly time, they were incrementally innovating on the shop-floor. When the Indian pharmaceutical firm Cipla reverse-engineered an HIV treatment, that it then manufactured and sold at one-twentieth the international price, they were implementing what is known effectively. There is little that is creative about these processes, but there is much that is hard and much that is innovative – that is new to the firm for its commercial advantage.

Effective *exploration* requires organizing for innovation quite differently. Table 9.1 lists terms and concepts we have used through the book that deal with being good at

Table 9.1   Exploitation and exploration skills in followers

Exploitation	*Exploration*
• Independence Technology World Reconnaissance Capability (ITWRC)	• Design
• R&D as learning	• R&D as research
• Technology keeping	• R&D as co-ordinating knowledge
• Independent Technology Learning Capacity (ITLC)	• Independent Technology Creating Capacity (ITCC)
• Sense of backwardness	• Self-reliance
• People involvement – Small Group Activity (SGA), suggestion scheme	• Capital goods as part of dynamic cluster
• Total Quality Management (TQM)	
• Get it right, first time	• Prototype and get it wrong, first time
• Make up for gaps in tacit knowledge from technology transferred	• Create new tacit knowledge
• Implementation	• Experimentation
• R&D as improving existing products	• Building international brands

either exploitation or exploration. The exploring firm has to foster experimentation and a culture of prototyping, being comfortable with getting it wrong first time. Building design skills takes, as we saw, a focus on aesthetics and understanding emotions. Telco's emotional Indica advertisement ('Isn't it time for some Indian engineering?') takes quite different skills to Hyundai's assembly-practice. The integrated design for manufacturability and marketing (IDMM) programme in India trying to get Godrej and Forbes Marshall engineers comfortable with making mistakes and 'wasting' prototypes represents a very different competence to Bajaj's quality circle eliminating waste. Titan trying to make 'Made in India' symbolize watches to Europeans takes creative brand-building far-removed from producing HP's calculators at 'lower cost than anyone else on the planet'. And Ranbaxy trying to develop and patent molecules for an anti-bacterial treatment that Americans would buy at American drug prices is quite different from Cipla producing AIDs treatments at world-beating cost.

Terms like creativity, and aesthetics, and research are inherently attractive, but it is not our intention to push exploration at the expense of exploitation. For a Japanese or Korean firm that has excelled at the hard slog of process innovation, the priority could well be exploration – to foster creativity and risk-taking. This may well take the advice (amusingly, the advice almost took the form of a directive at Samsung!) that Matsushita, Hitachi and Samsung have given their employees recently, of working fewer hours and dressing strangely – in the hope they will then experiment more and be more creative. But for an Indian firm with considerable slack in its operations, where implementing what is known is key, 'work less hard' would be strange advice indeed.

And if that Indian firm is Titan or Bajaj or Forbes Marshall, attempting simultaneously to absorb slack while moving to the proprietary product box, it is doubly hard. They need to get better at *both* exploitation and exploration at the same time. This will involve fostering a culture that reflects both columns of Table 9.1 and ultimately means getting comfortable with a schizophrenic existence. What is key is to get the balance right, and this balance will depend on *where* the firm is on our process–product–proprietary grid and *what path* it will choose to grow value-added. Talking of positions, paths and choice is all about strategy, which we turn to next.

Building a technology strategy for innovation

In building new capabilities, a strategic perspective may help firms understand the choices they must make. First, some vocabulary: assets, capabilities, position, trajectory, choice (see Box 9.6 for some more detail). Our mantra has been that for firms to move up the value-added ladder requires the hard slog of gradual improvement but then the need to graduate to proprietary and product. This transformation process involves building on old and building up new assets and capabilities. By *assets*, we mean a firm's specific assets, often intangible, that make it different from other firms and therefore give it its competitive advantage. By *capabilities* or *competencies*,* we mean those skills that make the firm good at using its assets or putting knowledge to work. Competencies are nothing if not used, and are therefore all about implementation, and often show up as the practices and routines by which firms get things done.

---

* We treat both as the same.

Since our focus is on improvement – *from* following *to* leading – two associated concepts are also useful – *position* and *trajectory*. Where a firm is *now* is its position – a result of previous building of assets and capabilities. Where a firm is *going* depends both on its current position and its past positions – which give it its trajectory. If it has been good at some things and bad at others in the immediate past, momentum – what economists call path-dependence – will determine its future direction. But firms also have *choices*: they make decisions, although those decisions are constrained by the firm's position (its current assets and competencies) and its trajectory (how its past assets and competences brought it to where it is). There is still room for manoeuvre and the choices made now will determine the firm's technical capability – and so its future competitiveness.

Box 9.6   Conceptual building blocks of strategy

Firm specific assets

A firm's competitive advantage is shaped by its assets. Assets are not just, or even primarily, fixed assets like plant and equipment, but those knowledge assets that are unique to each firm.[1] Such assets are:

- Technological assets, include assets that can be protected with intellectual property rights, but also the tacit knowledge that often determines a firm's competitiveness.
- Complementary assets, which we covered in Chapter 5, cover many non-technical functional areas and include brand, marketing, distribution, after-sales systems and financial resources.
- Institutional assets, including the public policy environment within which the firm operates, and the national innovation system within which it innovates.
- Locational assets, such as proximity to attractive markets and being part of a dynamic industrial cluster.
- Reputational assets, the image that others hold about a firm which is key to how it is seen in the outside world.

Some of our Chapter 5 firms built distinctive proprietary assets. Ispat, for example, has the asset of size and spread – it is the only multinational steel company with steel plants in countries like Kazakhstan. In 2000 it had manufacturing facilities in ten countries and marketing operations in 150 countries. Reliance has a vertically integrated chain extending from textiles to petrochemicals to the world's largest oil refinery to concessions for oil exploration. HLL and Bajaj have by far the most extensive distribution network in the world's largest or second largest market, a key complement to product innovation.

Capabilities or competencies

A firm's capability determines the effective use of its assets – its resources and knowledge. Capabilities include skills and functional competencies that allows the firm to take advantage of opportunities. They are the mix of skills and organizational routines and processes used to produce, to improve production and to introduce new products and processes.

Core competencies[2] are those that are unique to the firm. These competencies often feed into more than one business area – the common examples are 3M's in adhesives, Sony's in miniaturization and Honda's in engines. What matters is that the firm has a few crucial areas core to the firm's success where it is best in the world at doing things.

Although the concept was initially restricted to technology, we follow common practice of using it more broadly – indeed, in a follower, the core competencies will tend not to be technological. For Samsung the move from OEM to higher technology products, to own design ODM and to own proprietary equipment manufacturer involved building a strong engineering product design capability that cross-cut different types of product. In particular, it demonstrated its ability to produce prototypes and deliver product in record time. For process industry cases like Reliance and Posco, it is ability to complete plants before schedule and operate over capacity that is core to their success. Ispat's core competence is the ability to turn poorly managed plants into efficient low-cost producers (see Table 5.10) and spread best-practice rapidly around the group.

Positions and trajectories

At any point in time the sum total of a firm's assets and capabilities define its position. A firm's future direction is determined by its current position. Present position is itself shaped by past trajectory, and the path taken brings dependencies for future trajectory. The firm's routines constrain future behaviour.

Choice

The essence of strategy is choice: a firm must choose both what to do and what not to do. For example, a service firm must choose between serving a low-frills mass market and a more demanding but lower volume higher margin market. If it tries to do it all, then it might do more poorly than competitors at everything. So although position and trajectory constrain a firm's choices, it is choice which ultimately determines which direction the firm takes.

Let us now apply these strategic concepts to our process–product–proprietary grid. The grid shows the firm's current position, and the path it followed to get there. Where it goes from here will be constrained by its current assets and capabilities. Indeed, the firm can continue to be successful, at least in the short term, within the same quadrant. But jumping quadrants requires choice and the will to change position. Consider the questions facing firms at different points on the value-added spectrum that we have discussed in some detail in this book:

- Where does Tanzania Breweries, the leading brewer in a small country, go from an 80 per cent domestic market share?
- How does Hero Cycles, the world's largest bicycle manufacturer, meet Chinese competition?
- How does Vitro, an emerging player in the global glass industry, continue to close the value-added gap, after it has made many of the early gains?
- Is it enough, as the Indian software industry, to be one of the most unexpected success stories of the past twenty years, providing 400,000 plus high-paying jobs but with a 1:5 gap in value-added?
- How does Cemex, the global bench-mark firm in cement, stay ahead?
- How does Reliance, a firm with a dominant position in the Indian petrochemicals market, having exhausted potential for reverse-integration, keep growing rapidly?

Where these firms go from here will depend on where they want to go, and the choices they make now to build new assets and capabilities.

The choice of exports and new products

To grow sales beyond an 80 per cent domestic market share, TBL must either export or develop new products for the local market. As Table 9.2 shows, TBL has higher productivity than its parent South African Breweries. At the level of the firm, it seems that TBL is relatively competitive and could begin exporting. What is holding it back? Is it the perverse state policies that tax local production, including that for export, at a higher rate than imports? Or does South African Breweries not permit TBL to compete with it in export markets?

TBL's other possible trajectory is to add more products to its range (Figure 9.6a). That would take a product innovation capability it has not demonstrated in the past, and if TBL chooses this path then it must begin investment in product development

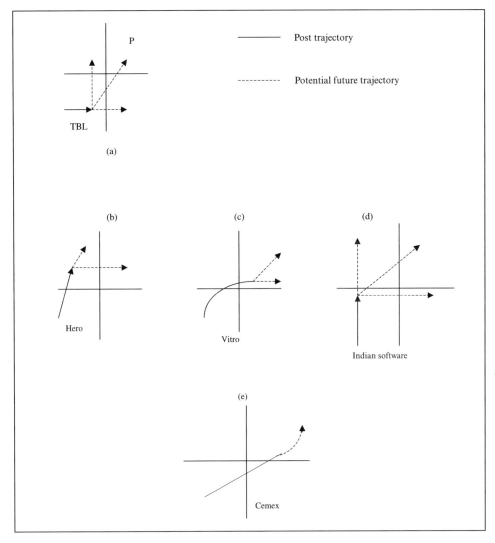

Figure 9.6   Future trajectories.

and local branding. Investment in design capability and fostering a culture of exploration would complement TBL's shop-floor competence.

The choice of design and proprietary products

Hero has the options of moving further up the value-chain with products or of going proprietary through new bicycle designs (Figure 9.6b).

Although comparative figures for international bicycle firms have been difficult to come by, there would seem to be a big gap in productivity with Taiwanese firms at least, which now manufacture bicycles mainly in China.* Certainly Hero has demonstrated its competence at hard-slog innovation for its standard Roadster and can even compete with imports from China at zero duty. A supply chain of 400 JIT suppliers and a distribution network of 3,000 dealers is a formidable asset. Being the world's largest manufacturer of bicycles is a useful complementary asset to any innovations in product, process or material technology.

However, the story is not as rosy for either exports or specials. Hero has seen Chinese exports replace its exports in the US and in Africa. India exports 1 million bicycles each year, with Hero at 400,000. China exports 20 million bicycles a year. China makes over 75 per cent of the 10 million bicycles imported into the US market each year, most of which are specials – geared, mountain or children's bikes. Hero is a relatively recent entrant into the specials market, and China is a threat to it in India itself, let alone overseas. There is a clear need to move up the value-chain with design to higher value-added segments, that competitors find difficult to match. Building volume in specials is key for exports, and Hero could also consider the expensive but ultimately lucrative option of establishing a brand in foreign markets. Finally, Hero's JIT supply chain has been enormously effective for the standard Roadster. What would it take to harness this JIT network more effectively for lower volume specials?

The choice of design

Vitro would seem still to have a big gap in sales per employee with Owens-Corning (Table 9.2), the leading US glass firm. But Vitro demonstrates that while position is important, it is even more important to be on a good trajectory. Vitro has rapidly been closing the gap – from one-seventh to one-third between 1991 and 2000. We would argue that Vitro is now just within the proprietary–product box, and it has the choice of competing mainly on glass-making or to move more heavily into proprietary products (Figure 9.6c). The East Asian Miracle option of moving to OBM via Own Idea Manufacturer may be useful in the glass industry, where the product concept could be suggested by Vitro as the supplier. Another option, that several Japanese and Korean firms used in electronics, is to buy US brands – LG bought Zenith and Acer bought Altos Computer, for example – to help enter the market with its own branded product.

---

* Comparative figures for international bicycle firms have been very difficult to come by (this is perhaps an indication of China's dominance of the industry – it has no data publicly or internationally available). The not strictly comparable figures we have found for the Taiwanese firm Giant indicate a huge difference in value-added (seven times) with Hero. A UK specialist bicycle producer, Tandem, shows a difference of around three times.

Table 9.2   Sales per employee ($US), comparing TBL, Hero, Vitro, Indian software and Cemex with world leaders

	Tanzania Breweries Ltd (TBL)	South African Breweries (SAB)	Heineken (H)	Ratio (SAB/TBL)	Ratio (H/TBL)
1995	11,480	55,159	134,039	5	12
1999	110,479	80,103	145,325	0.7	1.3
1995–99	×10	×1.5	×1.1		

	Hero cycles	Giant	Tandem Group	Ratio (Giant/Hero)	Ratio (Tandem/Hero)
1999	51,253	341,575	160,000 (2,000)	7	3

	Vitro	Owens-Corning (OC)	Ratio (OC/Vitro)
1991	22,266	160,867	7
2000	93,100	247,000	3
1991–2000	×4	×1.5	

	TCS	Infosys
1991	22,005	15,191
2000	44,589	54,770

	Cemex	Holderbank	Ratio Cemex/Holderbank
1991	39,986	106,962	3
2000	279,878	212,068	0.8
1991–2000	×7	×2	

Is there an argument for Vitro to have a stronger focus on design? It could certainly acquire design capability easier than technological capabilities.

The choice of saying no to jam today

Indian software firms have everything going for them, with a strong complementary asset in India's huge availability of low-cost technical manpower, sales growing at 50 per cent a year and profitability even faster. The key gap has been in moving to higher value-added activities. The better Indian firms – TCS, Infosys, Wipro, NIIT – have done so within services, attempting to build their own 'brand' as a reliable service provider. Certainly this is what Narayan Murthy, the head of Infosys, has been doing, through his very prominent presence representing Indian industry at meetings world-wide and so gaining access to the heads of the world's leading corporations, Infosys' target customers (most Indian software firms measure themselves on the percentage of Fortune 1000 firms they count as customers). But value-added per employee growth has been limited, even for these better performers (Table 9.2); more growth has come from adding people than productivity in the past five years.

And the industry as a whole is still projecting low value-added growth, regardless of talk about moving up the value-chain. What are the options for firms wishing to grow value-added faster (Figure 9.6d)?

Consider an Indian software services firm strong in financial services, with a record of developing some improved software development practices.* Opportunities include: expanding within services to integrate more financial service firms; entering new sectors such as telecommunications; through to developing own software products. Clarity about where the firm wants to be on the product–proprietary grid in the future improves clarity on its current choices. Most Indian software firms see their primary focus as gaining more large global clients. Jumping value-added produces more choices: the firm could open offices in new countries, hire professionals with background in a particular industry, invest in in-house learning mechanisms to capture project team experiences, or invest in a team to develop a product. These choices lead to a set of actions today to build the firm's future assets and capabilities. The firm could require that:

- It will simply not shop bodies, regardless of the immediately lucrative and riskless margin it earns;
- A fixed percentage of its professionals work on in-house specified projects rather than client driven ones;
- Take assignments only in particular fields, or seek an alliance with a foreign firm to enable development of product development capabilities.

As we discussed in Chapter 4, a neglected opportunity is for the software industry to target Indian industry. Seeing software as a capital good would simultaneously enable software to become more proprietary and Indian industry to become more competitive. This would require that software firms consciously choose less immediately lucrative contracts with Indian customers, and that Indian firms become more demanding and imaginative in the use of IT as a competitive tool, with huge and cheap development capabilities just down the road.

The choice of a whole new trajectory in a new industry

So far, we have described choices made within the same industry – we are still talking of beer, bicycles, glass and software. But firms might also choose to make much more dramatic – and much riskier – leaps into whole new industries. Nokia began in forest products. There are other equally dramatic company transformations, such as the Taiwanese firm that jumped from making stuffed dolls to calculators and Wipro, which still makes the vegetable oil it began life with in addition to software. If they

---

* As Indian software firms dominated the Y2K market, many of the better firms developed their own routines that enabled them to scan code that needed fixing quickly and accurately. In terms of our learning hierarchy this is *learning to improve production*.

had stuck to the standard management-consultancy advice of 'stick to the knitting', Nokia would not today be the world's largest mobile phone producer and Wipro would not be India's second largest software company. Not many firms can make these leaps into the unknown, but every follower-firm needs to choose to build new capabilities, to get to more attractive trajectories out of traditional positions.

In mid-2001, Indian streets were full of holes, thanks to Reliance's major investment in IT. Not for Reliance to be like every other large Indian group and start a software services company. Instead, Reliance invested in IT infrastructure – $5 billion in 20,000 km of underground fibre-optic cable around the country. The sheer scale of the investment is beyond the capacity of most firms. But did Reliance know anything about IT? No. Did it have any chance of succeeding? Yes. It argued that its key competence is in project execution. Laying 20,000 km of underground cable around the country took considerable project execution competence, including the ability to manage hundreds of local municipalities in every state around the country. No firm is better-placed to do that than Reliance. Having reached a position of dominance in petrochemicals, Reliance is moving into other attractive product areas: IT as above, power for many of the same reasons and even biotechnology.

The key strategic point in all these cases is choice: TBL must choose to export or build new product development capability. Hero must export, at whatever cost, to force either design capability or manufacturing efficiency in specials. This is difficult to do when you are the country's most successful firm in the industry or a hugely successful industry like Indian software – the choice has to be deliberate, and will probably make little economic sense in the short term. Ultimately, the choices firms make will depend on their view of the future, of where they want to be. Entrepreneurship will determine their success.

Policy implications

As we have gone through this book, we have made the case that followers can become leaders, first by doing things that make them efficient followers, catching up, and then choosing to do several different things that allow them to move ahead and lead. Making these choices takes vision and will. We will end this book with what the state can do to help followers become leaders.

That phrase 'help followers become leaders' reiterates our perspective throughout this book: industrial innovation happens in the firm, and therefore the focus of innovation policy must also be the firm. The role of the state is two-fold: first, it is to do things which help these exceptional firms become leaders, to create hundreds if not thousands of 'developed companies in developing countries', as the Forbes Marshall vision statement has it. Second, it is to foster a strong, internationally competitive industrial sector in general. Firms do not operate in vacuums, and more exceptions will emerge in a vibrant and successful industrial economy than in one rife with instability or with a stagnant economy.

We live in an increasingly liberalizing world and the kinds of infant industry policies that fostered industrial development in the US, Germany and Japan in the nineteenth century and Korea and Taiwan in the twentieth are not available to anything like the same extent to followers in the early twenty-first century. The state's room for manoeuvre is limited, but we would argue that there are three things it could aim to do. First, the essential role for the state is to make it cheap to do business in the country in general, and cheap to build technically capable firms in particular. Second, the state has a useful role in particular areas focused on technology. And finally there are some 'softer' roles for the state, which are no less important, such as articulating a vision of the future. We recognize that few states have either the capability or the will to do all this, so let us begin with the essential role for all states.

The essential role for the state: making it cheap for firms to do business and move up the chain

Making it cheap to do business is all about infrastructure, both physical and social. Schooling every child so that each shop-floor worker hired has finished primary and secondary education provides the base of skills of literacy and numeracy needed to continuously improve production. Providing higher technical education is more complex – research has shown that the benefits of higher technical education can be captured privately by the individual and there is less of what economists call a market failure. The role for the state is to ensure access to good technical education for all qualified students, though it does not have to provide or pay for it all.

Improving physical infrastructure includes reliable and cheap telecommunications, power, water, road transport and shipping. This sounds obvious and mundane but is not. For example, Forbes Marshall lost business to a Singapore firm because it took two days physically to walk a despatch through India's export formalities and transport the goods to Bombay as opposed to a routine of two hours in Singapore.

The state can play the key role in reducing the transaction costs of importing, exporting, despatching and getting paid. Liberalization has reduced regulation at the national level but not at the local level in many countries. In India, the reforms that took place between 1991 and 1993 were largely confined to the finance, commerce and industry ministries. What did not change was the local Inspector Raj, where several government inspectors could drop in on firms at will, each with absolute powers to demand they cease operations first, and challenge the order later.

On most such issues, there is complete agreement between industry and government – on the need to improve power or roads or education. And even a perverse bureaucrat would see no merit in delaying an export shipment. What is missing is the nitty-gritty of reform, the commitment to drive detailed change through at the local level. This is a considerable missed opportunity for reform, as the changes are far too detailed to be politically contentious.

As communications technology transforms entertainment and begins to transform industry, an emerging infrastructural role for the state is to make information cheap and accessible to all. Options to achieve this range afar. Telecoms deregulation is a minimum. At the other end of the scale is Singapore, where the state actively subsidizes internet access for every citizen. We are told that several state housing projects now have in their basements web access at 35 times the speed of a broad-band connection!

That is Singapore, a city, but what of India and China, which contain 500 Singapores, or Brazil and Mexico with 50 Singapores? The key way to make it cheaper to do business is to provide space for local and regional initiatives. A federal structure where one state competes with another in providing a more attractive business environment offers great potential in tackling the nitty-gritty of reform. The prominent success of reformist chief ministers in the Indian states of Andhra Pradesh, Madhya Pradesh and

Karnataka, could be the most positive political development for economic reform. China's export-processing zones, and especially its Hong Kong entrepôt connection, is precisely a way of lowering the cost of doing business.

Useful roles for the state: a few focused areas to help firms build technical capability

Normally, when one talks of innovation policy, thought immediately gravitates to doing research, to research institutes and indeed to state research institutes. As we have said in detail elsewhere, research supported by the state should be done within higher education as a way of improving the education students receive, and to attract the right staff into teaching. Doing research in autonomous institutions is largely a waste of scarce resources.

So is there no role for the state in industrial research? A common approach is tax policies to promote R&D. Studies have shown that this has led to activities being re-classified as R&D, but there is also evidence that it has raised the profile of R&D nationally. This in turn has attracted firms to do more R&D, key to building technical capability if properly focused, as we have discussed in this book.

A more direct role for the state is to support basic research in those fields where national firms are leaders or near leaders. A widespread programme of research in cement or glass-making in Mexico, for example, or of measuring quality in software development or certain areas of drug discovery in India, could provide industry with the well-springs of knowledge we spoke of in Chapters 1 and 6. What is key is to see research as following industrial development, not leading it. One first needs the successful industry at the frontier and *then* the research; research has no role for firms still well away from the frontier.

Bench-marking international best practices is key to firm innovation of the hard-slog variety, and the state can play a useful role in identifying and spreading generic best-practice. The Japanese government has long practised bench-marking, particularly for small firms. This can be especially effective in non-proprietary areas such as energy consumption. After the 1973 oil shock, the Japanese government launched a project to reduce industrial energy consumption that has also been very successful. They documented energy consumption by local firms, established the national best consumption norm for different processes, and compared this with international norms.

We said earlier that the state today has very limited scope for infant industry protection. If there is any intervention, it will have to be very limited – focused on a few carefully selected industries and for a credible short period. Again, this inter-vention has to be directed at the firm to be useful. Otherwise it is worse than useless.

Soft roles for the state: articulating visions, setting tones

Apart from these essential and useful focused roles for the state, there are some 'softer' roles. Perhaps the most important is the role the state can play in articulating a vision of the future.

Mahathir Mohammed may not be the darling of environmentalists but his vision of Malaysia 2020 – 'a car in every garage' – transmitted a vision to every citizen. When citizens are exhorted to forgo consumption today, or to work harder, or to save more so that one's children and grandchildren have more 'jam' tomorrow, a clearly articulated view of where the country is heading helps make present sacrifice seem more worthwhile. So does the state see several local multinationals competing globally in ten years? That makes competitiveness a more understandable objective to the ordinary citizen, justifying privatization or user charges to improve services.

More specifically with regard to technology, the state can set the tone for discourse on technology. For example, it can play a clear demonstrator role in avoiding the 'not invented here plus foreign is best' combination we spoke of in Chapter 8. The state can promote an openness to learning from the best everywhere – even from ideologically 'suspect' countries – and then promote the confidence to improve on it. Take two contemporary Indian examples: in 2001, a Hindu fundamentalist party objected to college students celebrating Valentine's Day, and the same party objected to McDonald's, questioning whether their french fries were cooked in beef fat. This fear of cultural pollution occurs in many countries. But if a state tackles it by spreading objective reasoning, by educating, by encouraging citizens to question and appreciate their own and other cultures, this sets the tone for a response to NIH–FIB.[3] Or consider another example: after the January 2001 earthquake in Gujarat, there was much questioning of construction in the city of Ahmedabad. Buildings collapsed, with great loss of life, which simply would not have happened with the right building standards. Ahmedabad – and other Indian cities – are now quite appropriately set on establishing a much more stringent building code. But there has been no attempt to learn from Japan or California, where codes that are now decades old have demonstrated their ability to save lives and property. The state could quite usefully practise avoiding NIH–FIB, by learning from these experiences world-wide, and then adapting and improving practice for India in the 2000s.

Our underlying message is the need for pragmatism to focus on what will work and how to bring down-to-earth the articulation of a long-term vision. There was no better statement of pragmatism than when Deng Hsao Peng was asked several years ago how he could square China's dramatic economic reforms with socialism: 'what does it matter if a cat is black or white, so long as it catches mice'.

All these roles for the state – whether useful or soft – involve will. We would be fortunate indeed if many states did demonstrate this will. Our expectations for firms, though, is higher: we should expect many firms to have the vision and will to attempt to close the gap and become leaders. This requires the kind of will we have seen in many firms in this book. At the top of the scale is Cemex, a firm that has closed the gap – it is the international leader. Cemex is ahead of the world's biggest cement firm in sales per employee. More important, its trajectory is dramatically different with sales per employee up seven times in ten years, compared with just twice for Holderbank (Table 9.2).

But writing of Cemex – you may be wondering why we left them out of our analysis of where it goes from here: How does the global bench-mark firm stay ahead? We are not going to answer that question. This book has been on how followers become leaders. Staying ahead as the leader is another book – a book about leaders.

Notes

1 Beneath the surface

1 *The Economist*, 28 September 2000.
2 As of May 2001, Mr Mittal was out of the top team. Trouble in the Kazakhstan plant led to a fall in profits and share prices in 2001.
3 W. Vincenti, *What Engineers Know and How They Know It: Analytical Studies from Aeronautical History,* Baltimore: Johns Hopkins University Press, 1991.
4 W. Faulkner, 'Conceptualizing knowledge used in innovation: a second look at the science–technology distinction and industrial innovation', *Science, Technology and Human Values,* 19, 1994, p. 429.
5 P. Patel and K. Pavitt, 'The continuing widespread (and neglected) importance of improvements in mechanical technologies', *Research Policy,* 23, 5, 1994, pp. 533–45.
6 R.R. Nelson, 'The roles of firms in technical advance: a perspective from evolutionary theory', in Dosi *et al.* (eds) *Technology and Enterprise in a Historical Perspective,* Oxford: Oxford University Press, 1992, p. 175.
7 R. Dore, 'Technological self-reliance: sturdy ideal or self-serving rhetoric', in M. Fransman and K. King (eds) *Technological Capability in the Third World,* London and Basingstoke: Macmillan, 1984.
8 World Bank, *The East Asian Miracle,* Oxford and New York: Oxford University Press 1993.
9 R. Nelson, *Understanding Technological Change as an Evolutionary Process,* Amsterdam: Elsevier, 1987.
10 D. Leonard-Barton, *Wellsprings of Knowledge: Building and Sustaining the Sources of Innovation,* Boston: Harvard Business School Press, 1995, p. 7.
11 A. Desai (ed.) *Technology Absorption in Indian Industry,* New Delhi: Wiley Eastern, 1989.
12 N. Rosenberg, 'Uncertainty and technological change', in Landau *et al.* (eds) *The Mosaic of Economic Growth,* Stanford: Stanford University Press, 1996.
13 R.E. McGinn, *Science, Technology and Society*, Englewood Cliffs, New Jersey: Prentice-Hall, 1991, p. 18.
14 S. Kline, 'Innovation styles in Japan and the United States: cultural bases, implications for competitiveness', *Report INN-3B,* Stanford University, 1989, p. 10.
15 Gibbons *et al.*, *The New Production of Knowledge,* London: Sage, 1994, p. 26.
16 OECD, *Technology and the Economy,* Paris, 1994, p. 17.
17 Ibid: p. 17.
18 Dore, op. cit., p. 67.
19 R. Dore, 'Technology in a world of national frontiers', *World Development,* 17, 1, 1989, p. 1673.
20 Niosi *et al.*, 'Technology transfer to developing countries through engineering firms: the Canadian experience', *World Development,* 23, 1995, pp. 1815–24.
21 D. Teece quoting Killing, 'The R&D and technology transfer activities of multinational firms', in R. Hawkins (ed.) *Technology Transfer and Economic Development,* Greenwich, CT. JAI Press, 1981, p. 88.
22 Dankbaar *et al.*, *Research and Technology Management in Enterprises: Issues for Community Policy,* Brussels: EC, 1992, p. 4.

23 I. Nonaka and H. Takeuchi, *The Knowledge Creating Company,* New York: Oxford University Press, 1995.
24 J. Bhagwati, *Protectionism,* Cambridge, MA: MIT Press, 1988.
25 See P. Adler, 1993, 'Time and motion regained', *Harvard Business Review,* January–February, pp. 97–108.
26 Teece, op. cit.
27 M. Tushman and R. Nelson, 'Introduction: technology, organizations and innovation', *Administrative Science Quarterly,* 35, 1990, p. 1.
28 H.E. Riggs, 'Innovations: a US–Japan perspective', paper presented to the US–Japan Project on High Technology, Stanford University, 1984, and published in shortened form in D. Okimoto and R. Rohlen (eds) *Inside the Japanese System,* Stanford: Stanford University Press, 1988.
29 R. Kaplinsky, 'Technique and system, the spread of Japanese management techniques to developing countries', *World Development,* 23, 1, 1995, pp. 57–71.
30 C. Freeman, 'Design and British economic performance', lecture given at Design Centre, London, 23 March 1983, quoted in Walsh *et al.,* 1992, p. 23.

2 Innovation success in follower-firms

1 P.A. Kattuman, 'The role of history in the transition to an industrial district: the case of the Indian bicycle industry,' in P. Cadene and M. Holmstrom (eds) *Decentralized Production in India: Industrial Districts, Flexible Specialization and Employment,* New Delhi: Sage, 1998.
2 M. Tewari, 'When the marginal becomes mainstream: lessons from a half century of small firm growth in Ludhiana, India', PhD Dissertation, MIT, Cambridge, 1996.
3 Kattuman, op. cit., pp. 238–9.
4 Interview with O.P. Munjal, Founder Director, Hero Cycles.
5 Interview with S.K. Rai, Works Director, Hero Cycles.
6 Kattuman, op. cit., p. 239.
7 S. Lall, *Building Industrial Competitiveness in Developing Countries,* Paris: OECD Development Centre, 1990.
8 A. Pita, *Competencias Medulares Taller de Liderazgo en Tecnología,* Vitro, Monterrey,1998.
9 S. Dheer and B. Viard, 'Tata Consultancy Services: globalization of software services', case study, Graduate School of Business, Stanford University, 1995.
10 Arora *et al.,* 'The Indian software services industry', *Research Policy,* 30, 2001, pp. 1267–87.
11 Arora *et al.,* op. cit., p. 9.
12 *The Times of India,* 6 December 2000.
13 *The Economic Times,* January 2001.
14 *Business Standard,* 4 January 2001.
15 Nasscom-McKinsey, *The Indian IT Strategy,* December 1999, p. 130.
16 *Business Standard,* 3/4 February 2001.
17 *Business World,* 25 December 2000.
18 *World Investment Report,* 1995.
19 *The Economist,* 17 June 1999.
20 'Cemex to buy Southdown for $2.6 bn', *Reuters News,* www.siliconcomment.com/headlines/financial/2000929/235689.html

3 Changing policies for science and technology

1 J. Bhagwati, *Protectionism,* Cambridge, MA: MIT Press, 1988.
2 A. Desai (ed.), *Technology Absorption in Indian Industry,* New Delhi: Wiley Eastern, 1989.
3 J. S. Mill, quoted by S. Lall, ' "The East Asian miracle" study: does the bell toll for industrial strategy?', *World Development,* 22, 2, 1994, pp. 645–54.
4 C. Johnson, *MITI and the Japanese Miracle,* Stanford: Stanford University Press, 1982, p.16.
5 R. Wade, *Governing the Market,* Princeton: Princeton University Press, 1990, p. 359.
6 Ibid., p. 361.
7 Bhagwati, op. cit.

8 A.H. Amsden, *Asia's Next Giant: South Korea and Late Industrialization,* New York and Oxford: Oxford University Press, 1989, p. 16.

9 S. Bum-shik, *Major Speeches by Korea's Park Chang Hee,* Seoul: Hollym, 1970, p. 305, quoted in Amsden, op. cit., p. 68.

10 H. Pack, 'Research and development in the industrial development process', in L. Kim and R.R. Nelson (eds), *Technology, Learning and Innovation,* Cambridge: Cambridge University Press, 2000, p. 80.

11 M. Hobday, 'East versus South East Asian innovation systems: comparing OEM- and TNC-led growth in electronics', in L. Kim and R.R. Nelson, ibid., 2000, pp. 134, 138, 162.

12 S. Young, 'Trade policies in Korea: background and prospect', paper for joint conference on Industrial policies of ROC and ROK, Seoul, Korea Development Institute, 1984.

13 Wade, op. cit., p. 119.

14 Wade, op. cit., p. 336.

15 M. Bell and K. Pavitt, 'Technological accumulation and industrial growth: contrasts between developed and developing countries', *Industrial and Corporate Change,* 2, 2, 1993, p. 193.

16 Ibid., p. 194.

17 Personal conversation, October 1999.

4   Innovation on the shop-floor

1 I.C. Magaziner and M. Patinkin, 'Fast heat: how Korea won the microwave war', *Harvard Business Review,* January–February, 1989, p. 89.

2 R.E. Cole, 'Some cultural and social bases of Japanese innovation: small group activities in comparative perspective', in S. Kumon and H. Rosovsky (eds) *The Political Economy of Japan, Vol. 3 Cultural and Social Dynamics,* Stanford University Press, 1992, p. 298.

3 From Chapter 2, p. 26.

4 R. Vernon, 'International investment and international trade in product cycles', *Quarterly Journal of Economics,* 80, 1999, pp. 190–207.

5 *The Economist,* 'The China Syndrome', 28 September 1996.

6 Doeringer and Watson note that 'firms show large differences in the time from fabric purchase through completion of manufacturing (79 days compared with 129 days), replenishment supply speeds (9 days compared with 26 days), and operating profits (10.5 per cent compared with 5 per cent)', P. Doeringer and A. Watson, 'Apparel', in D. Mowery (ed.) *US industry in 2000,* Washington, DC: National Academy Press, 1999, p. 345. Such qualitative differences are difficult for offshore competitors to match. American clothes-making is becoming a capital intensive business with speed and innovation winning over low labour rates.

7 South Korea did the same in the 1970s and early 1980s.

8 Tony Tan, interview, February 1996. Other data from Singapore Economic Report, various years, Singapore: Government of Singapore.

9 Hayes *et al., Dynamic Manufacturing: Creating the Learning Organization,* New York: Free Press, 1988, p. 53.

10 Quoted by A. Wilkinson and H. Willmott in *Making Quality Critical,* International Thomson, 1995.

11 R.E. Cole, *Managing Quality Fads: How American Business Learned to Play the Quality Game,* Oxford University, 1999, p. 84.

12 H.J. Harrington, *The Improvement Process: How America's Leading Companies Improve Quality,* Singapore: McGraw-Hill, 1987, p. 20.

13 Cole, op. cit., 1999, p. 66.

14 Cole, ibid., p. 69.

15 D.C. Mowery and N. Rosenberg, *Paths of Innovation,* Cambridge University Press, 1998.

16 J. Humphrey, 'Introduction' to Special Issue, *World Development,* 23, 1, 1995a, p. 1.

17 R. Kaplinsky, *Easternisation: The Spread of Japanese Management Techniques to Developing Countries,* Ilford: Frank Cass, 1994, pp. 219–20.

18 Ibid., p. 222.

19 Ibid.
20 Ibid., p. 226.
21 H. Schmitz, 'Small shoemakers and Fordist giants: tale of a supercluster', *World Development*, 23, 1, 1995, p. 11.
22 Ibid., p. 12.
23 Ibid., p. 12.
24 Ibid., pp. 13–14.
25 Cole, op. cit., 1992.
26 Ibid., p. 298.
27 R. Kaplinsky, 'Technique and system', *World Development*, 23, 1, 1995, pp. 58–9.
28 Ibid., p. 64.
29 B. McKern, and R. Malan, 'Posco's strategy in the development of Korea', Case No. S–1B–10, Graduate School of Business, Stanford: Stanford University, 1992. This was particularly true in the early years of the company.
30 R.H. Hayes and G.P. Pisano, 'Beyond world class: the new manufacturing strategy', *Harvard Business Review,* January–February, 1994, p. 82, describing lean production.
31 J. Humphrey, 'Industrial reorganization in developing countries: from models to trajectories', *World Development*, 23, 1, 1995b, p. 156.
32 H. Schmitz, 'Small firms and flexible specialization in developing countries', *Labour and Society,* 15, 3, 1990.
33 R. Rabellotti, 'Is there an "Industrial District Model"? Footwear districts in Italy and Mexico compared', *World Development*, 23, 1, 1995, p. 30.
34 Ibid.
35 M. Bell and M. Albu, 'Knowledge systems and technological dynamism in industrial clusters in developing countries?', *World Development*, 27, 9, 1999, p. 1723.
36 N. Rosenberg, 'Capital goods, technology and economic growth', in N. Rosenberg (ed.) *Perspectives on Technology*, Cambridge: Cambridge University Press, 1985, pp. 146–7.
37 Ibid., p. 148.
38 P. Barnevik, speaking at the Confederation of Indian Industry/World Economic Forum India Economic Summit, Delhi, December 2000.
39 Humphrey, op. cit., 1995b, p. 160.

5 From process to product and proprietary

1 *Hewlett Packard Singapore, Case Study*, Harvard Business School, Boston: Harvard Business School Press, 1994a.
2 From this chapter.
3 From this chapter.
4 See H.E. Riggs, 'Innovations: a US–Japan perspective', unpublished paper presented to the US–Japan Project on High Technology, Stanford University, 1984. An abridged version is reprinted in D. Okimoto and R. Rohlen (eds) *Inside the Japanese System,* Stanford University Press, 1988.
5 See P. Patel and K. Pavitt, 'The continuing widespread (and neglected) importance of improvements in mechanical technologies', *Research Policy*, 23, 5, 1994, pp. 553–45.
6 M. Hobday, *Innovation in East Asia: The Challenge to Japan,* Aldershot: Edward Elgar, 1995.
7 Taken from *Hewlett Packard, Case Study*, Harvard Business School, Boston: Harvard Business School Press, 1994a,b,c.
8 Ibid., 1994a, p. 7.
9 *The Economist*, 5 November 1998.
10 R.M. Buitelaar and R.P. Perez, 'Maquila, economic reform and corporate strategies', *World Development,* 28, 9, 2000, pp. 1627–42.
11 Buitelaar and Perez, op. cit., pp. 1635, 1638.
12 Humphrey *et al., Corporate Restructuring, Crompton Greaves and the Challenge of Globalization*, New Delhi: Response Books, 1998, p. 37.
13 Ibid., p. 40.

14 Ibid., p. 38.
15 Ibid., p. 77.
16 Ibid., p. 131.
17 Ibid., p. 133.
18 Ibid., p. 166.
19 Ibid., p. 173.
20 Ibid., p. 182.
21 Ibid., p. 89.
22 Ibid., p. 232.
23 Ibid., p. 45.
24 Ibid., p. 241.
25 *Business Standard,* 18 November 2000.
26 H. Pack, 'Research and development in the industrial development process', in L. Kim and R.R. Nelson (eds) *Technology, Learning and Innovation: Experiences of Newly Industrializing Economies,* Cambridge University Press, 2000.
27 L. Kim, *Imitation to Innovation,* Boston: Harvard Business School Press, 1997, pp. 111–12.
28 Ibid., p. 29.
29 Ibid., p. 107.
30 Ibid., p. 110.
31 Ibid., p. 112.
32 Ibid., p. 117
33 C.J. Dahlman, 'Foreign technology and indigenous techological capability in Brazil', in M. Fransman and K. King (eds) *Technological Capability in the Third World,* London: Macmillan, 1984, p. 319.
34 Ibid., p. 320.
35 Ibid., p. 321.
36 B. Lundvall, 'Commentary', in Kim and Nelson, op. cit., 2000, p. 100.
37 M. Hobday, 'East versus South East Asian innovation systems: comparing OEM- and TNC-led growth in electronics', in Kim and Nelson, op. cit., 2000, pp. 162–3.
38 Hobday, op. cit., 1995, p. 117.
39 *Business India,* June 1997.
40 *Business Standard,* November 2000.
41 D.J. Teece, 'Profiting from technological innovation: implications for intergration, collaboration, licensing and public policy', *Research Policy,* 15, 1986, pp. 285–305.
42 Interview with Xerxes Desai, managing director, Titan, in *Business Standard,* 18 October 2000.

6 Managing R&D in technology-followers

1 D. Mowery and N. Rosenberg, *Paths of Innovation: Technological Change in 20th Century America,* Cambridge University Press, 1998, p. 1.
2 R.R. Nelson and H. Pack, 'Firm competencies, technological catch-up and the Asian Miracle', in G.R. Saxonhouse and T.N. Srinivasan (eds) *Development, Duality and the International Economic Regime: Essays in Honour of Gustav Ranis,* Ann Arbor: University of Michigan Press.
3 A. Desai, 'The origin and direction of industrial R&D in India', *Research Policy,* 9, 1980, p. 81.
4 C. Edquist and S. Jacobsson 'State policies, firm strategies and firm performance: production of hydraulic excavators and machining centres in India and Republic of Korea', in A. Desai (ed.) *Technology Absorption in Indian Industry,* New Delhi: Wiley Eastern, 1989.
5 Ibid., p. 171.
6 Ibid., p. 169.
7 Ibid., p. 162.
8 Ibid., p. 167.
9 Ibid., p. 171.
10 Ibid., p. 169.

11 Ibid., p. 177.
12 *Business Asia,* 5 April 1999.
13 US Department of Commerce, National Trade Data Bank, 3 November 2000.
14 H. Pack, 'Research and development in the industrial development process', in L. Kim and R.R. Nelson (eds) *Technology, Learning and Innovation: Experiences of Newly Industrialising Economies,* Cambridge University Press, 2000.
15 L. Kim, *Imitation to Innovation,* Boston: Harvard Business School Press, 1997, pp. 135, 136. A.H. Amsden, *Asia's Next Grant: South Korea and Late Industrialization,* Oxford University Press, 1989, also provides some case studies, although her focus is not specifically on technological capability.
16 L. Kim, op. cit., p. 112.
17 Ibid., p. 113.
18 P. Reddy, 'New trends in globalization of corporate R&D and implications for innovation capability in host countries: a survey from India', *World Development,* 25, 11, 1997, p. 1822.
19 Ibid., p. 1828.
20 Pharmaceutical Product Development Inc. (PPDI), *Annual Report,* 1 March 2000.
21 www.cnpr.nus.edu.sg
22 P. Reddy, *Globalization of Corporate R&D: Implications for Innovation Systems in Host Countries,* London and New York: Routledge, 2000.
23 Ibid.
24 R.S. Rosenbloom and W.J. Spencer, 'Technology's vanishing wellspring', in Rosenbloom and Spencer (eds) *Engines of Innovation: US Industrial Research at the End of an Era,* Boston: Harvard Business School Press, 1996, p. 1.
25 Ibid.
26 G. Moore, 'Some personal perspectives on research in the semiconductor industry', in Rosenbloom and Spencer (eds) op. cit., pp. 168–71.
27 *The Economist,* 30 September 2000.
28 S.E. Smith, 'Opening up to the world: India's pharmaceutical companies prepare for 2005', *Occasional Papers,* Asia Pacific Research Center, Institute for International Studies, Stanford University Press, 2000, p. 16.
29 N. Rosenberg, 'Uncertainty and technological change', in Landau *et al.* (eds) *The Mosaic of Economic Growth,* Stanford: Stanford University Press, 1996, p. 334.
30 N. Rosenberg, 'The commercial exploitation of science by American industry', Working Paper, Stanford University, 1983.
31 Katz *et al.*, 'Productivity and domestic technological search efforts: the growth of a rayon plant in Argentina' in J. Katz (ed.) *Technology Generation in Latin American Manufacturing Industries,* Macmillan, 1987, p. 214.
32 L.A. Perez and J. Peniche, 'A summary of the principal findings of the case study on the technological behaviour of the Mexican steel firm Altos Homos de Mexico', in J. Katz, ibid., 1987, pp. 188–9.
33 L. Kim, op. cit., 1997.
34 R. Nelson, 'The roles of firms in technical advance', in G. Dosi, R. Giannetti and P.A. Toninelli (eds) *Technology and Enterprise in a Historical Perspective,* Oxford: Oxford University Press, 1992.
35 W. Cohen and D. Levinthal, 'Absorptive capacity: a new perspective on learning and innovation', *Administrative Science Quarterly,* 35, 1990, p. 128.
36 N. Rosenberg, 'Why do firms do basic research (with their own money)?', *Research Policy,* 19, 1990, pp. 165–74.
37 L. Kim, op. cit., 1997.
38 R. Dore, 'Technological self-reliance: sturdy ideal or self-serving rhetoric', in M. Fransman and K. King (eds) *Technological Capability in the Third World,* Macmillan, 1984, pp. 65–6.
39 L. Kim, 'National system of industrial innovation: dynamics of capability building in Korea', in R. Nelson (ed.) op. cit., 1993, p. 376.
40 L. Kim, op. cit., 1997, pp. 120, 143.
41 K. Pavitt, 'Innovating routines in the business firm: what matters, what's staying the same, and what's changing?', *SPRU Paper No. 45,* Brighton: University of Sussex, 2000.

Design in Caps

7 Design leadership for technology-followers

1 So too, of course, are scale economies – which require a degree of capital investment often beyond firms in NICs. The Korean chaebols are obvious exceptions.
2 C. Freeman, 'Design and british economic performance', lecture given at the Design Centre, London, 23 March 1983, Brighton: Science Policy Research Unit, Sussex University, quoted in Walsh *et al.*, *Winning by Design*, Oxford: Blackwell, 1992, p. 23.
3 V. Walsh, 'Design, Innovation and the boundaries of the firm', *Research Policy*, 25, 1996, p. 516.
4 A. Morita, *Made in Japan*, New York: Dutton, 1986.
5 *Financial Times*, quoted in *Business Standard*, 5/6 May 2001.
6 See D. Leonard-Barton and J.L. Doyle, 'Commercializing technology: imaginative understanding of user needs', in R.S. Rosenbloom and W.J. Spencer (eds), *Engines of Innovation*, Boston: Harvard Business School Press, 1996, for a description of these techniques
7 S. Lall, *Learning to Industrialize: The Acquisition of Technological Capacity in India*, London: Macmillan, 1987, p. 167.
8 L. Kim, *Imitation to Innovation*, Boston: Harvard Business School Press, 1997, pp. 113–14.
9 Ibid., p. 120.
10 We are grateful to Kiyoung Ko, student at Stanford University, for expert research assistance on the acquisition of design capability by Korean firms.
11 D. Patnaik and R. Becker, 'Needfinding: the why and how of uncovering people's needs', *Design Management Journal*, Spring 1999, pp. 39, 43.

8 Building a culture for innovation

1 See for example, R. Kaplinsky, *Easternisation: The Spread of Japanese Management Techniques to Developing Countries*, Ilford: Frank Cass, 1994, which has examples of JMTs used in India, Mexico, Dominican Republic and Zimbabwe.
2 J.C. Campbell, 'Culture, innovation borrowing, and technology management', in Liker *et al.* (eds) *Engineered in Japan: Japanese Technology–Management Practices*, New York: Oxford University Press, 1995, p. 311.
3 R. Dore, *Taking Japan Seriously: A Confucian Perspective on Leading Economic Issues*, Stanford University Press, 1987, pp. vi–vii.
4 Lewis *et al.*, *The Growth of Nations*, Bristol: Bristol Academic Press, 1996, p. 19.
5 R. Dore, *British Factory, Japanese Factory*, London: George Allen and Unwin, 1973.
6 Ibid., p. 70.
7 Ibid., p. 51.
8 Ibid., p. 260.
9 Ibid., p. 261.
10 Ibid., p. 262.
11 M.J. Wiener, *English Culture and the Decline of the Industrial Spirit, 1850–1980*, Harmondsworth: Penguin, 1985.
12 C. Barnett, *The Audit of War*, London: Macmillan, 1986, p. 237.
13 M. Vander Weyer, *Falling Eagle: The Decline of Barclays Bank*, London: Weidenfeld & Nicolson, 2000.
14 *The Economist*, 11 May 2000.
15 N. Rosenberg, 'Can Americans learn to become better imitators?', in N. Rosenberg, *Exploring the Black Box*, Cambridge: Cambridge University Press, 1994.
16 L. Kim, *Imitation to Innovation*, Boston: Harvard Business School Press, 1997, p. 14.
17 Ibid., p. 59.
18 Ibid., pp. 69–70.
19 Ibid., p. 71.
20 Ibid., p. 75.
21 L. Kim, 'Korea's system in transition', in L. Kim and R.R. Nelson (eds) *Technology, Learning and Innovation*, Cambridge: Cambridge University Press, 2000, p. 353.

22 G. Hofstede, *Culture and Organizations,* London: HarperCollins, 1991, p. 110.

23 Tidd *et al., Managing Innovation,* Chichester: Wiley, 1997, p. 326.

24 R. Dore, 'Technological self-reliance: sturdy ideal or self-serving rhetoric', in M. Fransman and K. King (eds) *Technological Capability in the Third World*, London and Basingstoke: Macmillan, 1984.

25 A. Gerschenkron, *Economic Backwardness in Historical Perspective*, New York: Praeger, 1962.

26 R. Dore, 'Reflections on culture and social change', in G. Gereffi and D.L. Wyman (eds) *Manufacturing Miracles,* Princeton: Princeton University Press, 1990, p. 361.

27 F. Zakaria, 'Culture is destiny: a conversation with Lee Kuan Yew', *Foreign Affairs,* 73, 6, 1994, p. 192.

28 D. Landes, *The Wealth and Poverty of Nations: Why Some are So Rich and Others So Poor,* London: Abacus, 1998, pp. 94–7.

29 M.E. Porter *et al., Can Japan Compete*, New York: Perseus, 2000.

30 *Business India*, December 1997.

31 *Business India,* July 1997.

32 *Business India,* September 1995.

33 *Business India,* December 1997.

34 Anil Ambani, *Business India,* December 1997.

35 *Business India,* December 1997.

36 Kaplinsky, op. cit., 1994, p. 173.

37 Ibid.

38 J.G. March, 'Exploration and exploitation in organizational learning', *Organization Science,* 2, 1, 1989, pp. 71–87.

39 H. Leibenstein, 'Allocative efficiency versus X-efficiency', *American Economic Review*, 1966.

40 Tidd *et al.*, op. cit., p. 326.

41 T. Rickards, *Stimulating Innovation: A Systems Approach,* London: Pinter, 1985.

42 J. Adams, *Conceptual Blockbusting,* New York: Perseus, 1990, p. 184.

43 R. Mitchell, 'Masters of innovation: how 3M keeps its new products coming', in J. Henry and D. Walker (eds) *Managing Innovation,* London: Sage, 1991.

44 I. Nonaka and H. Takeuchi, *The Knowledge Creating Company,* New York: Oxford University Press, 1995, p. 117.

45 Rickards, op. cit., p. 51.

9 Organizing for innovation

1 D.J. Teece *et al.*, 'Dynamic capabilities and strategic management', *Strategic Management Journal,* 18, 7, 1997, pp. 509–53.

2 C.K. Prahalad and G. Hamel, 'The core competence of the corporation', *Harvard Business Review*, May–June, 1990, pp. 79–91.

3 Perhaps India should aim to dominate the world market for Valentine's Day cards.

Bibliography

Abramovitz, M. and David, P. (1996) 'Convergence and deferred catch-up: productivity leadership and the waning of American exceptionalism', in R. Landau, T. Taylor and G. Wright (eds) *The Mosaic of Economic Growth,* Stanford: Stanford University Press.

Adams, J.L. (1990) *Conceptual Blockbusting*, Boston: Perseus.

Adler, P. (1993) 'Time and motion regained', *Harvard Business Review*, Jan–Feb: 97–108.

Adler, P. and Cole, R. (1993) 'Designed for learning: a tale of two auto plants', *Sloan Management Review*, Spring: 85–94.

Amendola, M. and Bruno, S. (1990) 'The behaviour of the innovative firm: relations to the environment', *Research Policy*, 19: 419–33.

Amsden, A.H. (1989) *Asia's Next Giant: South Korea and Late Industrialization*, New York and Oxford: Oxford University Press.

Archibugi, D. and Michie, J. (1995) 'The globalisation of technology: a new taxonomy', *Cambridge Journal of Economics*, 19: 121–40.

Archibugi, D., Howells, J. and Michie, J. (eds) (1999) *Innovation Policy in a Global Economy*, Cambridge: Cambridge University Press.

Arora, A., Arunachalam, V.S., Asundi, J. and Fernandes, R. (2001) 'The Indian software services industry', *Research Policy*, 30: 1267–87.

Bairoch, P. (1993) *Economics and World History: Myths and Paradoxes*, Chicago: University of Chicago Press.

Balassa, B. and Associates (1982) *Development Strategies in Semi-Industrialized Economies*, Baltimore: Johns Hopkins University Press.

Barnett, C. (1986) *The Audit of War*, London: Macmillan.

Bell, M. (1984) 'Learning and the accumulation of industrial technological capacity in developing countries', in M. Fransman and K. King (eds) *Technological Capability in the Third World*, London and Basingstoke: Macmillan.

Bell, M. and Pavitt, K. (1993) 'Technological accumulation and industrial growth: contrasts between developed and developing countries', *Industrial and Corporate Change, 2*, 2: 157–209.

Bell, M. and Albu, M. (1999) 'Knowledge systems and technological dynamism in industrial clusters in developing countries', *World Development*, 27, 9: 1715–34.

Bhagwati, J. (1988) *Protectionism*, Cambridge, MA: MIT Press.

Buitelaar, R.M. and Perez, R.P. (2000) 'Maquila, economic reform and corporate strategies', *World Development*, 28, 9: 1627–42.

Bum-Shik, S. (1970) *Major Speeches by Korea's Park Chung Hee*, Seoul: Hollym.

Cadene, P. and Holmstrom, M. (eds) (1998) *Decentralized Production in India: Industrial Districts, Flexible Specialization, and Employment,* New Delhi: Sage Publications.

Campbell, J.C. (1995) 'Culture, innovation borrowing, and technology management', in J.K. Liker, J.E. Ettlie and J.C. Campbell (eds) *Engineered in Japan: Japanese Technology – Management Practices,* New York and Oxford: Oxford University Press.

Cardoso, F.H. (1975) *Autoritarismo e democratizacao*. Rio de Janeiro: Paz e Terra.

Cardoso, F.H. and Faletto, E. (1979) *Dependency and Development in Latin America*, Berkeley: University of California Press.

Casanueve, C. (2000) 'Globalization and industrial restructuring in Mexico: the cases of the electronics and automotive industries', Working Paper, Instituto Tecnologico y Estudios Superiores de Monterrey, Mexico City Campus.

Casanueve, C. (2001) 'The acquisition of firm technological capabilities in Mexico's open economy, the case of Vitro', *Technological Forecasting and Social Change*, 66, 1: 75–85.

Centre for Monitoring Indian Economy (2000) *Industry: Market Size and Shares*, Bombay: Economic Intelligence Service.

Chandler, A.D., Jr (1990) *Scale and Scope: The Dynamics of Industrial Capitalism*, Cambridge, MA: Harvard University Press.

Cohen, W. and Levinthal, D. (1989) 'Innovation and learning: the two faces of R&D', *Economic Journal*, 99: 569–596.

Cohen, W. and Levinthal, D. (1990) 'Absorptive capacity: a new perspective on learning and innovation', *Administrative Science Quarterly*, 35: 128–52.

Cole, R.E. (1992) 'Some cultural and social bases of Japanese innovation: small group activities in comparative perspective', in S. Kumon and H. Rosovsky (eds) *The Political Economy of Japan, Vol. 3 Cultural and Social Dynamics*, Stanford: Stanford University Press.

Cole, R.E. (1999) *Managing Quality Fads: How American Business Learned to Play the Quality Game*, Oxford: Oxford University Press.

Cole, R. (1989) *Strategies for Learning: Small Group Activities in American, Japanese and Swedish Industry*, Berkeley: University of California Press.

Collinson, S. (1993) 'Managing product development at Sony: the development of the data-discman', *Technology Analysis and Strategic Management*, 5, 3: 285–306.

Cusumano, M. and Elenkov, D. (1994) 'Linking international technology transfer with strategy and management: a literature commentary', *Research Policy*, 23: 195–215.

Dahlman, C.J. (1984) 'Foreign technology and indigenous technological capability in Brazil', in M. Fransman and K. King (eds) *Technological Capability in the Third World*, London: Macmillan.

Dahlman, C.J. and Frischtak, C.R. (1993) 'National systems supporting technical advance in industry: the Brazilian experience', in R.R. Nelson (ed.) *National Innovation Systems: A Comparative Analysis*, Oxford: Oxford University Press.

Dankbaar, B., Kuhlmann, S. and Tsipouri, L. (1992) *Research and Technology Management in Enterprises: Issues for Community Policy*, Brussels: EC.

Desai, A.V. (1980) 'The origin and direction of industrial R&D in India', *Research Policy*, 9: 74–96.

Desai, A. (ed.) (1989) *Technology Absorption in Indian Industry*, New Delhi: Wiley Eastern.

Dheer, S. and Viard, B. (1995) 'Tata Consultancy Services: globalization of software services', case study, Graduate School of Business, Stanford University.

Doeringer, P. and Watson, A. (1999), 'Apparel', in D.C. Mowery (ed.) *US Industry in 2000: Studies in Competitive Performance*, Washington, DC: National Academy Press.

Dore, R. (1973) *British Factory, Japanese Factory*, London: George Allen and Unwin.

Dore, R. (1984) 'Technological self-reliance: sturdy ideal or self-serving rhetoric', in M. Fransman and K. King (eds) *Technological Capability in the Third World*, London and Basingstoke: Macmillan.

Dore, R. (1987) *Taking Japan Seriously: A Confucian Perspective on Economic Issues*, Stanford: Stanford University Press.

Dore, R. (1989) 'Technology in a world of national frontiers', *World Development*, 17, 1: 1665–75.

Dore, R. (1990) 'Reflections on culture and social change', in G. Gereffi and D.L. Wyman (eds) *Manufacturing Miracles*, Princeton: Princeton University Press.

Dosi, G. (1999) 'Some notes on national systems of innovation and production, and their implications for economic analysis', in D. Archibugi, J. Howells and J. Michie (eds) *Innovation Policy in a Global Economy,* Cambridge: Cambridge University Press.

Dosi, G., Giannetti, R. and Toninelli, P.A. (eds) (1992) *Technology and Enterprise in a Historical Perspective*, Oxford: Oxford University Press.

Drucker, P. (1986) 'The changed world economy', *Foreign Affairs*, Spring: 768–91.

DST – Department of Science and Technology (1999) *Research and Development Statistics,* New Delhi: Government of India Publications.

Dussauge, S., Hart, S. and Ramanansota, J. (1992) *Strategic Technology Management*, Chichester: John Wiley.

Economic and Social Research Foundation (ESRF) (1996) *Tanzania Breweries Limited Before and After Privatization,* mimeo, Dar Es Salaam.

Edquist, C. (eds) (1997) *Systems of Innovation: Technologies, Institutions and Organizations*, London and Washington: Pinter.

Edquist, C. and Jacobsson, S. (1989) 'State policies, firm strategies and firm performance: production of hydraulic excavators and machining centres in India and Republic of Korea', in A. Desai (ed.) *Technology Absorption in Indian Industry,* New Delhi: Wiley Eastern.

Evans, P. (1995) *Embedded Autonomy*, Princeton: Princeton University Press.

Faulkner, W. (1994) 'Conceptualizing knowledge used in innovation: a second look at the science–technology distinction and industrial innovation', *Science, Technology and Human Values*, 19, 4: 425–58.

Forbes, N. (1996) 'Technology in newly industrializing countries: managing innovation in nations and firms', in *UNIDO, 30 Years of Industrial Development, 1966–96*, Vienna: UNIDO.

Forbes, N. (2001) 'Should developing countries do science?' mimeo, Stanford University.

Forbes, N. (2002) 'Doing business in India: what has liberalisation changed?', in A.O. Krueger (ed.) *Economic Policy Reforms and the Indian Economy*, Chicago: University of Chicago Press.

Fransman, M. and King, K. (eds) (1984) *Technological Capability in the Third World*, London and Basingstoke: Macmillan.

Freeman, C. (1983) 'Design and British economic performance', lecture given at the Design Centre, London, 23 March, Brighton: Science Policy Research Unit (mimeo).

Freeman, C. (1987) *Technology Policy and Economic Performance: Lessons from Japan*, London: Francis Pinter.

Freeman, C. (1997) 'The "national system of innovation" in historical perspective', in D. Archibugi and J. Michie (eds) *Technology, Globalisation and Economic Performance*, Cambridge: Cambridge University Press.

Gereffi, G. and Wyman, D.L. (eds) (1990) *Manufacturing Miracles: Paths of Industrialization in Latin America and East Asia*, Princeton: Princeton University Press.

Gerschenkron, A. (1962) *Economic Backwardness in Historical Perspective*, New York: Praeger.

Gibbons, M. and Johnston, R. (1982) 'Science, technology and the development of the transistor', in B. Barnes and D. Edge (eds) *Science in Context*, Milton Keynes: Open University Press.

Gibbons, M., Limoges, C., Nowotny, H., Schwartzman, S., Scott, P. and Trow, M. (1994*) The New Production of Knowledge*, London: Sage.

Golub, S. (1995) 'Comparative and absolute advantage in the Asia-Pacific region', Working Paper No. PB95–09, Federal Reserve Bank of San Francisco.

Gourevitch, P., Bohn, R. and McKendrick, D. (2000), 'Globalization of production: insights from the hard disk drive industry', *World Development*, 28, 2: 301–17.

Hamilton, A. (1817) *The Soundness of the Policy of Protecting Domestic Manufactures*, Philadelphia: JRA Skerett.

Harrington, H.J. (1987) *The Improvement Process: How America's Leading Companies Improve Quality*, Singapore: McGraw-Hill.

Harrison, L.E. (1992) *Who Prospers? How Cultural Values Shape Economic and Political Success*, New York: Basic Books.

Harvard Business School (1994a, b, c) *Hewlett Packard Singapore, Case Study*, Boston: Harvard Business School Press.

Hayes, R.H. and Pisano, G.P. (1994) 'Beyond world class: the new manufacturing strategy', *Harvard Business Review*, January–February: pp. 77–86.

Hayes, R.H., Wheelwright, S.C. and Clark, K.B. (1988) *Dynamic Manufacturing: Creating the Learning Organization*, New York: Free Press.

Henry, J. and Walker, D. (eds) (1991) *Managing Innovation*, London: Sage.

Hewitt, T. and Wield, D. (1996) 'Technological capability and competitiveness', in *UNIDO 30 Years of Industrial Development, 1966–96*, Vienna: UNIDO.

Hobday, M. (1995) *Innovation in East Asia: The Challenge to Japan*, Aldershot: Edward Elgar.

Hobday, M. (2000) 'East versus Southeast Asian innovation systems: comparing OEM- and TNC-led growth in electronics', in L. Kim and R.R. Nelson (eds) *Technology, Learning and Innovation: Experiences of Newly Industrializing Economies*, Cambridge: Cambridge University Press.

Hofstede, G. (1991) *Cultures and Organizations*, London: HarperCollins.

Hounshell, D. (1996), 'The evolution of industrial research in the United States', in R.S. Rosenbloom, and W.J. Spencer (eds) *Engines of Innovation: US Industrial Research at the End of an Era*, Boston: Harvard Business School Press.

Howells, J. (1999) 'Regional systems of innovation', in D. Archibugi, J. Howells and J. Michie (eds) *Innovation Policy in a Global Economy*, Cambridge: Cambridge University Press.

Humphrey, J. (1995a), 'Introduction', *World Development*, 23, 1: 1–7.

Humphrey, J. (1995b), 'Industrial reorganization in developing countries: from models to trajectories', *World Development*, 23, 1: 149–62.

Humphrey, J., Kaplinsky, R. and Saraph, P.V. (1998) *Corporate Restructuring, Crompton Greaves and the Challenge of Globalisation*, New Delhi: Response Books.

Jacobsson, S. (1993) 'The length of the infant industry period: evidence from the engineering industry in South Korea', *World Development*, 21: 407–19.

Johnson, C. (1982) *MITI and the Japanese Miracle*, Stanford: Stanford University Press.

Jones, G. (1998) 'Knowledge management and management knowledge: old mistakes, new opportunities?', paper for the conference on Emergent Fields in Management: Connecting Learning and Critique, Leeds.

Jones, O., Green, K. and Coombs, R. (1994) 'Technology management: developing a critical perspective', *Technology Analysis and Strategic Management*, 9: 156–71.

Kaplinsky, R. (1994) *Easternisation: The Spread of Japanese Management Techniques to Developing Countries*, Ilford: Frank Cass and Tokyo: United Nations University Press.

Kaplinsky, R. (1995) 'Technique and system, the spread of Japanese management techniques to developing countries', *World Development*, 23, 1: 57–71.

Kattuman, P.A. (1998) 'The role of history in the transition to an industrial district; the case of the Indian bicycle industry', in P. Cadene and M. Holmstrom (eds) *Decentralized Production in India: Industrial Districts, Flexible Specialization, and Employment*, New Delhi: Sage.

Katz, J.M., Gutkowski, M., Rodrigues, M. and Goity, G. (1987) 'Productivity and domestic technological search efforts: the growth path of a rayon plant in Argentina', in J.M. Katz (ed.) *Technology Generation in Latin American Manufacturing Industries*, London: Macmillan.

Keck, O. (1993) 'The national system for technical innovation in Germany', in R.R. Nelson (ed.) *National Innovation Systems: A Comparative Analysis*, Oxford and New York: Oxford University Press.

Kelley, Augustus M. (1971) *The Social Intellectual and Historical Background of Nineteenth Century Britain (c. 1820–1900)*, Clifton, NJ: A.M. Kelley.

Kim, L. (1993) 'National system of industrial innovation: dynamics of capability building in

Korea', in R.R. Nelson (ed.) *National Innovation Systems, A Comparative Analysis,* Oxford and New York: Oxford University Press.

Kim, L. (1997) *Imitation to Innovation,* Boston: Harvard Business School Press.

Klevorick, A., Levin, R., Nelson, R. and Winter, S. (1995) 'On the sources and significance of interindustry differences in technological opportunities', *Research Policy,* 24: 185–205.

Kline, S. (1989) 'Innovation styles in Japan and the United States: cultural bases, implications for competitiveness', *Report INN-3B,* December, Stanford University.

Kline, S. (1991) 'Government technology policy: what should it be?', *Report INN-6,* Department of Mechanical Engineering, Stanford University.

Kline, S. and Rosenberg, N. (1986) 'An overview of innovation', in R. Landau and N. Rosenberg (eds) *Harnessing Technology for Economic Growth,* Washington, DC: National Academy Press.

Kuemmerle, W. and Coughlin, W. (2000) 'Infosys: financing an Indian software start-up,' Case Study Boston: Harvard Business School.

Lall, S. (1987) *Learning to Industrialize: The Acquisition of Technological Capacity in India,* London: Macmillan.

Lall, S. (1990) *Building Industrial Competitiveness in Developing Countries,* Paris: Development Centre, Organization for Economic Co-operation and Development.

Lall, S. (1994) ' "The East Asian miracle" study: does the bell toll for industrial strategy?', *World Development,* 22, 2: 645–54.

Lall, S. (1999) 'India's manufactured exports: comparative structure and prospects', *World Development,* 27, 10: 1769–86.

Lall, S. (2000) 'Technological change and industrialization in the Asian newly industrializing economies: achievements and challenges' in L. Kim and R.R. Nelson (eds) *Technology, Learning, and Innovation: Experiences of Newly Industrializing Economies,* Cambridge: Cambridge University Press

Landau, R., Taylor, T. and Wright, G. (eds) (1996) *The Mosaic of Economic Growth,* Stanford: Stanford University Press.

Landes, D. (1998) *The Wealth and Poverty of Nations: Why Some are So Rich and Others So Poor,* London: Abacus.

Leibenstein, H. (1966) 'Allocative efficiency versus X-efficiency', *American Economic Review.*

Leonard-Barton, D. (1995), *Wellsprings of Knowledge: Building and Sustaining the Sources of Innovation,* Boston: Harvard Business School Press.

Leonard-Barton, D. and Doyle, J.L. (1996) 'Commercializing technology: imaginative understanding of user needs', in R.S. Rosenbloom and W.J. Spencer (eds) *Engines of Innovation: US Industrial Research at the End of an Era,* Boston: Harvard Business School Press.

Lewis, M., Fitzgerald, R. and Harvey, C. (1996) *The Growth of Nations: Culture, Competitiveness and the Problems of Globalization,* Bristol: Bristol Academic Press.

Liker, J.K., Ettlie, J.E. and Campbell, J.C. (eds) (1995) *Engineered in Japan: Japanese Technology–Management Practices,* New York and Oxford: Oxford University Press.

List, F. (1855) *The National System of Political Economy,* Philadelphia: Lippincott.

Lowe, N. and Kenney, M. (1999) 'Foreign investment and the global geography of production; why the Mexican consumer electronics industry failed', *World Development,* 27, 8: 1427–44.

Lundvall, B.-A. (ed.) (1992) *National Systems of Innovation: Towards Theory of Innovation and Interactive Learning,* London: Francis Pinter.

Lundvall, B.-A. (2000) 'Commentary', in L. Kim and R.R. Nelson (eds) *Technology, Learning, and Innovation: Experiences of Newly Industrializing Economies,* Cambridge: Cambridge University Press.

McGinn, R.E. (1991) *Science, Technology and Society,* Englewood Cliffs, NJ: Prentice Hall.

McKern, B. and Malan, R. (1992), 'Posco's strategy in the development of Korea,' Case No. S–IB–10, Graduate School of Business, Stanford, Stanford University.

Magaziner, I.C. and Patinkin, M. (1989) 'Fast heat: how Korea won the microwave war', *Harvard Business Review,* January–February: 83–92.

Mahalingam, S. (1989) 'The computer industry in India: strategies for latecomer entry', *Economic and Political Weekly*, 21 October.

March, J.G. (1989) 'Exploration and exploitation in organizational learning', *Organization Science*, 2, 1: 71–87.

Massey, D., Quintas, P. and Wield, D. (1992) *High Tech Fantasies*, London: Routledge.

Mitchell, R. (1991) 'Masters of innovation: how 3M keeps its new products coming', in J. Henry and D. Walker (eds) *Managing Innovation*, London: Sage.

Moore, G.E. (1996) 'Some personal perspectives on research in the semiconductor industry', in R.S. Rosenbloom and W.J. Spencer (eds) *Engines of Innovation: US Industrial Research at the End of an Era*, Boston: Harvard Business School Press.

Morita, A. (1986) *Made in Japan*, New York: Dutton.

Mowery, D.C. and Rosenberg, N. (1998), *Paths of Innovation: Technological Change in 20th Century America*, Cambridge: Cambridge University Press.

Mytelka, L. (1989) 'The unfulfilled promise of African industrialization', *African Studies Review*, 32, 3: 77–137.

Mytelka, L. (1993) 'Rethinking development: a role for innovation networking in the other "two-thirds"', *Futures*, July–August, 694–712.

Nasscom-McKinsey (1999), *The Indian IT Strategy*, National Association of Software and Service Companies and McKinsey, 17 December 1999, New Delhi.

Nehru, J. (1937) *Inauguration of the Indian Science Congress*, address given to the Indian Science Congress.

Nehru, J. (1993) *Selected Works of Jawaharlal Nehru Part 1 (15 November 1949–8 April 1950) Volume 14*, New Delhi: Oxford University Press.

Nelson, R. (1987) *Understanding Technical Change as an Evolutionary Process*, Amsterdam: Elsevier.

Nelson, R.R. (1990) 'Capitalism as an engine of progress', *Research Policy*, 19: 193–214.

Nelson, R.R. (1992) 'The roles of firms in technical advance: a perspective from evolutionary theory', in G. Dosi, R. Giannetti and P.A. Toninelli (eds) *Technology and Enterprise in a Historical Perspective*, Oxford: Oxford University Press.

Nelson, R.R. (ed.) (1993) *National Innovation Systems: A Comparative Analysis*, Oxford: Oxford University Press.

Nelson, R.R. and Pack, H. (1999) 'Firm competencies, technological catch-up, and the Asian miracle', in G.R. Saxonhouse and T.N. Srinivasan (eds) *Development, Duality, and the International Economic Regime: Essays in Honor of Gustav Ranis*, Ann Arbor: University of Michigan Press.

Nelson, R.R. and Rosenberg, N. (1993) 'Technical innovation and national systems', in R.R. Nelson, (ed.) *National Innovation Systems: A Comparative Analysis*, Oxford: Oxford University Press.

Niosi, J., Hanel, P. and Fiset, L. (1995) 'Technology transfer to developing countries through engineering firms: the Canadian experience', *World Development*, 23: 1815–24.

Nonaka, I. and Takeuchi, H. (1995) *The Knowledge Creating Company*, New York: Oxford University Press.

Odagiri, H. and Goto, A. (1993) 'The Japanese system of innovation: past, present, and future', in R.R. Nelson (ed.) *National Innovation Systems: A Comparative Analysis*, Oxford: Oxford University Press.

Ohno, T. (1992) *Toyota Production System, Beyond Large-Scale Production*, Cambridge, Mass.: Productivity Press.

Okimoto, D.L. (1989) *MITI and the Market: Japanese Industrial Policy for High Technology*, Stanford: Stanford University Press.

Organization for Economic Co-operation and Development (OECD) (1994) *Technology and the Economy*, Paris: OECD.

Orsenigo, L., Pammolli, F. and Riccaboni, M. (2001) 'Technological change and network dynamics lessons from the pharmaceutical industry', *Research Policy*, 30, 3: 485–508.

Pack, H. (2000). 'Research and development in the industrial development process', in L. Kim and R.R. Nelson (eds) *Technology, Learning and Innovation: Experiences of Newly Industrializing Economies,* Cambridge: Cambridge University Press.

Patel, P. and Pavitt, K. (1994) 'The continuing widespread (and neglected) importance of improvements in mechanical technologies', *Research Policy*, 23, 5: 533–45.

Patnaik, D. and Becker, R. (1999) 'Needfinding: the why and the how of uncovering people's needs', *Design Management Journal,* Spring: 39, 43.

Pavitt, K. (2000) 'Innovating routines in the business firm: what matters, what is staying the same, and what's changing?' *SPRU Paper No. 45*, Brighton: University of Sussex.

Perez, L.A. and Peniche, J. (1987), 'A summary of the principal findings of the case-study on the technological behaviour of the Mexican steel firm Altos Hornos de Mexico', in J.M. Katz (ed.) *Technology Generation in Latin American Manufacturing Industries,* London: Macmillan.

Pietrobelli, C. (1994) 'Technological capabilities at the national level: an international comparison of manufacturing export performance', *Development Policy Review* 12: 115–148.

Pita, A. (1998) *Competencias Medulares Taller de Liderazgo en Tecnología*, Vitro, Monterrey, México, 10 March.

Porter, M.E. (1990) *The Competitive Advantage of Nations,* London: Macmillan.

Porter, M.E., Takeuchi, H. and Sakakibara, M. (2000) *Can Japan Compete*, New York: Perseus.

Prahalal, C.K. and Hamel, G. (1990) 'The core competence of the corporation', *Harvard Business Review,* May–June: 79–91.

Prebisch, R. (1950) *The Economic Development of Latin America and Its Principal Problems,* New York: United Nations.

Price, D.J. de Solla (1963) *Big Science, Little Science,* NY and London: Columbia University Press.

Rabellotti, R. (1995) 'Is There an "Industrial District Model"? Footwear districts in Italy and Mexico compared', *World Development*, 23, 1: 29–41.

Reddy, P. (1997) 'New trends in globalization of corporate R&D and implications for innovation capability in host countries: a survey from India', *World Development* 25, 11: 1821–37.

Reddy, P. (2001) *Globalization of Corporate R&D: Implications for Innovation Systems in Host Countries*, London and New York: Routledge.

Rickards, T. (1985) *Stimulating Innovation: A Systems Approach,* London: Pinter.

Riggs, H.E. (1984) 'Innovations: a US–Japan perspective', paper presented to the US–Japan Project on High Technology, Stanford University.

Riggs, H.E. (1988) 'Innovations: a US–Japan perspective', in D. Okimoto and R. Rohlen (eds) *Inside the Japanese System*, Stanford: Stanford University Press.

Rosenberg, N. (1982) 'How exogenous is science', in *Inside the Black Box,* Cambridge: Cambridge University Press.

Rosenberg, N. (1983) 'The commercial exploitation of science by American industry', Working Paper, Stanford University.

Rosenberg, N. (1985) 'Capital goods, technology, and economic growth', in N. Rosenberg (ed.) *Perspectives on Technology,* Cambridge University Press.

Rosenberg, N. (1990), 'Why do firms do basic research (with their own money)?', *Research Policy* 19: 165–74.

Rosenberg, N. (1994) *Exploring the Black Box*, Cambridge: Cambridge University Press.

Rosenberg, N. (1996) 'Uncertainty and technological change', in R. Landau, T. Taylor and G. Wright (eds) *The Mosaic of Economic Growth,* Stanford: Stanford University Press.

Rosenbloom, R.S. and Spencer, W.J. (1996) 'Technology's vanishing wellspring', Introduction to *Engines of Innovation: US Industrial Research at the end of an Era,* Boston: Harvard Business School Press.

Saxonhouse, G.R. and Srinivasan, T.N. (1999) 'Development, duality, and the international economic regime', in *Essays in Honor of Gustav Ranis,* Ann Arbor: University of Michigan Press.

Schmitz, H. (1990) 'Small firms and flexible specialization in developing countries', *Labour and Society,* 15, 3: 257–86.

Schmitz, H. (1995) 'Small shoemakers and Fordist giants: tale of a supercluster', *World Development,* 23, 1: 9–28.

Schlebrugge, K. von (ed.) (1995) *Research for Development – SAREC 20 years,* Stockholm, SAREC.

Schneider, B. R. (1987) 'Framing the state: economic policy and political representation in post authoritarian Brazil', in John D. Wirth, Edson de Oliveira Nunes and Thomas E. Bogenschild (eds) *State and Society in Brazil: Continuity and Change,* Boulder: Westview Press.

Semboja, H.H. and Kweka, J. (1997) 'Divestive impact and privatization process in Tanzania', paper presented at International Conference, Manchester University, July.

Sorensen, K. and Levold, N. (1992) 'Tacit networks, heterogeneous engineers, and embodied technology', *Science, Technology and Human Values,* 17, 1: 13–35.

Smith, S.E. (2000) 'Opening up to the world: India's pharmaceutical companies prepare for 2005', Occasional Papers, Asia/Pacific Research Center, Institute for International Studies, Stanford University.

SRI-International (1990) *Technology/Competitive Positioning for the Year 2000, Final Report Documentation, Grupo Vitro,* Menlo Park, CA.

SRI-International (1994) *Key Terms in Identifying Technical Core Competencies,* Menlo Park, CA.

Teece, D. (1981) 'The R&D and technology transfer activities of multinational firms', in R. Hawkins (ed.), *Technology Transfer and Economic Development,* Greenwich, CT: JAI Press.

Teece, D. and Pisano, G. (1994) 'The dynamic capabilities of firms: an introduction', *Industrial and Corporate Change,* 3: 537–56.

Teece, D.J., Pisano, G. and Shuen, A. (1997) 'Dynamic capabilities and strategic management', *Strategic Management Journal,* 18, 7: 509–33.

Tewari, M. (1996) 'When the marginal becomes mainstream: lessons from a half century of small firm growth in Ludhiana, India', PhD Dissertation, Department of Urban Studies and Planning, Massachusetts Institute of Technology, Cambridge, MA.

Tidd, J., Bessant, J. and Pavitt, K. (1997) *Managing Innovation: Integrating Technological, Market and Organizational Change,* Chichester: Wiley.

Toye, J. (1987) *Dilemmas of Development: Reflections on the Counter Revolution in Development Theory and Policy,* Oxford: Blackwell.

Trajtenberg, M. (2001) 'Innovation in Israel 1968–1997: a comparative analysis using patent data', *Research Policy,* 30, 3: 363–89.

Tushman, M. and Nelson, R. (1990) 'Introduction: technology, organizations and innovation', *Administrative Science Quarterly,* 35: 1–8.

UNCTAD (1995) *World Investment Report,* New York: United Nations Publications.

Vernon, R. (1999) 'International investment and international trade in product cycles', *Quartely Journal of Economics,* 80: 190–207.

Vincenti, W. (1991) *What Engineers Know and How They Know It,* Baltimore: Johns Hopkins University Press.

Wade, R. (1990) *Governing the Market,* Princeton: Princeton University Press.

Wade, R. (1998) 'The Asian debt and development crisis of 1997: causes and consequences', *World Development,* 26: 535–53.

Walsh, V. (1996) 'Design, innovation and the boundaries of the fiirm', *Research Policy,* 25: 509–29.

Walsh, V., Roy, R., Bruce, M. and Potter, S. (1992) *Winning by Design,* Oxford: Blackwell.

Wangwe, S. (1992) 'Building indigenous technological capability in African industry: an overview', in F. Stewart, S. Lall, and S. Wangwe, *Alternative Development Strategies in Sub-Saharan Africa,* Basingstoke and London: Macmillan.

Westphal, L.E., Rhee, Y.W. and Pursell, G. (1981) *Korean Industrial Competence. Where It Came From,* Washington, DC: World Bank.

Weyer, M. Vander (2000) *Falling Eagle: The Decline of Barclays Bank,* London: Weidenfeld & Nicolson.

Wiener, M.J. (1985) *English Culture and the Decline of the Industrial Spirit, 1850–1980,* Harmondsworth: Penguin.

Wilkinson, A. and Willmott, H. (1995) *Making Quality Critical,* London: International Thomson.

World Bank (1993), *The East Asian Miracle: Economic Growth and Public Policy,* Oxford and New York: Oxford University Press.

World Competitiveness Yearbook (2000) Lausane, Switzerland: International Institute for Management Development.

Young, S. (1984) 'Trade policies in Korea: background and prospect', paper for joint conference on industrial policies of ROC and ROK, Seoul: Korea Development Institute.

Zakaria, F. (1994) 'Culture is destiny: a conversation with Lee Kuan Yew', *Foreign Affairs,* 73, 6: 189–94.

Index